FENTON GLASS
COMPENDIUM
1985-2001

John Walk

4880 Lower Valley Road, Atglen, PA 19310 USA

Dedication

To Laurie & Richard Karman: without their kindness, help, and encouragement, this book—
and the other two Fenton compendiums—would never have been completed.

Copyright © 2003 by John Walk
Library of Congress Control Number: 2003101052

Designed by Bonnie M. Hensley
Cover design by Bruce Waters
Type set in Zapf Chancery Bd BT/Aldine 721 BT

ISBN: 0-7643-1811-X
Printed in China
1 2 3 4

Published by Schiffer Publishing Ltd.
4880 Lower Valley Road
Atglen, PA 19310
Phone: (610) 593-1777; Fax: (610) 593-2002
E-mail: Info@schifferbooks.com
Please visit our web site catalog at **www.schifferbooks.com**
We are always looking for people to write books on new and related subjects. If you have an idea for a book please contact us at the above address.

This book may be purchased from the publisher.
Include $3.95 for shipping.
Please try your bookstore first.
You may write for a free catalog.

In Europe, Schiffer books are distributed by
Bushwood Books
6 Marksbury Ave.
Kew Gardens
Surrey TW9 4JF England
Phone: 44 (0)20-8392-8585
Fax: 44 (0)20-8392-9876
E-mail: Bushwd@aol.com
Free postage in the UK. Europe: air mail at cost

Contents

Acknowledgments

Over the course of writing of this book, both of my parents, John W. and Bonnie Walk, have had their share of illnesses. In spite of that, they still tried to maintain the home front while I was out, doing research and taking pictures for this book. They will always have my undying gratitude. If it was not for them, these books would not have been completed. They both are always there when I need them, in spite of their health and limitations. They cared for me, listened to my fears and thoughts, and wholeheartedly supported me. Thank you from the bottom of my heart.

I also want to thank Doris Frizzell, Dorothy Hines, Helen Fiaoni, and Jane Warner Smith; if it was not for these women, I would not be in business today, let alone doing this book. Over the course of the years, they stood by me. They have been my friends, my inspiration, and my support in so many ways and actions. I will always be indebted to them.

John and Linda Flippen, again, with this book (as with the others), have been an invaluable help. Although they do not collect as much of the 1985-2000 items in Fenton, their presence is made know in this book. As always, they have made me welcome in their home, where we have spent many evenings going over details of this and other books, and glass in general.

Bobbie & Harold Morgan deserve special thanks for taking the time to pull many boxes of items out, unpack them, and help me photograph them. They are a special kind of collector: the kind that both love the glass so much and are always willing to share whatever information and items they have!

Thomas K. Smith of Indiana has become a very close friend since I started work on the first book. He is always there to offer ideas, help with research, and work out pricing. We have, over the past several years, traveled together a lot, doing both antique and glass shows. I have experienced and come to admire both his mind and his knowledge of all types of glass.

Jan Hollingsworth has been tremendously helpful in many different areas of this book, as she has in past books: giving me clues as to both the idiosyncrasies of different items in many patterns and to what was difficult to produce. Through many conversations she has become a close friend and confidante.

I have stated several times before that the pictures are the main part of any good reference book on glass. Sometimes the trouble comes in *locating* the items to *get* the photographs. In this book, Richard and Laurie Karman have went overboard, supplying me things to photograph and spent many days packing and unpacking, going over needs lists, confirming what they have, and helping me get the photographs completed. Also they, in a way, form the very basis of this book, as they provided me with the listings of what items were produced in the 1985-2000-time period. In many, many ways, I don't know what I would do without them. When we met almost twenty years ago, I never dreamed that our friendship would also turn into a continuing working relationship. But in the course of the past eight years, because of their unselfish assistance, sharing of information, and also of items to photograph, I have been able to present to the public with this series of books on Fenton Art Glass.

I want to extend a special thanks to Frank Fenton of the Fenton Art Glass Company, and Fenton Glass Museum, for help, advice, and support. Frank seemed to think that I was crazy to even attempt such a task as these books; but, he never tried to persuade me to drop it. He has done everything he could to help me. I am sure that the ordinary collector does not realize the dedication that he has for the glass that he and his family have produced for almost one hundred years. He is always ready to answer questions, supply information, and help in any way that he can. He has gone over several of my books, spending hours on them checking facts, ware numbers, etc., to verify the information that I have put in them. I, like so many other people, would be lost without his knowledge and first-hand insight as to when these items were made. Pam Dick, who is the assistant to the Historian, spent hours bringing out items from the back room of the Fenton Museum and getting them ready for me to photograph. I also want to thank Jennifer Maston, caretaker of the Fenton Glass Museum, who arranged for me to photograph the glass from the museum. She has always been ready to help whenever I needed a question answered or other information.

One who has gained a special place in my heart, not only because of the dedication that she has shown to me, but also of the love of glass that she has, is Millie Coty. Many times, she has helped out, going over manuscripts, checking for mistakes, inaccuracies, and gaps. At times I don't know what I would do with out her! She has been, over the past few years, a shoulder to lean on and sometimes to cry on. I can never express enough my thanks and gratitude to her.

So many other people have helped, giving both advice and support during the writing of this book. A few of these people are Dena & Allen Adden, Don Smith, Lee Garmon, Bonnie &

Frank Zeller, and Alex James & Mike Robbins of James Antiques.

I feel pictures are the main part of a reference book on antiques. It is true, a picture is worth a thousand words. If not for these people, who opened their homes and collections, this book would of not of been possible. I am awed and humbled by their generosity. The average person does not realize the efforts that these people go to in opening up their homes and lives to us so we can come in to take pictures. Sometimes, because of the amount of glass, we are there for several days at a time. My thanks go out to all of you who kept us and welcome us into your homes. Linda and John Flippen have not only become close friends, but have become family to us because of this. Betty & Ike Hardman have had us in a total of three times the past four years to take pictures. It is a wonder that you can keep digging through those rooms and still find items that you hadn't notice before! Pete & Shelia McMillian, of McMillian & Husband, not only opened up their home and shop so I could take whatever pictures I wanted, but also insisted that I stay the night with them! Bobbie and Harold Morgan spent a record ten-hour photo session in their home, bringing me glass to photograph. They work so well as a team, one bringing and the other carrying away, that I wish I could have them to go with me all the time!! Sharon and Alan Fenner have, several times, brought many items from a distance so that I could photograph them. The Williamstown Antique Mall (Fenton Heaven for those who have never been there) has always made their glassware accessible to us, most of the time during the height of their busy season. Diane Rohow also went out of her way, this time taking lists to different members of the Fenton Finders of the Twin Cities and arranging a special photo shoot at their meeting place. These are just a few of the people who opened their hearts and homes for us.

Others who opened up their hearts, lives, and collections to us included:

The Fenton Glass Museum
Maurice Myers of Myers Mystique
Jan Hollingsworth
Connie & Aaron Patient
Maurice Meyers

Melvin & Norma Lampton
Bev & Jon Spencer
Laurie & Richard Karman
Mala Foust
Diane & Tom Rohow
Kathy & Ernest Mathus
Trudy & Dick Green
Shelia & Pete McMillian
John & Mary Lou Tannery
Fran & Bill Ersham
Anne Musser
Rick & Tina Gaither
Sharon & Alan Fenner
Noralee & Ralph Rogers
Michael & Lori Palmer
Vickie Ticen
Cindy & Rick Blais
Dorothy Wiggins of Wiggins Gifts
Bob Depasilo
Phyllis & Terry Sterett
Luann & Atlee Beane
Chuck Bingham
Sarah Wells
Mildred & Roland Potter
Janet & Ken Wilke
Judy Henselman
Ruth Lawrence
Doris and Junior Devall
Donna Hatch
Lin & Rob Elbee
Joyce & Bob Stein
Dennis & Linda Sowers

Over the past several years, both The Fenton Finders Club of Greater Kansas City, during their Fenton Gala each September, and the National Fenton Glass Society, during their August convention, have allowed me to take pictures of their displays and many, many members of both groups have brought items for me, out of their homes, to photograph. It is because of the dedication of glass clubs and their members, such as these, that the desire for, and knowledge from, collecting glass exists.

Introduction

Many years ago, in the magazine the *Depression Glass Daze*, the late columnist Betty Bell made the statement that Fenton is a glass for everyone. That has seemed to hold true throughout the past twenty years since that statement was made. It is a glass for the advanced collectors—whether they are collectors of Carnival, Stretch Glass, or the art pieces from the early part of the twentieth century, or the ones, such as myself, who love the items that Fenton made in Opalescent, Crest, and Overlays throughout the 1940s and 1950s, or for the late baby boomer collectors, who have discovered the Carnival or Decorated Satin & Milk Glass of the 1970s. Fenton is even for the younger collectors who have discovered the glass the Fenton has produced within the last twenty years.

When I wrote the introduction to the *Fenton Glass Compendium: 1970-85*, I made the statement that I was surprised to be doing a volume on such a recent era of glassware. In this volume, I'm even more surprised, as much of that glass may still be found on Fenton dealers' shelves. To clarify this statement a bit further requires placing the whole collectibles market into context, especially the glass market. In the late 1960s, Depression Glass began to be noticed and collected by the American public. It hit full stride in the early 1980s; at that time, this glass was thirty to forty years old. This has seemed to hold true with much of the collectible glass made throughout the 1930s to the 1970s. Give or take a few years, most types of glassware seem to be noticed and to hit their stride as a popular collectibles within thirty or more years after their issue. Mostly this is due to the fact that the children or grandchildren of the original collectors grow interested in what their parents or grandparents had. While the Fenton Art Glass from 1985-2000 has yet to reach the thirty year mark, it has become attractive to collectors for other reasons.

I think the reasons that the items made by Fenton from 1985-2000 have become so attractive to collectors, both new and old alike, are:

1. They are well-made, beautiful, quality items.

2. The idea of collecting Fenton Art Glass is not new to the collecting public. It started in the 1960s with Carnival glass and became more widespread each pasting year, and throughout each year, encompassing more of their recent glass.

3. With the closure of so many glass companies over the past twenty years, and also the heighten awareness of antiques and collectibles; the public has become more interested in glassware, both new and old.

4. Due to several well establish collector's clubs, there is a large following for Fenton Art Glass, both older and newer, outside of what I call the "mainstream public."

5. Due to the presence of QVC™ on the cable TV stations, people have become more aware of Fenton Art Glass over the past fifteen years, not only the items that are sold on QVC, but also the items that are currently in Fenton's regular line. Many times the QVC items are made in the same treatments as Fenton regular line items, heightening awareness of both through the QVC advertising.

No matter what the reason, it is a guaranteed fact that the items produced by Fenton from 1985-2000 are just as highly regarded as their older counterparts. I have noticed, throughout my years of dealing in Fenton Art Glass, that there are several groups who collect this glass. There are what are referred to as the early collectors (collecting the items from prior to the 1940s); in the next group are the Baby Boomers (who collect the items from the World Ware II time period up to 1970); and then there are what many people in the Fenton collecting circles have called the "new collectors" (which are the people who collect the items from 1970-85). However, over the past several years I have noticed an even newer group of people who are interested in the even more recent items that Fenton has produced. Hopefully this volume will satisfy the thirst for knowledge among collectors of this time period, as my previous volumes have for the collectors of earlier Fenton.

Fenton: 1985-2000

As it had been almost forty years previous, when Frank M. and Bill Fenton took over the reins of the Fenton Art Glass Company, many people were nervous when George Fenton, the son of Frank M. Fenton, took over presidency of the company in the mid-1980s. Some time previous to this, several well establish glass companies had closed, including Imperial and Westmoreland. The country as a whole was not in the best shape economically. Due to good business sense and careful guidance, through his father and uncle, George Fenton was able to take the Fenton Art Glass Company and rise above some slow times in the 1980s to emerged as one of the leading glassmaking companies in the United States in the 1990s.

One thing that has led to the survival of Fenton Art Glass throughout the 1990s is the association with QVC. This association began in the late 1980s, when Fenton was approached to sell glass on the marketing giant cable TV channel. It is due to this advertising that many people, who had not even heard of Fenton before it was on QVC, have begun to collect the QVC items, the regular Fenton line, and even the older Fenton.

Due to their involvement with the QVC channel, Fenton sometimes had more orders than employees to fill them during the 1990s. Brisk sales to long-time dealers and collectors also helped the company to grow, despite at times. Troubles with the EPA developed due to the chemicals employed in making many long-time treatments.

As the 1990s progressed, Fenton wisely bought moulds and hired workers from many closing glass companies, causing them to be able to create items in shapes and, at other times, in colors and treatments that they had not been able to offer before.

As the 1990s drew to a close, and the beginnings of the twenty-first century appeared on the horizon, it was apparent that Fenton would be around for their one-hundredth birthday, and well after that.

Pricing

In past five years of observing Fenton prices throughout the U.S., I have found that prices are fairly standard in the mainstream market. Some areas are higher then others, while some are much lower.

This book is intended to be only a guide. I can assure you that you will find pieces priced both higher and lower than what is listed here. I am also sure that some of the readers will not agree with my pricing, but this is a compilation of an intense price survey, including what is realized from dealers selling their glass and also from what people have stated that they would be willing to pay for rare pieces. The ultimate guide is you and what your are willing to pay for a piece, how long you can do without that piece in your collection, and how much higher a piece will go while you are looking for a more reasonable price.

All prices listed here are retail for mint condition glassware. Some pieces will be listed as UND if the items have proven to be too rare to establish value.

It is not the intention of this author to control or establish prices. As I am also in the business of selling, I know that prices can sometimes be too high and that overpriced items will not sell.

Measurements

All measurements and terms are either from factory catalogs or from actual measurements of the pieces. Actual measurements tend to vary widely from factory catalogs with handmade glass.

When measurements are listed in Fenton catalogs, keep in mind that the measurements listed for baskets, bowls, and top hats represent the diameter of the piece. The measurement listed for a vase represents the height of the item.

Glossary

The following are terms and phrases used in the glassmaking business.

Batch: A mixture of sand, soda ash, lime, and other chemicals that modify the color or characteristics of the glass. The batch is inserted into the pot furnace or day tank and heated to 250 degrees Fahrenheit, thereby fusing into molted glass.

Blank: A blank is a piece of glass which has been formed, shaped, sent through the lehr, and which is now ready to be processed by cutting, sand carving, or decorating, either by the company producing the blank, by a glass decorating company, or a glass cutting shop. It is a piece that is ready to be processed further.

Blocker: The person who shapes the glass, fresh from the furnace, and blows the first bubble of air through a blow pipe into the glass.

Blower: The person who manipulates the glass into shape and plunges it into a mould. He then forces it throughout the mould by blowing into it.

Carrying-in Worker: The person who takes finished articles to the lehr for final cooling.

Carry Over Worker: The person who carries over pieces of glass just pressed from the mould to the glory hole for reheating so the finisher can put on a final crimp and shape in the glass.

D.C.: Term used for pieces that have a second, larger crimp besides the smaller, tight ruffle on pieces of Fenton Art Glass. (It might be noted that a crimping mould usually makes the first crimp, while the second crimp is made by pulling the glass down by hand with a tool for that purpose.)

Day Tanks: Direct fire furnaces in which glass is exposed to direct flames. A day tanks melt glass in twelve hours, which lets it be worked in the daytime, and melt a new batch at night … or the other way around.

Finisher: The skilled worker who changes the shape of the piece after it has come from the mould into its final form, which may be flared, crimped, cupped, or changed into one of many different shapes.

Frit: Small pieces of crushed glass used in making Vasa Murrhina.

Gather: The still unformed glob of glass, fresh from the furnaces or day tank.

Gatherer: The worker who gathers glass from the day tank and takes it to the mould.

Glory Hole: A small furnace heated to a temperature to about 2,500 degrees Fahrenheit which is used to reheat the glass so it can be reshaped by the finisher.

Hand Swinging: The process of reheating a tumbler, bowl, or other item of glass to the point where it is so molten that it can be twirled on the end of the pipe like a baton so that centrifugal force will stretch the piece out into what we call a swung vase.

Handler: The worker who applies handles for baskets, jugs, etc.

Hot Metal Works: The area where furnaces are located in the glass factory.

Jobbers: Wholesalers who do not make the glass but who act as distributors for the glass company to the retail stores. The jobber may sell the regular Fenton, have glass made from the jobber's own moulds, or may have special glass made by the glass company from its moulds—sometimes in different colors or shapes. Then the jobber distributes the glass to retailers throughout the jobber's territory.

Lehr: A long annealing oven heated to about 1,000 degrees in which the glass is placed after it has been made in the Hot Metal Department. The glass is placed on a conveyor belt inside the oven. The stresses and strains that have been put into the glass during the process of heating and chilling are relieved by bringing all parts of the glass piece to the same temperature. Then the conveyor belt moves the glass to a cooler temperature and gradually cools it down to room temperature.

Mould Blown: Glass that is force blown into mould, either by mouth or air pressure.

NIL (Not in Line): An item that was not sold in the regular line of a certain treatment or color, nor was it offered in any of Fenton's catalogs. Usually it was a Sample (experimental) item, to test the market, or an item that was produced by special order, either for an individual, another company, or a jobber.

Off Hand Ware: Glass that is blown without moulds, and shaped by the glass worker with hand tools.

Opaline Glass: Partially opaque glass that is translucent. It looks opaque but will transmit light. It is glass that is about halfway between transparent glass and opaque glass.

Opaque Glass: Glass that allows a limited amount of light to pass through it, showing little fire or translucence when held to light.

Overlay Glass: Cased glass in which one layer is poured over another.

Pressed Blown: Glass pressed into the mould and then forced to fill out the mould by blowing into it, either by mouth or air pressure.

Presser: The skilled glassworker who controls the temperature of the mould, cuts off the glass when it is dropped by the gathers, controls the weight of the glass that goes into the mould, and pulls the lever of the press which brings the plunger down to force the glass into each part of the press mould. He removes the plunger and opens the mould to remove the glass.

Ringer: The worker who spins a thin ring of different colored molten glass to the edge of the piece, thereby forming the glass that we call Crest glass.

Spot mould: Sometimes called an optic mould. This mould is used to create an inner pattern in the glass. The mould itself has a pattern that is transferred to the glass. After reheating, the glass is then blown into a second plain mound with no pattern. When the piece is made from opalescent or other heat sensitive glass, by chilling and reheating, the patterns becomes opaque while other parts remain clear.

Turn: Four hours of production will constitute a turn's work. The number of pieces made in that four-hour period depends on the size, complexity, and the shape of the piece.

Warming-In Worker: The person who reheats the glass in the glory hole, removes it, and takes it to the finisher for further shaping.

Years of Production

Through the help of Frank Fenton, and others, plus references through old catalog pages, we have attempted to show the readers of this book, the exact years that a piece was made.

Hopefully the collector will soon see why one piece in a certain color is so much rarer than the same piece in another color. This research will show that the rare piece simply was not produced for as many years, and in some cases, it was produced for only a few months.

The years in production, will be included in most cases in the caption beside each picture. (Example: Vase, 5.5", 389, YOP: 1940-48, $45-55.)

Ware Number Description

In July 1952, Fenton began to assign individual ware numbers to each item. After that time, the ware number included six digits: four numerals and two letters. The letters indicate the color or decoration, and the numerals indicate pattern and shape. Before July 1952, the mould numbers represented pattern or mould shape and needed a word description following the number to describe shape and color. (Example: All Hobnail pieces have the same number, 389. All melon-shaped pieces were 192.) All sizes and shapes from the same shaped or patterned mould carried the same number.

Logos

The now famous "Fenton" in Script in an oval logo was first used in 1970, only on Carnival Glass. Between 1972 and 1973, it was placed on Hobnail and other items. By 1975, almost all items made by Fenton had this logo.

In 1980, a small 8 was added to show the decade of the '80s.

A small F in a logo was used in moulds that were acquired from McKee or moulds purchased from other glass companies. This practice started in 1983.

The sand blasted logo was used on blown items or limited edition items where other logos could not be seen. Also, this logo was used on off hand items and paste mould items. The sand blasted logo was used from 1980 to 1984.

The fancy script F logo was first sand blasted on Artisan and Connoisseur items in 1984. It is used on items that do not have the regular logo impressed in the mould. Beginning in 1994, it replaced the regular logo on all items that had not been previously marked. These items were primarily blown.

In 1990, a small 9 was added to the moulds to show the decade of the '90s. In some cases, one has to look closely, as the numeral is so small that it looks like an 8.

In 2000, a small 0 was added to the moulds to show the 2000s decade.

Other markings include the 75th mark above the Fenton logo, to designate the seventy-fifth anniversary items. This practice was continued for each anniversary issue thereafter.

The reader must keep in mind, that even though items made throughout the 1970s, and after, were to have been marked, there are many, many instances in which the logo is either fired out or so faint that it is easier to detect by rubbing it with your finger than by seeing it with the naked eye. The type of glass in which the logo was fired out was mostly cased blown ware such as Cranberry. Sometimes the logo is so faint on these items that all you can make out is part of the oval!

Family Signature Series/ Historic Collection

Two of the more popular ongoing series of glass that have been issued throughout the 1990s are the Family Signature series and the Historic Collection.

The Family Signature series was first issued in 1993. Each year, a number of different items from several different lines would have a facsimile signature of a different family member. These signed items would be the ultimate in whatever mould, treatment, decoration, or color they were made. Over the years, these items have caught on with collectors, who sometimes only collect certain family members' signatures. These items have been included in whatever pattern, color, or treatment they were made in. They are indicated with notations such as: Frank Fenton's Signature.

The Historic Collection was created from glassware items originally produced in the early 1980s for Levay and other companies. During the initial early 1980s production, Fenton would issue full color pamphlets, displaying whatever pattern or treatment was made for those companies at that time, and this series would be labeled as being made for the Antique Trade. Later, after Fenton split with Levay, this series was called the Collector's Extravaganza. One of the first issues in this line was Green Opalescent in 1985 (shown in the *Fenton Compendium 1970-85*); after that, Pink Opalescent in Hobnail (often called Peaches 'n' Cream) was issued in 1988, followed by items in Persian Blue Opalescent in 1989 and items in Sapphire Blue Opalescent in 1990. In the early 1990s, this series name was changed to the Historic Collection. Throughout the following ten years, many different treatments would be issued. At times, one issue would be out for a single year beginning in January, another would debut in June and would consist of a grouping of limited numbered items. This series is included in the following pages, and will be noted as part of the Historic Collection. The limited number items will be noted as to how many were made (i.e.: Limited to 1500).

Colors/Treatments

Carnival

Throughout the late 1980s and on into the 1990s some of the most beautiful and also unusual colors of Carnival glass were produced by Fenton. In the late 1980s, a Marigold Iridescent Spray, usually used over Amber Glass, was tried on both Cobalt and Teal Royale. Both treatments stayed in the Fenton line for several years. In the early 1990s, when Fenton began to issue the Historical Collection, many different colors of Carnival Glass were developed for that series. Also in the early 1990s Red Carnival Glass was issued for several years, followed by Plum Carnival and then later Spruce Green.

In a marketing strategy that had been employed by Fenton earlier in the 1970s with their Original Formula Carnival Glass, each item, in each color, would only be available for one year (and sometimes less), thereby making each item scarce, and also collectible, from the time of its issue.

Cobalt Marigold NK 1985-87

First produced in 1984 (see *Fenton Compendium 1970-85* for earlier items), Cobalt Marigold is literally Cobalt Glass that was sprayed with a Marigold Spray, which was usually used on Amber Glass. It makes unusually bright iridescences on the glass when hit with bright light.

Many moulds made on this treatment had been previously bought from McKee several years before. Also keep in mind that this is one of the first instances when the "F" in the oval logo was used.

Items Not Pictured:

Basket, 8335, Open Edge, YOP: 1987, $55-65
Bowl, 8289, Orange Tree & Cherries, YOP: 1986, $45-55
Comport, 9279, Marquette, YOP: 1986, $40-45

Nut Bowl, 6", 2-Handled, 8629, $35-40; Basket, 9234, Butterfly & Berry, YOP: 1986, $65-75; Votive, Toothpick, 9292, YOP: 1986, $25-35; Pitcher, 9269, Quintec, YOP: 1986, $75-85. *Courtesy of Norma & Melvin Lampton.*

Pitcher, 9269, Quintec, YOP: 1986, $75-85; Rose Bowl, 3022, Wavy Hobnail, YOP: 1987, $30-35; Candy, Covered Footed, 9284, Rose, YOP: 1987, $65-75. *Courtesy of Bobbie & Harold Morgan.*

Pitcher, 9461, Plytec, YOP: 1987, $75-85; Comport, 9276, Innovation, YOP: 1986, $40-45. *Courtesy of Norma & Melvin Lampton.*

Crackle Sea Mist Green L4 1992-93/
Crackle Pink P8 1992-93/Crackle Twilight Blue T6 1992-93

Crackle glass, which had been a long time favorite with glass collectors, was made briefly at Fenton in the early 1990s. Crackle glass is produced by taking hot glass that is still on the end of a blow pipe and plunging it into cold water, thereby producing fine cracks throughout the glass. The glass is then reheated to seal the cracks on the outside of the glass. Fenton added an iridescent spray, when finished, which made for a remarkable looking line. Most items in this treatment are very scarce to rare and hardly ever appear on the open market.

Item Description	Ware Number	Pink Crackle	Twilight Blue Crackle	Sea Mist Green Crackle
Basket, 11"	7576	$100-110	$90-100	$80-90
Basket, 8"	7463	$80-90	$70-80	$70-80
Pitcher, 10.5"	7483	$150-175	$125-150	$125-150
Pitcher, 4"	7648	$80-90	$70-80	$70-80
Vase, 4.5"	7645	$40-50	$35-40	$35-40
Vase, 5"	7644	$60-70	$50-60	$50-60
Vase, Pinch, 8.5"	7647	$80-90	$70-80	$70-80
Vase, 9.5"	7649	$80-90	$70-80	$70-80
Vase, 10.5"	7479	$100-110	$90-100	$80-90
Vase, 14"	7477	$100-110	$90-100	$80-90
Vase, 14.5"	7476	$100-110	$90-100	$80-90

Baskets, 8", 7463 (Notice the difference in crimps): Vase, Pinch, 8.5", 7647; Basket, 11", 7576. See tables for values when they do not appear in the captions. *Courtesy of Bobbie & Harold Morgan.*

Pitcher, 4", 7648.

Vase, Pinch, 8.5", 7647.

Pitcher, 10.5", 7483.

Vase, 10.5", 7479; Vase, Pinch, 8.5", 7647.

Gold Pearl GP 1992

Gold Pearl appeared in Fenton's line for the Historic Collection in 1992. Due to the Cerium that was used in the formula to produce the color (which reacted with the bone ash to produce the Opalescent), the glass became very brittle when cooled, making this line extremely difficult to produce. Two items, the Owl Figural and the Covered Swan Box, are extremely rare today, as not many of them were produced intact.

Items Not Pictured:

Swan Box with cover, 4600, UND

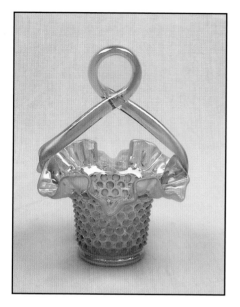

Basket, Looped Handled, 3335, $100-125. *Courtesy of Laurie & Richard Karman.*

Cruet, 3863, $125-150. *Courtesy of Williamstown Antique Mall.*

Vase, 6", Hand, 3355, $125-150. *Courtesy of Norma & Melvin Lampton.*

Epergne, 4801, Diamond Lace, $250-300. *Courtesy of Kansas City Fenton Finders.*

Water set, 5 piece, 3908: Pitcher:, $125-150; Tumblers:, $35-40 ea. *Courtesy of Lin & Rob Elbee.*

Light Amethyst Carnival DT 1991

Produced for the Historic Collection in 1991, this pattern made used of many moulds that Fenton had bought from both U.S. Glass and McKee, along with the Westmoreland moulds that they were using in a royalty agreement with Levay. The McKee Fruit Water Set in this color proved very difficult to produce and was quickly discontinued, being replaced with the Westmoreland Panel Grape Water Set. Also scarce are the Good Luck Plate, and the covered Eagle Box.

Items Not Pictured:

Bowl, 10", Oval, 4618, $75-80
Butter, 8680, Regency, $65-70
Cuspidor, 3-toed, 4643, Innovation, $45-50
Toothpick, 4644, Diamond & Paneled, $20-25

Basket, 7", 3-toed, 4617, Innovation, $65-70.
Courtesy of Norma & Melvin Lampton.

Water Set, 4650, Paneled Grape Pitcher, $150-200; Tumbler, $45-55. (This set replaced the Mckee Fruit 5 piece Water Set, 4609, which proved to be too difficult to produce.) *Courtesy of Sharon and Al Fenner.*

Punch Bowl Set, 4601, Paneled Grape, $350+. *Courtesy of Phyllis & Terry Sterett.*

Covered Box, Eagle, 4679, $80-90. *Courtesy of Norma & Melvin Lampton.*

Persian Pearl XV 1992-93

Persian Pearl is unique in the sense that this is one of the first times that Fenton ever attempted to make one of their Opalescent colors iridescent. In this case, they took Persian Blue, which had been in their line for several years before, and put a light Clear Spray over it. This color proved quite popular, and remained in Fenton's line for several years, making it one of the few Historic Collections to do so.

Items Not Pictured:

Bowl, 8454, Curtain, YOP: 1993 only, $55-60
Candy Box, Footed, 3784, Hobnail, YOP: 1992 only, $45-55
Punch Bowl Set, 4601, Panel Grape, YOP: 1992 only, $350+
Punch Cup, 4642, Panel Grape, YOP: 1992 only, $20 ea.
Swan, 5127, YOP: 1993 only, $35-45
Vase, 6.5", Tulip, 3183, Hobnail, YOP: 1992 only, $45-55

Plate, 4611, Good Luck, $65-75. *Courtesy of Norma & Melvin Lampton.*

Bell, 9065, Sables Arch, $35-40; Basket, Looped Handled, 4646, Innovation, $80-85; Plate, 4611, Good Luck, $65-75; Bowl, 10", 4619, Good Luck, $65-75; Covered Box, Eagle, 4679, $80-90. *Courtesy of Bobbie & Harold Morgan.*

Basket, 7", 2725, Button & Arch, $45-50; Basket, 11", Spiral, 3077, $75-80; Basket, 4", 2728, Button & Arch, $60-65. *Courtesy of Sarah Wells.*

Basket, Footed Ribbon Candy Edge, 9435, Drapery, YOP: 1993 only, $65-70. *Courtesy of Sarah Wells.*

Epergne, Mini, 3801, Hobnail, YOP: 1993 only, $100-125; Epergne, 3701, Hobnail, $125-150; Candleholder, 6", 3674, Hobnail, YOP: 1992 only, $35-40 ea. *Courtesy of Sarah Wells.*

Bowl, 12", 3938, YOP: 1992 only, $55-60. *Courtesy of Sarah Wells.*

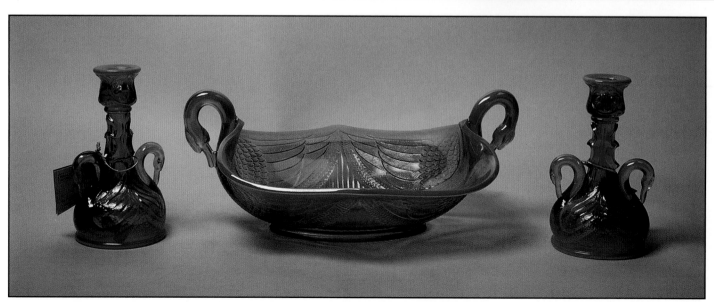

Bowl, 2754, Swan, YOP: 1993 only, $75-80; Candleholders, 5172, Swan, YOP: 1993 only, $35-40 ea. *Courtesy of Sarah Wells.*

Pitcher, 1875, Fern, $150-175; Tumblers, 1876, Fern, $45-50 ea. *Courtesy of Sarah Wells.*

Water Set, Mini, Button & Arch Creamer, 2726, Button & Arch, $20-25; Tumbler, 2727, Mini Button & Arch, $10-15 ea. *Courtesy of Bobbie & Harold Morgan.*

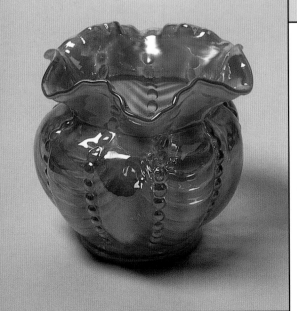

Vase, 5", 2056, Curtain, $45-55. *Courtesy of Sarah Wells.*

Pink Pearl HZ 1991-94

Made in the early 1990s for several years, Pink Pearl is an iridescent version of Fenton's popular Petal Pink color. This color was usually used at Easter for their series of covered animals, but also used in other shapes that were offered in the Fenton catalog. With this, and many other patterns/treatments that appear in this book, one would think that since they are so recent it would be easy for the collector to find them to buy. I have found that is not the case; in fact, I thought it would be a breeze, doing this volume, as I would find items for the pictures a whole lot easier to come by than with previous books. It seems these newer patterns & treatments are *harder* to find! I think one reason for this is many people who were not Fenton collectors bought the regular line items, such as Pink Pearl and many other treatments from this time period, for use in their homes and they have not come onto the secondary market yet! I have realized while doing this book that the "Fenton Collector" bought items such as the Limited Edition series, Connoisseur Items, and a lot of the Holiday items, as they were special issue, and many times ignored items in Fenton regular catalogs. It will take several years for items to come out now and to see what will be the more collectible and harder to find pieces from this time period, the Special Issue/Limited Edition items, or the regular line Catalog items.

Items Not Pictured:

Atomizer, Oval, 5315, YOP: 1991 only, $30-35
Atomizer, Beaded, 5316, YOP: 1991 only, $30-35
Basket, 5.5", 4631, YOP: 1991-92, $45-55
Basket, 7", 4632, Wildflower, YOP: 1992 only, $45-55
Puff Box, 6570, Paneled Grape, YOP: 1992 only, $25-35
Trinket Box, 9687, Hexagonal, YOP: 1994 only, $20-25
Candleholder, 2-way, 9596, YOP: 1992 only, $15-20 ea.
Clock, 8698, YOP: 1991-92, $20-25
Comport, 6981, Teardrop, YOP: 1991 only, $30-35
Comport, 6988, Teardrop, YOP: 1992 only, $30-35
Picture Frame, 4690, YOP: 1991-92, $20-25
Ring Holder, 9144, Fine Cut & Block, YOP: 1992 only, $10-15
Toothpick, 8294, Paneled Daisy, YOP: 1992 only, $15-20
Vase, 8", 6564, Elite, YOP: 1992 only, $30-35

Trinket Box, 5786, Hummingbird, YOP: 1991-92, $20-25. *Courtesy of Linda & Dennis Sowers.*

Perfume, 1940, YOP: 1992 only, $55-65. *Courtesy of Mildred & Roland Potter.*

Slipper, 9295, Rose, YOP: 1991-92, $15-20. *Courtesy of Mildred & Roland Potter.*

Plum Carnival PX 1997-98

Perhaps one of the most dramatic and beautiful Carnival colors that has been made by Fenton is the Plum Carnival color. The base color of Plum is quite close to the Fenton Amethyst color that was used in the Original Formula Carnival Glass. Plum Carnival was made for two years in a multitude of items. Many of the moulds used in this color had not been in Fenton's line for a long while.

Items Not Pictured:

Perfume with Stopper, 5305, YOP: 1997 only, $65-75
Vase, 7.5", 7653, Daffodil, YOP 1988 only, $55-60

Basket, 3-toed, 6838, $65-75; Basket, 7.5", 5731; Basket, 6", 2035, Ruffles, $55-60. *Courtesy of Laurie & Richard Karman.*

Basket, 7", 5731, Hummingbird, YOP: 1997 only, $75-80; Basket, 9.5", 1535, Diamond Paneled, YOP 1997 only, $65-70. *Courtesy of Laurie & Richard Karman.*

Candy, 6780, Paisley, YOP: 1997 only, $65-70; Basket, 9.5", 1535, Diamond Paneled, YOP 1997 only, $65-70; Pitcher, 9.5", 6869, YOP: 1997 only, $125-150; Box with Cover, 2970, $100-124. *Courtesy of Norma & Melvin Lampton.*

Jug, 9014, Aztec, YOP: 1998 only, $100-125. *Courtesy of Myers Mystique.*

Bowl, 7677, Viking, YOP: 1998 only, $100-125; Candlesticks, 7676, Viking, YOP: 1998 only, $45-55 ea. *Courtesy of Myers Mystique.*

Bowl, 7677, Viking, YOP: 1998 only, $100-125; Box, Square, 7640, Beaded Grape, YOP: 1998 only, $55-60. *Courtesy of Laurie & Richard Karman.*

Vase, 10", 8769, Thistle, YOP: 1997 only, $200-225. *Courtesy of Bev & John Spencer.*

Vase, 9458, Swan, YOP: 1997 only, $100-125. *Courtesy of Norma & Melvin Lampton.*

Rose Pearl DN 1992-94

As Pink Pearl is the iridescent version of Petal Pink, Rose Pearl is the iridescent of Dusty Rose. Sometimes it is difficult to tell the difference of these two colors unless they are side by side.

Items Not Pictured:

Trinket Box, 5783, Rose, $25-30
Trinket Box, 5786, Hummingbird Heart, YOP: 1993-94, $25-30
Candy, Covered, 8.5", 9185, Paneled Daisy, YOP: 1993 only, $40-45
Comport, 6", 9102, Fine Cut & Block, YOP: 1993 only, $30-35
Comport, 9120, Fine Cut & Block, YOP: 1993 only, $30-35
Hat, 2.5", 1992, Daisy & Button, YOP: 1993 only, $20-25
Slipper, 1995, Daisy & Button, YOP: 1993 only, $20-25
Vase, Mini, 6569, Jacqueline, YOP: 1992-93, $20-25
Vase, Mini, 7151, Beaded Melon, YOP: 1992-93, $30-35
Vase, 8", 6564, Elite, YOP: 1993 only, $30-35

Red Carnival RN 1990-96

For many years, after the initial production of Fenton's Carnival Glass in the early 1900s, Red Carnival was the color that captured many people imagination due to its brilliance and its rarity. When it was reintroduced for a short time in the 1970s, it sold briskly. In 1990, it was made again and was in the Fenton line for several years. It seems that a collecting cult formed while it was being made and, due to that fact, hardly any pieces of it appear on the market today.

Items Not Pictured:

Basket, 5.5", 6573, Peacock & Dahlia, YOP: 1992 only, $65-70
Basket, 10.5", 5488, Hearts & Flowers, YOP: 1994 only, $100-125
Bonbon, 8230, Butterfly, YOP: 1992 only, $45-55
Bowl, 6", 2927, Wild Rose Bowl, YOP: 1995 only, $55-60
Rose Bowl, 8429, Water Lily, YOP: 1994 only, $45-55
Candy, Covered, 9280, Butterfly, YOP: 1994 only, $50-55
Alarm Clock, 8691, YOP: 1990 only, $50-55
Comport, 9422, Persian Medallion, YOP: 1994 only, $50-55
Comport, 9120, Fine Cut & Block, YOP: 1992 only, $50-55
Nut dish, 4.5", 2926, YOP 1995 only, $30-35
Slipper, 2931, Beauty, YOP: 1995 only, $30-35
Slipper, 1995, Daisy & Button, YOP: 1991 only, $25-30
Vase, 7.5", 2857, Wild Rose, YOP: 1995 only, $55-60
Vase, 8", 6564, Elite, YOP: 1993 only, $40-45

Basket, 8", 9137, Fine Cut & Block, YOP: 1993 only, $30-35; Basket, 6", 2731, Lamb's Tongue, YOP: 1993 only, $40-45. *Courtesy of Laurie & Richard Karman.*

Perfume, 1940, YOP: 1993 only, $55-65. *Courtesy of Laurie & Richard Karman.*

Basket, 7.5, 1231, Spanish Lace, YOP: 1996 only, $65-70. *Courtesy of Laurie & Richard Karman.*

Basket, 9074, Grape & Cable, YOP: 1990 only, $100-125. *Courtesy of Williamstown Antique Mall.*

Basket, 8", 1937, Daisy & Button, YOP: 1995 only, $65-70. *Courtesy of Connie & Aaron Patient.*

Basket, 8.5", 7538, Ribbon Tie Interior/Lily of the Valley Exterior, $65-70. *Courtesy of Mala Foust.*

Basket, 7.5", 2734, Button & Arch, $45-55; Basket, 5.5", 6573; Basket, 6.5", 9240, Rose, YOP: 1990 only, $65-70; Basket 8233, Orange Tree & Cherry, YOP: 1992-93, $65-70. *Courtesy of Laurie & Richard Karman.*

Basket, 2779, Lion & Leaf, YOP: 1994 only, Tom Fenton Signature Piece, $80-85; Basket, 7", 5730, Rose, YOP: 1991 only, $65-70; Vase, 8", Tulip, 3356, Hobnail, YOP: 1994, $55-65. *Courtesy of Norma & Melvin Lampton.*

Boot, 1990, Daisy & Button, YOP: 1991 only, $25-30; Slipper, 9295, Rose, YOP: 1990 only, $25-30; Tobacco Jar, 9188, Grape & Cable, YOP: 1996 only, $225-250; Basket, 7.5", 2733, Vintage, YOP: 1993 only, $65-70; Basket, 7", 5730, Rose, YOP: 1991 only, $65-70. *Courtesy of Bobbie & Harold Morgan.*

Candy, Covered, 9185, Paneled Daisy, YOP: 1992 only, $55-60; Basket, 7.25", 8335, Open Edge, YOP: 1991 only, $60-65; Vase, 6", 2557, Beaded Melon, YOP: 1991 only, $55-60. *Courtesy of Norma & Melvin Lampton.*

Epergne, 4801, Diamond Lace, YOP: 1991 only, $300-350. *Courtesy of Linda & Dennis Sowers.*

Candy Box, 8489, Lily of the Valley, YOP: 1993 only, $85-90. *Courtesy of Mala Foust.*

Pitcher, 9666, Sandwich, YOP: 1991 only, $45-55; Creamer, 2726, Button & Arch, YOP: 1993 only, $30-35. *Courtesy of Ann Musser.*

Pitcher, 6 oz., 3762, Hobnail, YOP: 1994 only, $65-70. *Courtesy of Bobbie & Harold Morgan.*

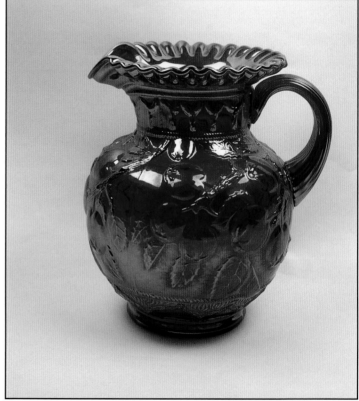

Pitcher, 6575, Apple Tree, YOP: 1995 only, $225-250. *Courtesy of Ruth Lawerance.*

Tumbler, 6576, Apple Tree, YOP: 1995 only, $40-45 ea. *Courtesy of Myers Myerstique.*

Candy Box, 9480, Chessie, YOP: 1991 only, $125-150. *Courtesy of Sarah Wells.*

Trinket Box, 9384, Floral, YOP: 1990 only, $30-35.

Comport, 8625, Puritan, YOP: 1990 only, $65-70. *Courtesy of Norma & Melvin Lampton.*

Candy, Covered, 9185, Paneled Daisy, YOP: 1992 only, $55-60; Fairy Light, 3 piece, 1167, Hobnail, YOP: 1994 only, $100-124; Rose Bowl, 8223, Orange Tree, $65-70. *Courtesy of Bev & John Spencer.*

Vase, 8.25", 8654, Sun Burst, YOP: 1991 only, $55-65; Bowl, 9", 9529, Verlys, YOP: 1996 only, $80-100. *Courtesy of Norma & Melvin Lampton.*

Hen on Nest, 5182, YOP: 1996 only, $55-65. *Courtesy of Norma & Melvin Lampton.*

Pear Box, 2980, YOP: 1995 only, $30-35; Slipper, 9295, Rose, YOP: 1990 only, $25-30; Vase, 9", 2752, Alpine Thistle, YOP: 1993 only, Frank Fenton Signature, $200-225; Trinket Box, 9384, Floral, YOP: 1990 only, $30-35; Pitcher, 9666, Sandwich, YOP: 1990 only, $45-55; Vase, 10.5", 8256, Mitre & Circle, YOP: 1991 only, $55-65; Perfume, 8.5", 1940, YOP: 1993 only, $75-80. *Courtesy of Norma & Melvin Lampton.*

Vase, 7.5", 9752, Daffodil, YOP: 1990 only, $55-60. *Courtesy of Anne Musser.*

Vase, 8253, Vessel of Gems, YOP: 1994 only, $80-90. *Courtesy of Williamstown Antique Mall.*

Vase, 9", 5750, Rose, YOP: 1992 only, $55-60; Vase, 9752, Daffodil, YOP: 1990 only, $55-60; Basket, 7", 2725, Button & Arch, $65-70; Vase, 7.5", Footed, 4655, Daffodil, YOP: 1992 only, $55-60. *Courtesy of Bev & John Spencer.*

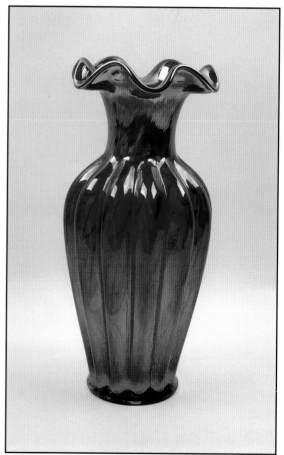

Vase, 11", Spiral, 3161, YOP: 1994 only, $90-100. *Courtesy of Bev & John Spencer.*

Vase, 6.5", 5150, Atlantis, YOP: 1992 only, $100-125; Planter, 8254, Mermaid, $250-300. *Courtesy of Bev & John Spencer.*

Sea Green Satin GE 1998

Sea Green Satin, a very unusual Opaque Carnival glass, was made for the Historic Collection in 1998. This color of glass was first used in sixteenth century China to imitate Celadon porcelain. As with others of the Historic Collection, this pattern employed moulds that had not been in use for some time, including the Mandarin and Empress vases, the square box with the Fish Finial (that is from the 1930s), and the Verleys Swallows Bonbon Box.

Items Not Pictured:

Candlesticks, 8.5", 9071, $40-45 ea.
Cat Slipper, 5290, $25-30
Vase, 8", 9458, Swan, $90-100

Bonbon with Cover, 6840, Butterflies, $100-125. *Courtesy of Myers Mystique.*

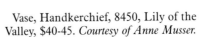

Vase, Handkerchief, 8450, Lily of the Valley, $40-45. *Courtesy of Anne Musser.*

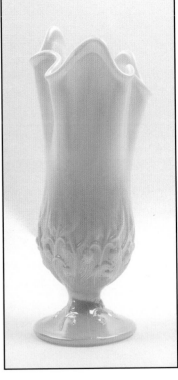

Epergne, 7601, $350+. *Courtesy of Myers Mystique.*

BACK: Vase, 8251, Mandarin, $80-90; Vase, 8252, Empress, $75-85; FRONT: Sunfish, 5167, $30-35; Basket, 2731, Lamb's Tongue, $65-70; Box, Square with Fish Finial, 9080, $55-60. *Courtesy of Myers Mystique.*

Perfume, Oval, 5301, $75-80. *Courtesy of Bobbie & Harold Morgan.*

Sea Mist Green Iridescent EZ 1991-94

Sea Mist Green Iridescent is one of the many Sea Mist Green color treatments that were made by Fenton in the early 1990s. This color, which was mostly use to produce covered Animal Boxes for Fenton's Easter series, was also used to make this series of dresser items and vases.

Items Not Pictured:

Atomizer, 5315, YOP: 1991 only, $30-35
Atomizer, 3 oz., Beaded, 5316, YOP: 1991 only, $30-35
Heart Trinket Box, 5786, Hummingbird, YOP: 1994 only, $20-25
Vase, Mini, 6569, Jacqueline, YOP: 1992-93, $20-25

Vase, Mini, 7151, Beaded Melon, YOP: 1992-93, $30-35. *Courtesy of Diane & Tom Rohow.*

Shell Pink PE 1988-91

Shell Pink is a very unusual color treatment in which a very light pink milk glass is sprayed with an iridescent spray, causing the glass to have a mother of pearl look much like the pinker inside of a clam. This treatment proved quite popular to both collectors and buyers in the late 1980s and was in Fenton's line for several years.

Items Not Pictured:

Basket, 7.25", Open Edge, 8335, $35-40
Trinket Box, Oval, 5783, Rose, $20-25
Hurricane Candle, 8376, Valencia, YOP: 1988-89, $25-30
Candy, Covered, 9185, Paneled Daisy, YOP: 1988-89, $35-40
Clock, 4638, Victorian, YOP: 1991 only, $25-30
Comport, 9223, Rose, $30-35
Slipper, 1995, Button & Daisy, $15-20
Toothpick, 8294, Paneled Daisy, YOP: 1988-89, $20-25
Bud Vase, 9256, Rose, $20-25
Vase, 9752, Daffodil, YOP: 1990-91, $30-35
Vase, 9", 5750, Rose, $30-35

Candy Box, 9480, Chessie, YOP: 1990-91, $100-124. *Courtesy of Bobbie & Harold Morgan.*

Basket, 7", 5730, Rose, $35-40; Basket, 6.5", 9240, Rose, $35-40. *Courtesy of Laurie & Richard Karman.*

Slipper, 9295, Rose, YOP: 1990-91, $20-25. *Courtesy of Chuck Bingham.*

Pearly Sentiments PT 1988-94/Rose Corsage MP 1989

Pearly Sentiments PT

Both Pearly Sentiments and Rose Corsage were unusual in the fact that each item had a porcelain rose applied to it. The Rose Corsage items were made on Shell Pink and a tiny blue garland was painted streaming around the applied rose. The Pearly Sentiments items were made on Iridescent Opal, affixed with the Porcelain Rose and small pink ribbon, and then sold with a small cardboard card which had either a saying or greeting on it.

Items Not Pictured:

Basket, 9539, Leaf, YOP: 1989-91, $30-35
Heart Box, 5780, Rose, YOP: 1988-94, $20-25
Paperweight, 8751, Heart, YOP: 1989 only, $15-20
Vase, 6", 9656, Paneled, YOP: 1989 only, $30-35

Comport, 9780, Heart, YOP: 1989 only, $30-35. *Courtesy of Mildred Potter.*

Basket, Mini, 6560, Diamond, YOP: 1994 only, $20-25. *Courtesy of Laurie & Richard Karman.*

Slipper, 9295, Rose, YOP: 1990-93, $20-25; Bell, 9763, Heart, YOP: 1989-94, $30-35. *Courtesy of Marilyn Bingham.*

Rose Corsage MP 1989

Items Not Pictured:

Trinket Box, 9384, Floral, $20-25
Hurricane Candle, 8376, Valencia, $20-25
Bud Vase, 9056, $20-25
Vase, 4", Basket weave, 9357, $20-25
Vase, 7", 7691, Aurora, $30-35

Comport, Open Edge,
8324, $30-35. *Courtesy of
Laurie & Richard Karman.*

Basket, 6.25", Paneled, 9239, $30-35.
Courtesy of Doris & Junior Devall.

Spruce Carnival US 1999

Spruce Carnival was Fenton's Carnival offering for 1999. This was one of the few times that a green based Carnival glass had been offered by the company. Quite beautiful, and vivid in color, this treatment proved to be very popular with collectors. Items to watch for in this pattern are the Grape & Cable Tobacco Jar, the Alley Cat, and the Mini Hand Vase.

Items Not Pictured:

Basket, 8.5", 2779, Lion, $55-65
Basket, 5930, Strawberry, $55-65
Pitcher, 8.5", 6869, $100-125

Alley Cat, 5177, $80-90; Tobacco Jar, 9188, Grape & Cable, $100-125; Hand Vase, Mini, 5153, $30-35; Duck Box, Covered, $55-65.
Courtesy of Myers Mystique.

Hand Vase, Mini, 5153, $30-35. *Courtesy of Diane & Tom Rohow.*

31

Stretch Glass, for those who do not realize it, is glass that while still warm is sprayed with a special metallic salt and then reheated; the edges are pulled, giving them a pulled and satin appearance. Fenton and other companies first used this procedure in the 1920s. After that, Fenton reissued Stretch several times, most notably in 1980 for their 75th Anniversary. This issue of Stretch was for the Historic Collection in 1994.

Items Not Pictured:

Basket, 9", Footed, 5551, $65-75
Basket, 7", Footed, 5555, $55-65
Rose Bowl, 3.5", 2759, $35-40
Bowl, 12", 5552, $75-80
Candle Holders, 4", 5526, $30-35 ea.
Urn, 4602, Diamond, $70-80
Vase, 7", JIP, 5553, $45-55

Bowl, 8", Open Edge, 2773, $85-90; Lion Box, 2799, $80-90. *Courtesy of Myers Mystique.*

Logo, 9799, $35-40; Epergne, 2 piece, 4802, Diamond Lace, $100-125.

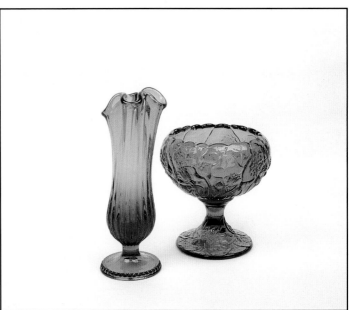

Vase, 8", Handkerchief, 5559, $45-55; Comport, 5.5", 5554, $45-55.
Courtesy of Shelia & Pete McMillian.

Epergne, 7601, $350+. *Courtesy of Bobbie & Harold Morgan.*

Jug, 8", 5562, $225-250; Goblets, 5562, $35-40 ea. *Courtesy of Myers Mystique.*

Teal Marigold OI 1988-89

Perhaps the most unusual Carnival glass treatment by Fenton was made in the late 1980s by taking Teal Royale and covering it with a Marigold Spray. This gave it a very unusual shine that has proved appealing to many people.

Items Not Pictured:

Bowl, 8283, Orange Tree & Berry, YOP: 1989 only, $40-45
Bowl, 6.5", Open Edge, 8323, YOP: 1988 only, $30-35
Bowl, 8428, Butterfly & Berry, YOP: 1988 only, $40-45
Comport, Footed, 8234, YOP: 1988 only, $30-40

Epergne, 4801, Diamond Lace, YOP: 1989 only, $125-150.

Basket, 6.25", Rose Footed, 9240, $55-60 NIL; Basket, Open Edge, 8335, YOP: 1988 only, $45-55. *Courtesy of Chuck Bingham.*

Candy, Covered, 9185, Paneled Daisy, YOP: 1989 only, $45-55; Comport, 8227, Pinwheel, YOP: 1989 only, $30-40; Basket, 8", 9137, Fine Cut & Block, YOP: 1989 only, $40-45. *Courtesy of Chuck Bingham.*

Vase, 9251, Mandarin, YOP: 1989 only, $90-100; Candy Box, 9480, Chessie, YOP: 1988 only, $125-150; Slipper, 1995, Daisy & Button, YOP: 1988 only, $15-20; Bowl, 8223, Leaf & Orange Tree, YOP: 1988 only, $30-40. *Courtesy of Chuck Bingham.*

Vase, 9251, Mandarin, YOP: 1989 only, $90-100. *Courtesy of Dorothy Wiggins.*

Candy Box, 9480, Chessie, YOP: 1988 only, $125-150. *Courtesy of Bobbie & Harold Morgan.*

Candy, Covered, 9185, Paneled Daisy, YOP: 1989 only, $45-55; Boot, 1990, Daisy & Button, YOP: 1989 only, $15-20; 5151, Bear Cub, YOP: 1988 only, $45-55; Pitcher, 36 oz., 8464, Water Lily, YOP: 1989 only, $65-75; 8406, Heart Fairy Light, YOP: 1988 only, $65-75.

Violet Satin XK 1999

Inspired by Fenton's Orchid color from the 1920s, Violet Satin was made for the Historic Collection in 1999. This color, a light lavender, was sprayed with metallic salts to make it look almost like a cross between stretch glass and carnival.

Items Not Pictured:

Water Set, 4650, Paneled Grape Pitcher, $150-200; Tumbler, $45-55

Perfume, 5320, $75-80

Vase, 8", 4559; Lance, $65-75

Cat Slipper, 5290, $25-30. *Courtesy of Myers Mystique.*

Epergne, 5 piece, 7601, $350+; Vase, 7", JIP, 2963 $60-65. *Courtesy of Phyllis & Terry Sterret.*

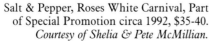

Salt & Pepper, Roses White Carnival, Part of Special Promotion circa 1992, $35-40. *Courtesy of Shelia & Pete McMillian.*

Opalescent/Opaline

Fenton returned to Opalescent Glass in a huge way in the early 1990s, after making hardly any of it for almost twenty years. Cranberry Opalescent was reintroduced in the early 1990s into Fenton line at the same time Fenton made several Opalescent lines for their Historic Collection. In the late 1990s Fenton introduced Champagne Satin and Misty Blue Opalescent (both Iridescent Opalescent lines), which proved quite popular.

Autumn Gold Opalescent AO 6/93-12/94

Throughout the past sixty years, whenever a certain treatment or color that had been produced by Fenton turns out not to be a sales success, it seems that later on the collectors become aware of it and it becomes one of the more sought after treatments. This was the way of the Honeysuckle color in the Coin Dot pattern, and also several of the Vasa Murrhina colors. It is too soon to tell with this Autumn Gold Opalescent, but it also wouldn't surprise me if it did become one of the more collected treatments in the next twenty years! Taking Autumn Gold produced this color, and casing it with French Opalescent, much like the way that Cranberry is produced. In this treatment, the Rib Optic mould was used, making a line of striking and beautiful items.

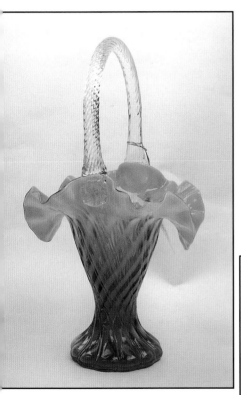

Basket, 11", Frank Fenton Signature, 1217, $70-75. *Courtesy of Laurie & Richard Karman.*

Vase, 7", Fine Ribbed, 1549, $45-50; Vase, 9.5", Fine Ribbed, 1559, $55-60; Vase, 7", Fine Ribbed, 1549 (Sample: Note Difference in Crimp), $65-70; Vase, 8", Feather Ribbed, 1218, $55-60; Pitcher, 32 oz., Fine Ribbed, 1569, $45-50; Vase, 7.5", 1558, Fine Ribbed, $55-60; Vase, 5", Fine Ribbed, 1599, $30-35. *Courtesy of Laurie & Richard Karman.*

Basket, 8", Fine Ribbed, 1531, $45-50. *Courtesy of Laurie & Richard Karman.*

Champagne Satin PQ 1997-

Fenton did not produce a true pink opalescent until the past fifteen years; in that time, two different pink opalescents were made. The first was Peaches 'N' Cream, which was produced in the late 1980s, and then ten year later, Champagne Satin was introduced into the Fenton line. This treatment, along with Misty Blue Satin, was one of several Opalescent treatments to be made with an iridescent finish, making for an unusual type of opalescent glass.

Items Not Pictured:

Basket, 6", 2731, $30-35
Trinket Box, Quilted, 5589, $20-25
Trinket Box, Rose, 5783, $20-25
Trinket Box, Humming Bird, 5786, $20-25
Box, Covered Dolphin, 9080, $20-25
Comport, Cactus, 3429, YOP: 1997, $25-30
Comport, 9120, Fine Cut & Block, 1998, $25-30
Ring holder, 9144, $10-15
Open Swan, 5127, 1999, $20-25
Slipper, 2931, $20-25
Slipper, 1995, Daisy & Button, 1998, $20-25
Bud Vase, Faberge, 9451, $15-20
Votive, 2 Way Leaf, 9596, 1998, $15-20
Vase, 11", 2782, Feather, 1997, $40-45

Trinket Box, 9384, Floral, $20-25.

Rose Bowl, Lily of the Valley, 8453, $20-35; Candlesticks, Lily of The Valley, 8475, $25-30 ea.; Basket, 8", Lily of the Valley, 6835, $30-35; Vase, 8450, Lily of the Valley, 1997, $25-30; Candy, Lily of the Valley, 8484, $35-40; Basket, Lily of the Valley, 8437, $35-40; Bell, 8265, Lily of the Valley, $30-35. *Courtesy of Mala Foust.*

Basket, 6", 2035, Ruffles, 1998, $35-40.
Courtesy of Laurie & Richard Karman.

Vase, Peacock, 8257, $55-60; Rose Bowl on Brass Stand, 5731, $25-30. *Courtesy of Laurie & Richard Karman.*

Vase, 5.5", Daffodil, 7759, $25-30; Vase, 7", Daffodil, 9752, $25-30. *Courtesy of Donna Hatch.*

Cranberry Opalescent CR 1970-1994

In the late 1970s, when Cranberry Opalescent was discontinued from the Fenton line, it was hardly noticed due to the fact that people at that time were more interested in the Satin Decorated items and Carnival Glass items the company was producing. It was over ten years later before another true run of Cranberry Opalescent would again be produced by Fenton. By that time, many people had discovered the older Cranberry Hobnail and Coin Dot from the 1940s and '50s, and welcomed this production with open arms. Since the early 1990s Cranberry Opalescent has been a mainstay in all Fenton catalogs, including pieces in many different optics and patterns, including their famous Hobnail and Coin Dot pattern.

Fern Optic, a pattern that Fenton had produced for many years in Cranberry for L.G. Wright, was one of the new patterns that had been developed for their Cranberry line. In an agreement with the L.G. Wright company, Fenton would not use any of their shapes, and would also change the pattern so it could be distinguished from the older L.G. Wright Daisy & Fern. This change was done by making the flowers with curved petals instead of straight petals.

Items Not Pictured:

Basket, 8.5", 3346, Hobnail, YOP: 1994 only, $65-75
Pitcher, 32 oz., 1872, Fern, YOP: 1991 only.
Pitcher, 10", 1873, Fern Optic, YOP: 1995, $125-150
Pitcher, 4.5", 2071, Drapery Optic, YOP: 1991-93, $65-70
Vase, 6", 1799, Diamond Optic, YOP: 1990 only, $55-65
Vase, JIP, 7.5", 3356, Hobnail, YOP: 1994 only, $85-90

Basket, 8", 1531, Rib Optic, YOP: 1995-96, $85-90; Basket, 6", 3133, Spiral, YOP: 1990-91, $75-80; Basket, 7", 1739, Diamond Optic, YOP: 1990-93, $85-90. *Courtesy of Laurie & Richard Karman.*

Cruet, 2095, Drapery Optic, YOP: 1990-93, $125-150. *Courtesy of Linda & John Flippen.*

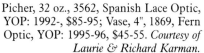

Picher, 32 oz., 3562, Spanish Lace Optic, YOP: 1992-, $85-95; Vase, 4", 1869, Fern Optic, YOP: 1995-96, $45-55. *Courtesy of Laurie & Richard Karman.*

Vase, 7", 1354, Dot Optic, YOP: 1990-93, $45-50; Cruet, 2095, Drapery Optic, YOP: 1990-93, $125-150; Vase, 4", 1784, YOP: 1991-93, $45-55. *Courtesy of Laurie & Richard Karman.*

Pitcher, 8", 3064, Spiral Optic, YOP: 1996, $125-150; Vase, Tulip, 10", 1353, Fine Dot, YOP: 1990-93, $100-125; Bowl, 10", 1726, Diamond Optic, YOP: 1990-93, $80-90; Basket, 7", 1739, Diamond Optic, YOP: 1990-93, $85-90. *Courtesy of Sarah Wells.*

Pitcher, 70 oz., 1874, Fern Optic, YOP: 1991-93, $175-200; Tumbler, 9 oz., 1840, Fern Optic, YOP: 1991-92, $7. *Courtesy of Phyllis & Terry Sterett.*

Vase, 7", 1843, Fern Optic, YOP: 1990, $65-70. *Courtesy of Laurie & Richard Karman.*

Basket, 7.5", 3346, Hobnail, YOP: 1994 only, $85-90. *Courtesy of Laurie & Richard Karman.*

Rose Bowl, 4.5", 3861, Hobnail, YOP: 1994 only, $45-50; Cranberry Opalescent CR, Fairy Light, 3 piece, 3380, Hobnail, YOP: 1994 only, $150-175; Pitcher, 5.5", 3366, Hobnail, YOP: 1994 only, $55-65. *Courtesy of Laurie & Richard Karman.*

Vase, Feather, 9.5", 1854, Fern Optic, YOP: 1995-96, $80-90; Vase, 11", 1852, Fern Optic, YOP: 1990-93, $150-200. *Courtesy of Laurie & Richard Karman.*

Pitcher, 16 oz., 3163, Spiral, YOP: 1990-91, $55-60; Vase, 11", 3161, Spiral, YOP: 1990-93, $100-125; Vase, 7", 1555, Rib Optic, YOP: 1997, $70-75; Vase, 9", 1554, Rib Optic, YOP: 1995-96, $90-95; Vase, 5", 1599, Rib Optic, YOP: 1996-96, $45-55. *Courtesy of Laurie & Richard Karman.*

Left: Tulip Vase, 10", 1353, Fine Dot, YOP: 1990-93, $100-125. *Courtesy of Phyllis & Terry Sterett.*

Right: Vase, 11", 3161, Spiral, YOP: 1990-93, $100-125. *Courtesy of Chuck Bingham.*

Left: Vase, 11", ???? Sample, $125-150. *Courtesy of Emogene Snyder.*

Right: Vase, 9", 8354, Basket weave, YOP: 1991 only, $100-125. *Courtesy of Laurie & Richard Karman.*

Vase, Tulip, 11.5", 3053, Rib Optic Vase, YOP: 1996, $100-125. *Courtesy of Laurie & Richard Karman.*

French Cream FO 1986-87/Minted Cream EO 1986-87/
Peaches 'N' Cream UO 1987-88

French Cream (French Opalescent) and Minted Cream, along with Peaches 'N' Cream (Pink Opalescent), were introduced in the mid-1980s. Both French Cream and Minted Cream were not the success that Fenton had hoped they would be, and they were discontinued in a little over a year's time. Some of the pieces that had been produced in these colors were later sold through the Gracious Touch party plan (see *Fenton Special Orders* books).

The Minted Cream color proves somewhat confusing to the collector, as it resembles the same shade of the later issued Persian Blue Opalescent. Keep in mind that most pieces of Persian Blue were issued in blown moulds such as Fern Optic and Coin Dot, whereas most of the items in Minted Cream were issued in pressed moulds. Also the color of Minted Cream seems to be softer and more muted than Persian Blue does.

Peaches 'n' Cream, was perhaps the most popular of the three Opalescent colors that were produced during this time. It was in the Fenton line for several years, and later on became one of the first colors used for their Historic Collection (see also Peaches 'n' Cream this chapter).

Item Description	Ware Number	Peaches 'n' Cream	Minted Cream	French Cream
Basket, 4.5", Rose	9535	$20-25	$20-25	$10-15
Basket, Butterfly & Berry	9234	$45-55	$40-45	$25-30
Basket, 7"	6634	$35-40	$30-35	$25-30
Basket, 7.5", Open Edge	8335	$35-40	$30-35	
Basket, 8", Vulcan	9544	$30-35	$25-30	$15-20
Bowl, Sheffield	6625	$20-25	$20-25	
Bowl, 5.5"	6626	$20-25	$20-25	$15-20
Bowl, 6.5", Open Edge	8323	$20-25	$20-25	
Bowl, 11"	6624	$25-30	$25-30	$20-25
Trinket Box, Teardrop	9685	$20-25	$20-25	$10-15
Trinket Box, Hexagonal	9687	$25-30	$20-25	$10-15
Candleholder	6672	$15-20 ea.	$15-20 ea.	$10-15 ea.
Candleholder/ Nut Vase	9571	$20-25	$15-20	$10-15
Heart Candy	9519	$20-25	$20-25	$15-20
Candy, Vulcan	9556		$25-30	
Candy, Sheffield	6688	$25-30	$25-30	
Small Hen on Nest	5186	$40-45	$35-40	
Comport	8234	$25-30	$20-25	
Slipper, Daisy & Button	1955	$20-25	$15-20	
Toothpick, Paneled Daisy	6688	$15-20	$15-20	
Toothpick	9572	$15-20	$15-20	
Vase, 4"	3952		$20-25	
Bud Vase, 6"	6650	$15-20	$15-20	
Vase, 7"	3195	$30-35	$30-35	$25-30
Vase, 11"	6654	$35-40	$40-45	$20-25
Vase, 13"	3196	$45-55	$40-45	$25-30
Vase, 14", Rib Optic	3197	$45-55	$40-45	$25-30
Votive	6655		$15-20	$10-15
Votive with Candle & Cup	6657	$15-20	$15-20	$10-15
Votive, 2.5"	9576	$15-20	$15-20	$10-15
Votive/Vase	9555	$15-20	$15-20	$10-15
Votive, 6"	9557	$15-25	$15-20	$10-15

Small Hen on Nest, 5186, 1986-87; Trinket Box, 9687, Hexagonal, YOP: 1986-87; Basket, 7", 6634, YOP: 1986-87. See table for values. *Courtesy of Wiggins Gifts.*

Small Hen on Nest, 5186, 1986-87. *Courtesy of Barbara & Harold Morgan.*

Trinket Box, 9865, Tear Drop, YOP: 1986-87. *Courtesy of Wiggins Gifts.*

Votive/Vase, 9555, YOP: 1986-87; Votive, 6", 9557, YOP: 1986 only; Bowl, 5.5", 6626, YOP: 1986-87; Candy, 6688, Sheffield, YOP: 1987 only; Basket, 7", 6634, YOP: 1986 only; Candleholders, 6672, YOP: 1986-87; Votive/Vase, 9555, YOP: 1986-87; Votive, 6", 9557, YOP: 1986 only. *Courtesy of Donna Hatch.*

Bowl, 5.5", 6626, YOP: 1986-87; Slipper, 1959, Daisy & Button, 1987-89; Heart Candy, 9519, YOP: 1986-87.

Votive, 6.5", 6657, YOP: 1986 only. *Courtesy of Linda & Dennis Sowers.*

Heart Candies, 9519, YOP: 1986-87. *Courtesy of Kansas City Fenton Finders.*

Trinket Box, 9687, Hexagonal, YOP: 1986-87; Basket, 7", 6634, Sheffield, YOP: 1986-87.

Slipper, 1955, Daisy & Button, YOP: 1987 only. *Courtesy of Lin & Rob Elbee.*

Fushia EH 1994

Fuchsia, possibly the most beautiful Opalescent color produced during the 1990s, also turned out to be the most difficult to produce and was only made for one year. Made by casing Gold Ruby (Cranberry) over Rose Magnolia, it proved to be both a successful and striking color.

Basket, 8", 2031, Drapery, $100-125; Basket, 6.5", 2033, Drapery, $100-125. *Courtesy of Laurie & Richard Karman.*

Vase, 6", 2058, Drapery, $70-75; Bowl, 10", 2025, Drapery, $100-125; Vase, 8.5", JIP, 2059, $80-90; Vase, 7", 2052, Drapery, $80-90; Pitcher, 6", 1215, Spiral, $100-125. *Courtesy of Laurie & Richard Karman.*

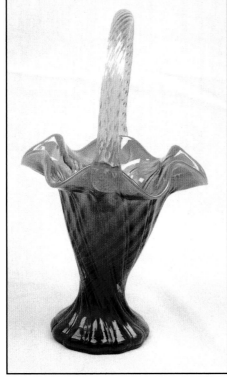

Basket, 11", 2077, Spiral, $125-150. *Courtesy of Laurie & Richard Karman.*

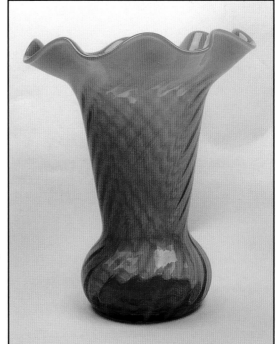

Vase, 10", Spiral, 1216, George Fenton Signature, $175-200. *Courtesy of Laurie & Richard Karman.*

Misty Blue Satin LR 1997-2000

Made as a champagne color to Champagne Opalescent, this color, like Champagne Opalescent and also Topaz Opalescent (from the same time period), had an Iridescent Satin finish on it. Misty Blue Satin proved quite popular with collectors and remained in Fenton's line for several years.

Items Not Pictured:

Basket, 5.5", 2919, YOP: 1999, $25-30
Basket, 8.5", 6630, Ribbed, YOP: 1999, $30-35
Rose Bowl, 6", with Brass Stand, 5371, YOP: 1998, $25-30
Rose Bowl, 8", 2929, Wildflower, YOP: 1998, $20-25
Trinket Box, 5783, Rose, $20-25
Trinket Box, 5786, Humming Bird, $20-25
Candy, Lily of the Valley, 8484, YOP: 1997, $35-40
Clock, 4.5", 8691, YOP: 1998, $20-25
Clock, 3.5", 8698, YOP: 1998, $20-25
Ring holder, 9144, Fine Cut & Block, YOP: 1998, $10-15
Bud Vase, 9451, Faberge, $20-25
Vase, 7.5", 4655, Daffodil, YOP: 1998, $20-25

Candy with Cover, 8454, Lily of the Valley, $35-40; Vase, 8450, Lily of the Valley, $25-30; Bell, 8265, Lily of the Valley, $30-35; Rose Bowl, 8453, Lily of the Valley, $20-25. *Courtesy of Mala Foust.*

Open Swan, 5127, 1997, $15-20; Votive, 2 Way Leaf, 9596, 1998, $20-25; Cat Slipper, 5290, 1998, $15-20. *Courtesy of Connie & Aaron Patient.*

Basket, 9.5", 1535, Diamond Paneled, $30-35. *Courtesy of Williamstown Antique Mall.*

Basket, 7.5", Silverton, 6830, 1997, $30-35. *Courtesy of Myers Mystique.*

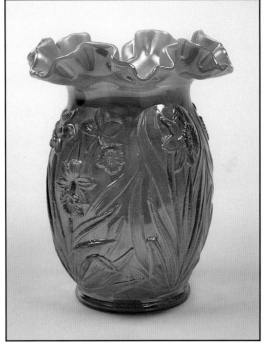

Left: Vase, 7.5", 7653, Daffodil, 1999, $30-35.

Right: Vase, 7.75", 9752, Daffodil, $30-35.

Opaline TG 1996

Opaline is one of Fenton's green colors from the 1990s that has proved to be somewhat difficult to tell apart from Minted Cream, Persian Blue Opalescent, and Sea Mist Green Opalescent. This treatment, though, has a decidedly blue cast to it, close to Fenton's Blue Opalescent from the 1950s.

Opaline was made for one year in 1996 as part of the Historic Collection. Many items made in this color were decorated with a Rose design and called Blush Rose (see Decorated section), but a line of Diamond Lace items were made, also in Opaline, plus the Cactus Cruet, which is quite scarce now.

Item Not Pictured:

Epergne, 10", 4808, Diamond Lace, $125-150

Basket, 9.5", 4835, Diamond Lace, $65-75; Logo, Oval, 9499, $50-55; Comport, 4854, Diamond Lace, $55-65. *Courtesy of Laurie & Richard Karman.*

Epergne, Mini, 4086, Diamond Lace, $45-55. *Courtesy of Kansas City Fenton Finders.*

Epergne, Mini, 4086, Diamond Lace, $45-55; Basket, 9.5", 4835,
Diamond Lace, $65-75; Logo, Oval, 9499, $50-55; Basket, 6",
Diamond Lace, 4833, $55-65. *Courtesy of Laurie & Richard Karman.*

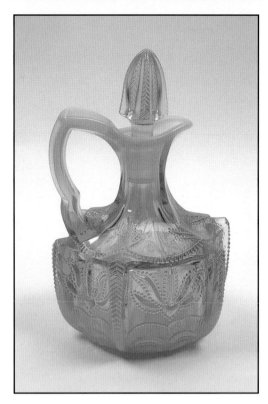

Cruet, 3463, Cactus, $150-200. *Courtesy of Bev
and Jon Spencer.*

Peaches 'N' Cream (Pink Opalescent) UO 1986-89

Peaches 'N' Cream Opalescent led a long and varied life in
Fenton's line throughout the late 1980s. First introduced to go
along with the quickly discontinued Minted Cream and French
Cream (see Minted Cream/French Cream/Peaches 'N' Cream
section), it later on was made in a line of Hobnail items, which
were sold by Fenton as one of the first Historic Collections. It
was also during this time that other items in Hobnail that were
not in the Historic Collection were made in Peaches 'N' Cream
for the Gracious Touch party plan.

Epergne, Mini, 3801, YOP: 1988 only, $100-125; Epergne, 3701,
YOP: 1988 only, $125-150. *Courtesy of Kansas City Fenton Finders.*

Basket, 10", 3830, Hobnail, YOP: 1988 only, $75-80; Basket, Looped
Handled, 3335, Hobnail, YOP: 1988 only, $45-55. *Courtesy of Laurie
& Richard Karman.*

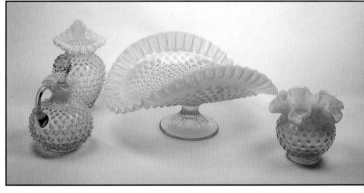

Vase, 6.5", Jack In the Pulpit, 3362, YOP: 1988 only, $35-40; Cruet,
3863, YOP: 1988 only, $85-90; Banana Boat, 3720, YOP: 1988 only,
$75-85; Vase, 4.5", 3854, YOP: 1988 only, $25-30. *Courtesy of Laurie
& Richard Karman.*

Basket, 4.5", 3834, YOP: 1988 only, $30-35; Water Set, 7 piece, 3908, YOP: 1988 only: Pitcher, $100-125; Tumblers, $20-25 ea.; Bonbon, 7.5", 3937, YOP: 1988 only, $25-30; Rose Bowl, 4.5", 3861, YOP: 1988 only, $25-30; Vase, 4", 3952, YOP: 1987-89, $25-30; Toothpick Holder, 3795, YOP: 1988 only, $15-20. *Courtesy of Laurie & Richard Karman.*

Pitcher, 52 oz., YOP: 1988 only, Pitcher, $100-125. Sold with Bowl, 12", 3000, $65-70 (Not Pictured). *Courtesy of Laurie & Richard Karman.*

Water Set, 7 piece, 3908, YOP: 1988 only, Pitcher, $100-125; Tumblers, $20-25 ea. *Courtesy of Phyllis & Terry Sterett.*

Punch Bowl Set, 3712, YOP: 1988 only, $300+. *Courtesy of Phyllis & Terry Sterett.*

Persian Blue Opalescent XC 1989-6/89

Made as one of the first Historic Collection treatments, this color has proved frustrating to the collector, both in trying to tell it from Fenton's other's Green and Blue Opalescent colors, and also, due to the fact, that's it's plain hard to locate!

Persian Blue, while very close in appearance to Minted Cream and Sea Mist Green Opalescent, still maintains a Blue appearance. Keep this in mind when looking for this color, plus the fact that most pieces in Persian Blue were made either in Coin Dot, Hobnail, or Fern Optic.

Items Not Pictured:

Butter, 9580, Button & Arch, $65-75
Comport, 8231, Multi-Fruit, $45-55
Epergne, 4801, Diamond Lace, $125-150

Basket, 7", Open Edge, 8330, Basket weave, $45-55. *Courtesy of Jan Hollingsworth.*

Basket, 7", with Looped Handle, 3334, Hobnail, $65-75; Basket, 4.5", 3834, Hobnail, $30-35. *Courtesy of Laurie & Richard Karman.*

Basket, 5.5", 1830, Fern Optic, $65-70; Basket, 5", Top Hat, 1435, Coin Dot, $45-55; Basket, 3-Toed, 9638, Grape, $45-55. *Courtesy of Laurie & Richard Karman.*

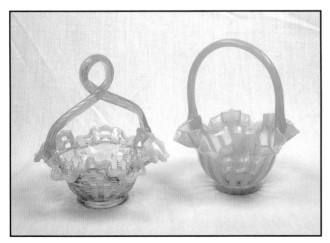

Basket, 7", Open Edge, 8330, Basket weave, $45-55; Basket, 7", 3138, Spiral Optic, $65-75. *Courtesy of Laurie & Richard Karman.*

Bowl, 10", 2323, Double Wedding Ring Optic, $65-70. *Courtesy of Sarah Wells.*

Bowl, DC, 9027, Grape & Cable, $80-85. *Courtesy of Sarah Wells.*

Water Set, 7 piece, 3908: Hobnail Pitcher, $125-150; Tumblers, $30-35 ea.; Water Set, 7 piece, 1404: Coin Dot Pitcher, $125-150; Tumbler, $35-40 ea. *Courtesy of Laurie & Richard Karman.*

Punch Set, 3712, Hobnail, $450+. *Courtesy of Laurie & Richard Karman.*

Cruet, 1865, Fern Optic, $100-125; Vase, Tulip, 10", 1353, Fine Dot, $75-80; Cruet, 3863, Hobnail, $75-80; Creamer, 1461, Coin Dot, $30-35; Top Hat, 1492, Coin Dot, $30-35. *Courtesy of Laurie & Richard Karman.*

Vase, Tulip, 10", 1353, Fine Dot, $75-80; Basket, 5.5", 1830, Fern Optic, $65-70. *Courtesy of Sarah Wells.*

Provincial Blue OO 1987-89

Provincial Blue was the color that was brought in to replace Minted Cream. This color, due to the similarities to Sapphire Blue Opalescent, has proved somewhat confusing to collectors. Keep in mind that Provincial Blue, when placed next to Sapphire Blue, seems more washed out and not as vivid as Sapphire Blue.

Items Not Pictured:

Trinket Box, Oval, 4.5", 5783, Rose, YOP: 1988-89, $25-30
Bowl, 13", 1627, Wide Rib, $30-35
Bowl, 6.5", Open Edge, 8323, $20-25
Candle Holder, 2 Way, 9569, $20-25 ea.
Hurricane Candle, 11", 8376, Valencia, $25-30
Alarm Clock, 8691, $30-35
Comport, 6.5", 9223, Rose, $30-35
Slipper, 1995, Daisy & Button, $20-25
Toothpick, 8294, Paneled Daisy, $20-25
Bud Vase, 9256, Rose, $25-30
Vase, 4", 3952, $25-30
Vase, 5", 7620, Aurora, $25-30
Vase, 7", 2057, Curtain, $30-35
Vase, 9752, Daffodil, $40-45
Vase, 11", 1677, Melon, $55-65

Swan, 5127, $25-30; Basket, 6.75", Open Edge, 8335, YOP: 1988-89, $35-40.

Basket, 9537, Strawberry Footed, $35-40; Basket, 6.75", Open Edge, 8335, YOP: 1988-89, $35-40. *Courtesy of Laurie & Richard Karman.*

Trinket Box, 5", 8304, Valencia, $30-35; Nut Dish, 9531, Strawberry, $25-30.

Basket, 7.5", 9237, Rose, $45-55; Swan, 5127, $25-30; Candy, Footed, 9284, Rose, $40-45. *Courtesy of Bobbie & Harold Morgan.*

Comport, 7.75", 9222, Rose, $30-35; Vase, 9", 5750, Rose, YOP: 1988-89, $35-40; Bud Vase, 9256, Rose, $20-25; Candy, Footed, 9284, Rose, $40-45. *Courtesy of Donna Hatch.*

Heart Candy, 9519, $20-25. *Courtesy of Janet & Ken Wilke.*

Comport, Open Edge, 8324, $30-35.

Rose Magnolia RV 1993-94

Rose Magnolia was in the Fenton Historic Collection in 1994. This color, which is more intense than Peaches 'N' Cream, was made from neodymium, a rare earth element, which also causes this glass to change hues under certain types of lighting. Scarce items in this treatment are the Hobnail Punch Set and Cruet.

Items Not Pictured:

Basket, Mini, 6556, Aztec, YOP: 1994 only, $25-30
Basket, 2728, Button & Arch, YOP: 1994 only, $45-50
Comport, 2742, Grape, YOP: 1994 only, $35-40
Cruet, 3863, Hobnail, YOP: 1993 only, $70-80
Vase, 7.5", Tulip, 3356, Hobnail, YOP: 1993 only, $45-50
Vase, 4.5", 3854, Hobnail, YOP: 1993 only, $30-35

Basket, 7", 3337, Hobnail, $55-65; Basket, 4.5", 3834, Hobnail, YOP: 1993 only, $35-40; Basket, 8460, Lily of the Valley, YOP: 1994 only, $55-65. *Courtesy of Laurie & Richard Karman.*

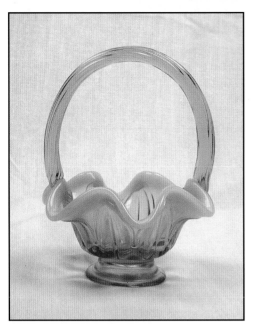

Basket, 2731, Lamb's Tongue, YOP: 1994 only, $45-50. *Courtesy of Laurie & Richard Karman.*

Epergne, 3701, Hobnail, YOP: 1993 only, $150-200. *Courtesy of Phyllis & Terry Sterett.*

Puff Box, 6570, Paneled Grape, YOP: 1994 only, $35-40. *Courtesy of Connie & Aaron Patient.*

Vase, 6.25", with Bow, 9754, Caprice, YOP: 1994 only, $45-55; Slipper, 9295, Rose, YOP: 1994 only, $25-30; Candy Box, Footed, 3784, Hobnail, YOP: 1993 only, $65-70. *Courtesy of Laurie & Richard Karman.*

Master Punch Set, 3712, Hobnail, YOP: 1993 only, $350+. *Courtesy of Phyllis & Terry Sterett.*

Pitcher, 54 oz., 3764, Hobnail, YOP: 1993 only,
$125-150; Tumblers, 9 oz., 3949, Hobnail,
YOP: 1993 only, $30-35. *Courtesy of Phyllis &*
Terry Sterett.

Vase, Handkerchief, 8450, Lily of the Valley, YOP: 1994 only, $45-50;
Basket, 8460, Lily of the Valley, YOP: 1994 only, $55-65; Rose Bowl,
8453, Lily of the Valley, YOP: 1994 only, $55-65; Bell, 8265, Lily of the
Valley, YOP: 1994 only, $30-35; Vase, Handkerchief, 8450, Lily of the
Valley, YOP: 1994 only, $45-50. *Courtesy of Mala Foust.*

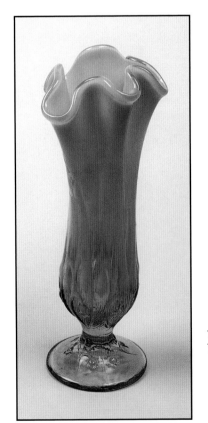

Vase, Handkerchief, 8450, Lily of the Valley,
YOP: 1994 only, $45-50.

Sapphire Blue Opalescent BX 1990-6/90

Sapphire Blue was Fenton's choice for their Historic Collection in 1990. This color was made in a line of blown optic items, in the Fern pattern, and also a line of pressed pieces in the Lily of the Valley pattern, plus several other pressed items. The Lily of the Valley items prove somewhat confusing to collectors, as several items in Lily of the Valley were also produced in Provincial Blue for Fenton's Gracious Touch party plan.

Bowl, 10", 8229, Heart & Flowers, $75-80. *Courtesy of Sarah Wells.*

Basket, 5.5", 1820, Fern, $45-55; Basket, 7", 1832, Fern, $65-75. *Courtesy of Sarah Wells.*

Bud Vase, 8458, Lily of the Valley, $30-35; Candy Box, 8489, Lily of the Valley, $65-75; Basket, 8437, Lily of the Valley, $55-65. *Courtesy of Sarah Wells.*

Rose Bowl, 8453, Lily of the Valley, $40-45. *Courtesy of Sarah Wells.*

Water Set, 1802: Fern Pitcher, $125-150; Tumbler, $35-45; Bowl, 10", 1826, Fern, $125-150 with Holder; Vase, Tulip, 10", Fern, $75-85; Cruet, 1860, Fern, $125-150. *Courtesy of Sarah Wells.*

Epergne, 4801, Diamond Lace, $150-175. *Courtesy of Sarah Wells.*

Vase, 3.5", 8652, Regency, $25-30.

Table Set, Mini, 4 piece, 9700, $100-125. *Courtesy of Sarah Wells.*

Sea Mist Green Opalescent LO/Jade Opaline AP 1991-93

First known as Jade Opaline (AP), then Sea Mist Green Opalescent, this color, while similar to Minted Cream, Opaline, and Persian Blue Opalescent, has a decidedly Green cast to it. Made from the popular transparent color of Sea Mist Green, Sea Mist Green Opalescent stayed in Fenton's line for several years.

Items Not Pictured:

Candleholder, 2 way, 9596, $25-30
Clock, 891, $30-35
Comport, 6.5", 9223, Rose, $35-40
Vase, 4.5", 9157, Fine Cut & Block, $25-30
Vase, 8", 9758, Stylized, $45-55
Vase, 9", 8354, Basket weave, YOP: 1991 only, $45-55
Vase, Swung, 2753, Stylized, YOP: 1993 only, $35-45
Bud Vase, 11", 9256, Rose, YOP: 1993 only, $25-30

Color comparison of Sea Mist Green Opalescent (L) and Persian Blue Opalescent (R).

Basket, 7.25", 9237, Rose, YOP: 1993 only, $45-50. *Courtesy of Laurie & Richard Karman.*

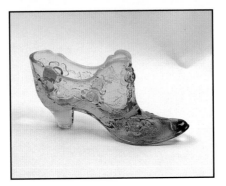

Slipper, 9295, Rose, $25-30.

Covered Candy, 9280, Butterfly,
$35-45. *Courtesy of Bobbie &
Harold Morgan.*

Tumbler Basket, 9249, Rose, $40-45.
Courtesy of Donna Hatch.

Stiegel Blue Opalescent BO 1991-6/91

Stiegel Blue Opalescent was named for William Henry Stiegel, a glassmaker from the eighteenth century noted for the different vibrant colors that he produced. This color of Blue Opalescent was made from the same formula that was used throughout the 1930s to the 1950s to produced Blue Opalescent at Fenton. Many of the items made in this issue were from Westmoreland moulds that Fenton was using with an agreement from Levay Importing.

Items Not Pictured:

Butter, 4667, Panel Grape, $55-65
Cake Plate, 11", Opened Edge, 4671, Ring & Petal, $55-65
Candle Stick, 3", Opened Edge, 4672, Ring & Petal, $30-35 ea.
Comport, Covered, 4612, Saw tooth, $55-65
Creamer & Sugar, 4673, Peacock, $45-$55 pr.
Water Set, 4650, Panel Grape Pitcher, $125-150; Tumblers, $45-55 ea.
Vase, 9", Tulip, 4653, Panel Grape, $55-65

Basket 7", 4632, Wildflower, $45-55.
Courtesy of Sarah Wells.

Basket, 6", 4633, Paneled
Grape, $30-35; Water Set,
Mini, 4614, Pitcher, $35-45;
Tumblers, $15-20 ea.
Courtesy of Sarah Wells.

Basket, 4613, Mini, Paneled Grape, $30-35. *Courtesy of Bobbie & Harold Morgan.*

Punch Set, 4601, Panel Grape, $350-400. *Courtesy of Phyllis & Terry Sterett.*

Bowl, 10.25", Open Edge, 4627, Ring & Petal, $65-75. *Courtesy of Sarah Wells.*

Compote, 6.5", Footed, 4693, Colonial, $45-55. *Courtesy of Shelia & Pete McMillian.*

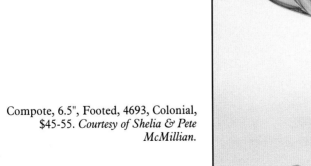

Topaz Opalescent TO 1988

There is one thing to remember when collecting Topaz (Vaseline) Opalescent (besides the fact that it glows under a black light) that has been made by Fenton: that there are actually four time periods during which this color was produced! The first three of these time periods amounted to two years in length each (1940-42; 1959-61; 1979-81). This issue of Topaz Opalescent was only in Fenton's line for six months! I have found items in this line of Topaz Opalescent are also the hardest to find, due to the short run of the color at this time.

Basket, 9435, Drapery, $125-150; Basket, Butterfly & Berry, 9134, $125-150; Basket, Looped Handled, 9436, Drapery, $125-150. *Courtesy of Laurie & Richard Karman.*

Nappy, 3-footed, 8442, $45-50. *Courtesy of Kill Creek Antiques.*

Basket, Butterfly & Berry, 9134, $125-150; Bowl, Butterfly & Berry, 8428, $125-150; Hat, Butterfly & Berry, 9495, $80-90. *Courtesy of Kill Creek Antiques.*

Bowl, Footed, Drapery, 9425, $75-80; Bowl, Curtain, 8454, $75-80. *Courtesy of Kill Creek Antiques.*

Breakfast Set, Regency, 8603: includes Butter, $200-225; Creamer, $65-70; Sugar, $65-70; and Spooner, $65-70. *Courtesy of Kill Creek Antiques.*

Butterfly on Stand, 5171,
$85-90.

Water Set, 3407, Cactus, Pitcher,
$300-350; Tumblers, $55-65 .
*Courtesy of Laurie & Richard
Karman.*

Topaz Opalescent TS 1997

I did not include this run of Topaz Opalescent in the section above simply due to the fact that the purist in this color, many times, ignores this run due to the iridescent satin finish it has. This color was the 1997 entry to the Historic Collection. The fact is, whether you hate it because of its finish or love it, it is a beautiful and exceptionally hard color to find.

Items Not Pictured:

Nut Dish, 8248, Scroll & Eye, $30-35
Slipper, 9295, Rose, $25-30

Epergne, 5 piece, 7601, $350+. *Courtesy of Kansas
City Fenton Finders.*

Basket, 8.5", 1158, Hobnail, $55-60; Vase, 8.5", 2851, Wild
Rose, $45-55; Basket, 5.5", 2919, Paneled Grape, $45-55.
Courtesy of Connie & Aaron Patient.

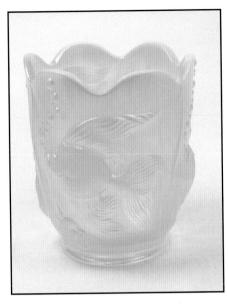

Vase, 5150, Alantis, $75-80. *Courtesy of John & Mary Lou Tannery.*

Vase, 5150, Alantis, $75-80; Basket, 5.5", 2919, Panel Grape, $45-55. *Courtesy of Bobbie & Harold Morgan.*

Punch Bowl Set, 10 piece, 9750, $350+. *Courtesy of Williamstown Antique Mall.*

Overlay

Throughout the twentieth century, Fenton was one of the few U.S. glass companies that had the capacities to produce Overlay glass. Ruby Overlay had been produced by Fenton since the 1940s. In the early 1980s its name was changed to Country Cranberry. In the late 1980s Fenton made another attempt to produce Mulberry Overlay, which had been attempted in the early 1940s. This time it was cased with Twilight Blue, giving it a somewhat paler cast than the original Mulberry. It was again produced in the late 1980s, after the original formula was re-discovered and the Ocean Blue Color was developed to produce it with. In the late 1990s, two new types of Overlay were tried: the first was Royal Purple, which was Ruby Glass cased with Cobalt, making for more of a darker and intense Mulberry style treatment. This treatment was used mostly in decorated ware until the Lifestyles (see the Special Series chapter.) line premiered in the late 1990s. The second treatment was Tranquility, which was Cobalt cased with Aquamarine, which actually made for an odd but unique color combination. This treatment remained in Fenton's line for several years in the late 1990s.

Country Cranberry CC 1985-94

Country Cranberry, which was originally Ruby Overlay, is possibly the longest running treatment, ever produced by Fenton. It was first issued in 1942, in the Diamond Optic pattern, along with the original issue of Mulberry. Since that time, it has been in the Fenton line, in several different optics, or one shape or another, till the present day. The name was changed to Country Cranberry in the early 1980s and is now simply called Cranberry. Made in virtually every blown mould that Fenton has in their inventory, the listings for this time period seem endless!

Items Not Pictured:

Bowl, 6", 1506, with Crystal Base, YOP: 1997, $65-75
Bowl, 9.5", 9723, Caprice, YOP: 1987-91, $45-50
Rose Bowl, 9126, Poppy, YOP: 1994 only, $45-65
Candy Box, 4.5", 6080, Wave Crest, YOP: 1991-93, $100-125
Cruet, 2095, Drapery Optic, YOP: 1991-92, $100-125
Pitcher, 32 oz., 1432, Coin Dot, YOP: 1982-94, $65-75
Vase, 5", 2056, Curtain, YOP: 1993-94, $80-90
Vase, Fan, 6", 3238, Wide Rib, YOP: 1992-93, $35-55
Vase, 8", 1218, Feather Rib, YOP: 1994 only, $65-75
Vase, 8", 1648, Reverse Melon, $65-75
Vase, 8", Swan, 9458, $80-90
Vase, 8", 3559, Spanish Lace, YOP: 1997, $45-55
Mandarin Vase, 8251, YOP: 1990 only, $100-125
Vase, 8354, Basket weave, YOP: 1994 only, $80-90

Basket, 7.5", 7139, Melon, $65-75; Basket, 6", 1731, Diamond, $35-40; Basket, 8.25", 9434, Jacqueline, YOP: 1989-91, $80-90. *Courtesy of Laurie & Richard Karman.*

Basket, 8.5", 2762, Poppy, YOP: 1994 only, $100-125; Basket, 9.5", 9730, Caprice, YOP: 1987-91, $75-80. *Courtesy of Laurie & Richard Karman.*

Basket, 7", 2534, Daisy, YOP: 1985-87, $65-70; Vase, 8", Drape, $55-65; Vase, 8.5", 1478, Coin Dot, YOP: 1987-94, $55-65. *Courtesy of Dorothy Wiggins.*

Basket, 8.5", 9464, Jacqueline, YOP: 1989-94, $65-70; Basket, 11", 7435, YOP: 1985-89, $100-125; Vase, 4", 1557, $25-30; Basket, 8.5", 1445, Coin Dot, YOP: 1987-88, $90-100. *Courtesy of Laurie & Richard Karman.*

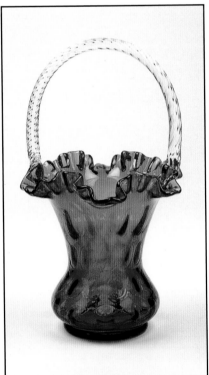

Basket, 8.5", 1445, Coin Dot, YOP: 1987-88, $90-100. *Courtesy of Trish & Harvey Holton.*

Jug, 6", 2566, Daisy, YOP: 1990-91, $40-45; Vase, 6", 2257, Daisy, $30-35; Vase, 6.5", 1553, Rib Urn, YOP: 1988-92, $35-40. *Courtesy of Laurie & Richard Karman.*

Basket, 9.5", 1735, Beaded Melon, YOP: 1988-89, $55-75. *Courtesy of Mildred & Roland Potter.*

Bowl, 10", 1728, Diamond, YOP: 1988-94, $65-75. *Courtesy of Phyllis & Terry Sterett.*

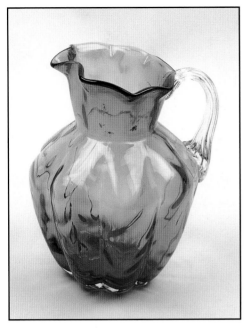

Pitcher, Melon, 1866, Fern,
YOP: 1985-92, $55-65. *Courtesy
of Myers Mystique.*

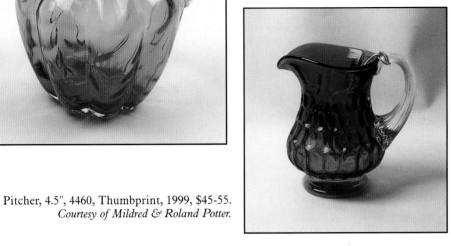

Pitcher, 4.5", 4460, Thumbprint, 1999, $45-55.
Courtesy of Mildred & Roland Potter.

Cruet, 7063, $75-80.

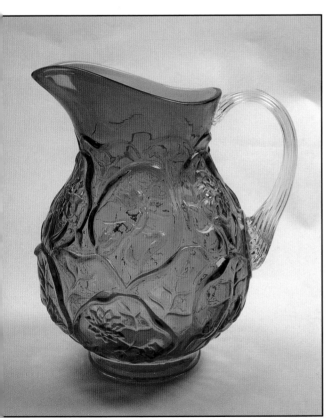

Salt & Pepper, 9500, Leaf, YOP: 1990-
92, $65-70. *Courtesy of Shelia & Pet
McMillian.*

Pitcher, 8464, Waterlily, 1997, $90-100. *Courtesy of Mildred
& Roland Potter.*

Pitcher, 4.5", 9760, Caprice, YOP: 1987-92, $45-55; Basket,
8.5", 9732, Caprice, YOP: 1987-91, $55-65; Vase, 4.5", 9753,
Caprice, $30-35; Vase with Bow, 6.25", 9754, Caprice, YOP:
1988-92, $35-40; Rose Bowl, 8", 9751, Caprice, YOP: 1987-88,
$40-45. *Courtesy of Mildred & Roland Potter.*

Pitcher, 4.5", 2071, Empress, YOP: 1991-93, $35-40; Basket, 7.5", 7139, Melon, $65-75; Pitcher, Sandwich, 5", 9666, YOP: 1990-92, $65-70; Basket, 8.75", 3132, YOP: 1985-94; Vase, 4.5", 9452, Jacqueline, YOP: 1989-90, $30-35; Basket, 8", 1434, Coin Dot, YOP: 1997, $55-65. *Courtesy of Mildred & Roland Potter.*

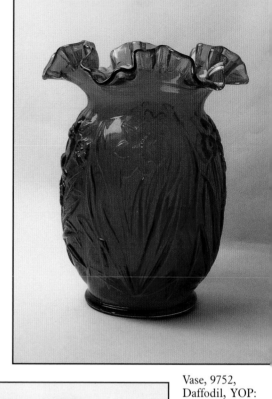

Vase, 9752, Daffodil, YOP: 1987-94, $45-55.

Vase, 8.5", 1478, Coin Dot, YOP: 1987-94, $55-65; Vase, 11", 3161, Spiral, YOP: 1985-94, $80-90; Bowl, 9.5", 9442, Jacqueline, YOP: 1989-94, $65-70; Vase, 8", 1743, Beaded Melon, YOP: 1988-89, $45-50. *Courtesy of Laurie & Richard Karman.*

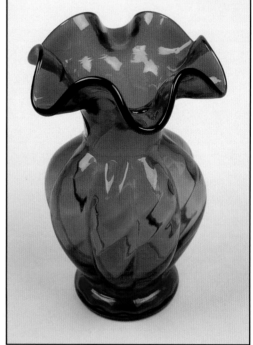

Vase, 6", 1222, Swirl Vase, YOP: 1993-94, $45-55. *Courtesy of Diane & Tom Rohow.*

Vase, 6", 3167, $30-35.

Vase, 9050, Dot & Flute, $45-55; Vase, 4.5", 9753, Caprice, YOP: 1987-88, $40-45; Vase, Melon, 6", 1214, YOP: 1994 only, $45-55. *Courtesy of John & Mary Lou Tannery.*

Empress Vase, 8252, YOP: 1990 only, $80-90; Bell, 6590, Spiral, YOP: 1992-94, $35-40; Vase, Melon, 6", 1214, YOP: 1994 only, $45-55; Pitcher, 1860, Fern, YOP: 1990 only, $55-60; Vase, 6.5", 3183, Tulip, YOP: 1992-94, $45-55. *Courtesy of Bobbie & Harold Morgan.*

Vase, 8", 2750, Melon, YOP: 1997, $40-45.

Vase, 7.5", 2054, YOP: 1985-87, $25-30; Vase, 8", Reverse Melon, 1646, YOP: 1998, $30-35; Vase, 11", 2782, Feather, $65-70; Vase, 5.5", 7793, Daffodil, $40-45; Vase, 8.5", 1498, Coin Dot, YOP: 1994 only, $55-60; Vase, 6.5", 3290, Rib, $40-45. *Courtesy of Mildred & Roland Potter.*

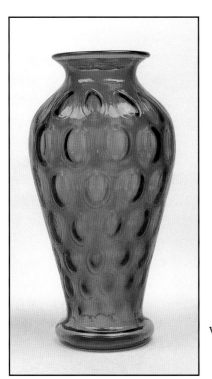

Vase, 9", 1433, Coin Dot, $75-80.

Vase, Wheat, 5858, YOP: 1985-87, $75-80. *Courtesy of Vickie Ticen.*

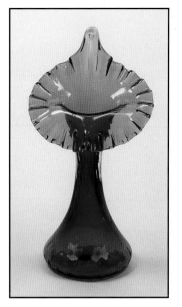

Vase, 10", Tulip, 1353, Fine Dot, YOP: 1991-94, $80-90. *Courtesy of Phyllis & Terry Sterett.*

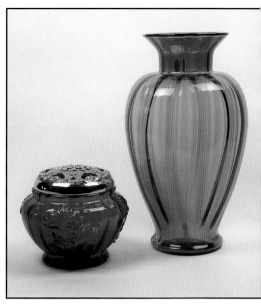

Box with Metal Cover, 5", 1589, $55-60; Vase, 10.5", 1552, Rib Urn, YOP: 1988-89, $70-80.

Vase, 10.5", 1443, YOP 1990-91, $90-100. *Courtesy of Bev & John Spencer.*

Cranberry Opaline KH 1990/JADE OPALINE AG 6/90-12/90

Both of these colors were made in 1990. Cranberry Opaline is very close in appearance to what would be call a deep, deep Peach Blow, while there is no mistaking the green hue of Jade Opaline.

Item Description	Ware Number	Cranberry Opaline	Jade Opaline
Bowl, 14"	7727	$100-125	$100-125
Bud Vase, Tulip, 6"	7373	$60-65	$55-60
Vase, 7"	7371	$90-100	$80-90
Vase, Basket weave, 8"	8354	$90-100	$80-90
Vase, 13"	7372	$125-150	$100-125

Bud Vase, Tulip, 6", 7373.

Bowl, 14", 7727. $60-65. *Courtesy of Phyllis & Terry Sterett.*

Vase, 7", 7371.

Vase, 8354, Basket weave.

Mulberry MG 1989-92

The Mulberry treatment, though quite popular with collectors, has been possibly one of the hardest colors for Fenton to produce. First introduced in 1942, it was quickly taken out of Fenton's line because the consistency of the color could not be contained from item to item. This treatment was not tried again until the late 1980s when it was discovered that the original formula to produced Mulberry had been lost. This time it was done with Gold Ruby and a blue color known as Twilight Blue, which was in Fenton's line at that time. Though similar to the original Mulberry, the color did not strike as well, and did not have the same hue and depth as the original. Several years later, Mulberry was again experimented with using the Salem Blue color, which was closer in color to the Blue that was used in the 1940s for both Mulberry and Aqua Crest. With this formula, Fenton has been able to produce a true and vibrant Mulberry, which has since 1996 been used in the Connoisseur line and Historic Collection line several times.

Items Not Pictured:

Vase, 7.5", 9655, $75-80
Vase, 11.5", 1797, Diamond Quilted, YOP: 1989 only, $100-125

Basket, 8", 1434, Coin Dot, $100-125; Basket, 6", 1731, Diamond, $65-70; Basket, 8.5", Jacqueline, 9464, YOP: 1991-92, $100-125. *Courtesy of Laurie & Richard Karman.*

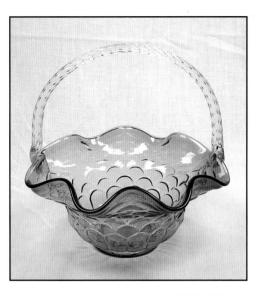

Basket, 10.5", 9139, Jacqueline, YOP: 1989-91, $100-125. *Courtesy of Laurie & Richard Karman.*

Vase, 4.5", 9452, Jacqueline, $65-70; Vase, 6.25", with Bow, 9754, Caprice, $75-80; Vase, 7.5", 9655, $70-75; Vase, 7.75", 9752, Daffodil, $75-80; Tulip Vase, 10", 1353, Fine Dot, $100-125; Cruet, 2095, Drapery Optic, YOP: 1991-92, $125-150. *Courtesy of Chuck Bingham.*

Bowl, 9.5", 9442, Jacqueline, $75-80; Pitcher, 32 oz., 1432, Coin Dot, $100-125. *Courtesy of Bobbie & Harold Morgan.*

Vase, 7.5", 9655, $70-75; Vase, 6", 2557, Daisy, $65-70; Vase, 11", Spiral, 3163, YOP: 1991-92, $125-150; Jug, 6", 2566, Daisy, $75-80; Pitcher, 4.5", 2071, YOP: 1991-92, $75-80. *Courtesy of Laurie & Richard Karman.*

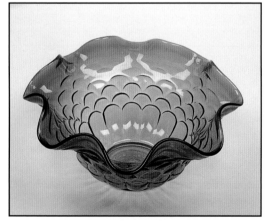

Bowl, 9.5", 9165, Jacqueline, YOP: 1989 only, $70-90. *Courtesy of Laurie & Richard Karman.*

Tulip Vase, 10", 1353, Fine Dot, $100-125. *Author's Collection.*

Vase, 4", 1784, $45-50. *Courtesy of Donna Hatch.*

Transparent

"As many colors as in the rainbow" is an apt description of Fenton's production of Transparent colors throughout the late 1980s and 1990s. Many different shades of blue, green, and pink were developed, mainly to have as base colors for their other lines of Carnival, Overlays, and Opalescent Glass.

Among the most popular of Fenton's Transparent colors produced in the 1990s was Dusty Rose. It was not only the most popular, but also the longest lived. From its introduction in 1984, till it was discontinued in 1997, this color was made in almost as many items as Country Cranberry had been produced in. It was replaced in 1997 with Empress Rose, a deeper and richer pink color, which is still in the Fenton line. Ruby, another long produced color, figured prominently in Fenton's catalog line, and also in items produced especially for the Christmas season.

Aquamarine AA 1999

Items Not Pictured:

Basket, 5", 4838, Diamond Lace, $15-20
Rose Bowl with Brass Stand, 5371, 1999, $35-40
Trinket Box, Hummingbird, 5786, $20-25
Clock, 3.5", 8698, 1999, $25-30
Ring holder, 9144, Fine Cut & Block, 1999, $5-10
Slipper, 1995, Daisy & Button, 1999, $10-15
Vase, 11", Tulip, 6155, 1999, $35-40

AQUAMARINE AA, YOP: 1999:
Basket, Ribbed, 6630, $35-40;
Trinket Box, Rose, 5783, $20-25.
Courtesy of Connie & Aaron Patient.

AQUAMARINE AA, YOP: 1999: Swan, 5127, $15-20; Butterfly, 5271, YOP: 1999, $30-35; Fairy Light, 9404, Faberge, 1999, $40-45; Bell, 9265, Butterfly, 1999, $20-25; Basket, 9", 6480, 1999, $35-40; Slipper, 1995, Daisy & Button, $20-25. *Courtesy of Myers Mystique.*

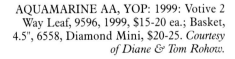

AQUAMARINE AA, YOP: 1999: Votive 2 Way Leaf, 9596, 1999, $15-20 ea.; Basket, 4.5", 6558, Diamond Mini, $20-25. *Courtesy of Diane & Tom Rohow.*

Autumn Gold AM 6/93-12/93

Items Not Pictured:

Basket, 8", Vulcan, 9544, $10-15
Candy, Barred Oval, 8388, $15-20
Clock, Alarm, 8691, $15-20
Comport, Empress, 9229, $10-15
Slipper, Daisy & Button, 1995, $10-15
Vase, 11", 3161, $25-30
Vase, 5", Aurora, 7620, $10-15
Vase, Flute & Dot, 9050, $10-15

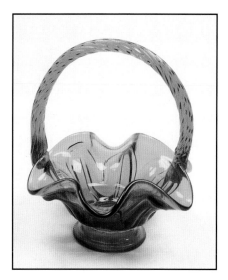

AUTUMN GOLD AM, YOP: 6/93-12/93: Basket, Lamb's Tongue, 2731, $20-25. *Courtesy of Laurie & Richard Karman.*

Blue Royale KK 1988-90

Items Not Pictured:

Basket, 8.5", Caprice, 9732, $35-40
Bowl, 9.5", Caprice, 9723, YOP: 1988-89, $25-30
Rose Bowl, 8", Caprice, 9751, YOP: 1988 only, $20-25
Candleholder, 8.5", 9071, YOP:1989-90, $25-30 ea.
Compote, 6.75", Open Edge, 8324, YOP: 1988-89, $20-25
Wine, 9244, 5.5", Empress, 9244, YOP: 1989-90, $15-20
Goblet, 6.75, Empress, 9245, $15-20
Pitcher, 4.5", Caprice, 9760, YOP: 1988 only, $25-30
Slipper, Daisy & Button, 1995, $20-25
Toothpick, Paneled Daisy, 8924, YOP: 1988-89, $15-20
Vase, 4", 3952, YOP: 1988-89, $20-25
Vase, 4.5", Caprice, 9753, YOP: 1988 only, $20-25
Vase, 6.25" with Bow, Caprice, 9754, YOP: 1988-89, $25-30
Vase, 6.5", Rib Urn, 1553, YOP: 1988-89, $30-35
Vase, 7.75", Daffodil, 9752, $25-30
Vase, 10.5", Rib Urn, 1552, YOP: 1988 only, $40-45
Vase; Flute & Dot Vase, 9050, $20-25

BLUE ROYALE KK, YOP: 1988-90: Basket, 6437, $45-55. *Courtesy of Bobbie & Harold Morgan.*

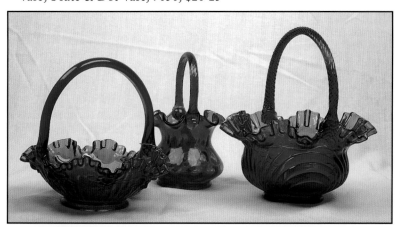

BLUE ROYALE KK, YOP: 1988-90: Basket, 7.25", Rose, 9237, $35-40; Basket, 8", 1434, Coin Dot, $35-40; Basket, 9.5", Caprice, 9730, YOP: 1988-89, $35-40. *Courtesy of Laurie & Richard Karman.*

BLUE ROYALE KK, YOP: 1988-90: Pitcher, 32 oz., Coin Dot, 1432, $45-50; Vase, 8", Swan, 9458, YOP: 1988 only, $45-50. *Courtesy of Melvin & Norma Lampton.*

BLUE ROYALE KK, YOP: 1988-90: Pitcher, 32 oz., Coin Dot, 1432, $45-50; Vase, 11", 3161, YOP: 1988-89, $40-45. *Courtesy of Diane & Tom Rohow.*

BLUE ROYALE KK,
YOP: 1988-90: Vase,
Handkerchief, 8450, Lily
of the Valley, YOP: 1994
only, $30-35. *Courtesy of
Mala Foust.*

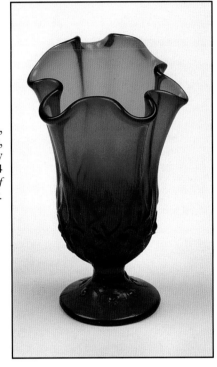

BLUE ROYALE KK, YOP: 1988-90:
Tulip Vase, 10", 1353, Fine Dot, $40-45.
Courtesy of Shelia & Pete McMillian.

BLUE ROYALE KK, YOP:
1988-90: Vase, 8", Wheat,
$45-50; Basket, 8", Coin Dot,
1434, YOP: 1988-89, $40-45.

BLUE ROYALE KK, YOP: 1988-90: Vase, 9", 1433, Coin Dot, $55-60.

Dusty Rose DK 1984-94

DUSTY ROSE DK, YOP: 1984-96: Basket, 7", 2725, Button & Arch, $25-30; Basket, Mini, 6558, Diamond, YOP: 1992-94, $15-20. *Courtesy of Laurie & Richard Karman.*

DUSTY ROSE DK, YOP: 1984-96: Candy, 9280, Butterfly, $35-45. *Courtesy of Myers Mystique.*

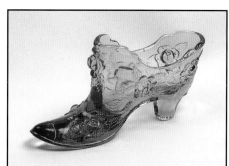

DUSTY ROSE DK, YOP: 1984-96: Slipper, 9295, Rose, YOP: 1990-94, $20-30. *Courtesy of Diane & Tom Rohow.*

DUSTY ROSE DK, YOP: 1984-96: Basket, Mini Footed, 6563, YOP: 1992-94, $25-30; Basket, 6.5", 9537, Strawberry, $35-40; Basket, 9.5", 4835, Diamond Lace, $45-50; Basket, 9544, Vulcan, YOP: 1992-94, $40-45.

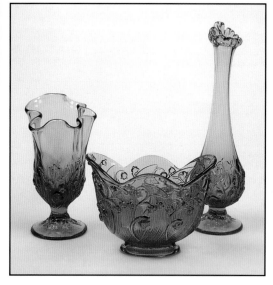

DUSTY ROSE DK, YOP: 1984-96: Vase, Handkerchief, 8450, Lily of the Valley, YOP: 1994 only, $35-40; Bowl, Oval SAMPLE Lily of the Valley, UND; Bud Vase, 8458, Lily of the Valley, $25-30. *Courtesy of Mala Foust.*

DUSTY ROSE DK, YOP: 1984-96: Perfume, 1940, YOP: 1992-94, $45-55. *Courtesy of Laurie & Richard Karman.*

DUSTY ROSE DK, YOP: 1984-96: Bud Vase, Faberge, 9453, $15-30; Vase, 9", 5750, Rose, YOP: 1988-94, $40-45; Slipper, 9295, Rose, YOP: 1990-94, $20-30; Vase, 6", 2557, Beaded Melon, YOP: 1987-94, $30-35; Basket, Footed, 9454, Strawberry, YOP: 1984-94, $30-35; Welcome Light, Pineapple, 9408, $40-45; Candleholder, 8.5", 9071, YOP: 1992-94, $25-30 ea. *Courtesy of Wiggins Gifts.*

Empress Rose CP 1997-

Items Not Pictured:

Slipper, 1995, Daisy & Button, $15-20.

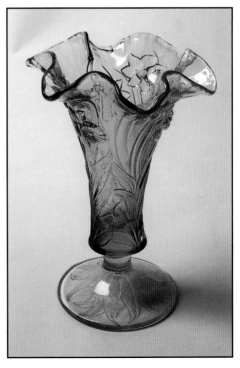

EMPRESS ROSE CP, YOP: 1997-99: Basket, 8.5", Ribbed, 6630, $30-35. *Courtesy of Laurie & Richard Karman.*

EMPRESS ROSE CP, YOP: 1997-99: Basket, 5", 4838, Diamond Lace, $20-25; Basket, 9", 6480, 1999, $25-30. *Courtesy of Laurie & Richard Karman.*

EMPRESS ROSE CP, YOP: 1997-99: Open Swan, 5127, 1997, $20-25; Cat Slipper, 5290, $20-25; Puff Box, 6570, Panel Grape, 1998, $25-30; Slipper, 1995, Daisy & Button, $15-20. *Courtesy of Myers Mystique.*

EMPRESS ROSE CP, YOP: 1997-99: Vase, 6855, Silverton, 1998, $25-30.

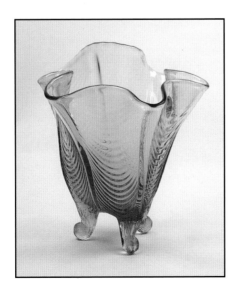

EMPRESS ROSE CP, YOP: 1997-99: Vase, Footed, 7.5", 7653, Daffodil, $30-35.

Petal Pink PN 1990-94

Items Not Pictured:

Basket, 7.25", 9237, Rose, YOP: 1990-91, $25-30
Basket, 5.5", 9243, Rose, YOP: 1990-94, $25-30
Basket, Mini, 6556, Aztec, YOP: 1992-93, $10-15
Basket, Mini, 9562, Vulcan, YOP: 1992-93, $10-15
Trinket Box, 9685, Tear Drop, YOP: 1990 only, $15-20
Bonbon, 8", 4435, Thumbprint, YOP: 1992 only, $10-15
Candleholder, 2 way, 9596, YOP: 1991-94, $10-15 ea.
Candleholder, 4", 4470, Thumbprint, YOP: 1992 only, $15-20 ea.
Candle Holder, 8.5", 9071, $20-25 ea.
Candy Box, Oval, 4486, Thumbprint, YOP: 1992 only, $20-25
Candy, 6780, Paisley, YOP: 1991-94, $25-30
Alarm Clock, 8691, YOP: 1990-94, $20-25
Comport, Footed, 4429, Thumbprint, YOP: 1992 only, $15-20
Comport, 9229, Empress, YOP: 1990-91, $25-30
Comport, 9780, Heart, YOP: 1990-94, $25-30
Ring Holder, 9144, Fine Cut & Block, YOP: 1994 only, $5-10
Vase, 4.5", 9157, Fine Cut & Block, YOP: 1994 only, $15-20
Vase, 5", 7620, Aurora, YOP: 1990-93, $20-25
Vase, 5.5", 9050, Flute & Dot, YOP: 1991-93, $20-25
Vase, 7.5", 4655, Daffodil, YOP: 1991-94, $20-25
Vase, 8", 9758, Stylized, YOP: 1990-94, $25-30
Vase, 9", 8354, Basket weave, YOP: 1991 only, $30-35

PETAL PINK PN, YOP: 1990-94: Basket, 9544, Vulcan, YOP: 1990-94, $20-25; Rose, 6.5", 9240, Basket, YOP: 1990 only, $25-30. *Courtesy of Laurie & Richard Karman.*

PETAL PINK PN, YOP: 1990-94: Vase, 6", 2557, $25-30; Comport, 4854, Diamond Lace, $55-65; Slipper, 9295, Rose, $10-15; Bell, 9560, Temple Bells, $30-35. *Courtesy of Laurie & Richard Karman.*

PETAL PINK PN, YOP: 1990-94: Vase, Handkerchief, 8458, Lily of the Valley, YOP: 1994 only, $35-40. *Courtesy of Mala Foust.*

Plum PL 1993-94

Items Not Pictured:

Basket, 2731, Lamb's Tongue, $30-35
Basket, 8", 2787, 1997, $30-35
Trinket Box, Hexagonal, 9687, $15-20
Candy, 9551, Vulcan, $20-25
Candleholder, 8.5", 9071, $20-25 ea.
Comport, 9229, Empress, $25-30
Ring Holder, 9144, Fine Cut & Block, $10-15
Slipper, 9295, Rose, $15-20
Bud Vase, 9454, Strawberry, $15-20
Vase, 5", 7620, Aurora, $20-25
Vase, 5", 2751, $25-30
Vase, 6", 1789, Melon, $25-30
Vase, 8", 1785, Diamond, $25-30
Vase, 10", 1786, Melon, YOP: 1993 only, $30-35
Votive, 2 way Leaf, 9578, $15-20 ea.

PLUM PL, YOP: 1993-94: Basket, 4.5", 6558, Diamond Mini, $20-25; Basket, 9544, Vulcan, $20-25; Basket, 2728, Button & Arch, $30-35. *Courtesy of Laurie & Richard Karman.*

PLUM PL, YOP: 1993-94: Vase, Mini, 7151, Beaded Melon, $25-30.

PLUM PL, YOP: 1993-94: Vase, Melon Rib, 11", 1792, Diamond, $40-45. *Courtesy of Connie & Aaron Patient.*

Ruby RU 1985-2000

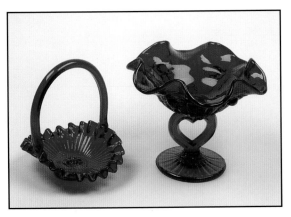

RUBY RU, YOP: 1985-2000: Basket, 4.5", 9535, Rose, YOP: 1987-88, $15-20; Comport, 9780, Heart, YOP: 1989-92, $30-35. *Courtesy of Diane & Tom Rohow.*

RUBY RU, YOP: 1985-2000: Comport, 9780, Heart, YOP: 1989-92, $30-35. *Courtesy of Bobbie & Harold Morgan.*

RUBY RU, YOP: 1985-2000: Pitcher, 32 oz., 1432, Coin Dot, YOP: 1989-90, $30-35.

RUBY RU, YOP: 1985-2000: Bell, 6761, Paisley, $20-25; Candy, 6780, Paisley, YOP: 1988-94, $20-25; Basket, 8", Spiral, 3131, YOP: 1989-90, $30-35; Basket, Mini, 6560, Diamond, YOP: 1992-94, $10-15; Swan, Open, 5127, $20-25; Slipper, 9295, Rose, YOP: 1990-94, $15-20. *Courtesy of Jan Hollingsworth.*

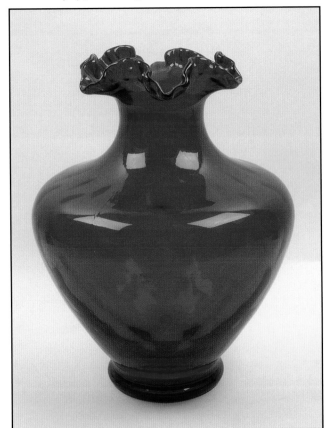

RUBY RU, YOP: 1985-2000: Vase, 9", 1433, Coin Dot, $75-80. *Courtesy of Bev & Jon Spencer.*

RUBY RU, YOP: 1985-2000: Basket, 11.5", 2917 PY, Diamond Flute, $35-40.

RUBY RU, YOP: 1985-2000: Vase, Handkerchief, 8450, Lily of the Valley, YOP: 1994 only, $35-40. *Courtesy of Mala Foust.*

Salem Blue SR 1990-92

Items Not Pictured:

Atomizer, Oval, 5315, YOP: 1991-92, $30-35
Atomizer, Beaded, 5316, YOP: 1991 only, $30-35
Basket, Mini, 6562, Vulcan, YOP: 1992 only, $10-15
Basket, Footed Mini, 6563, YOP: 1992 only, $10-15
Basket, 9544, Vulcan, $15-20
Basket, 8342, Valencia, $20-25
Basket, 12", 9036, Priscilla, $40-45
Bowl, 10.5", 9068, Priscilla, $25-30
Candy, Covered, 9280, Butterfly, YOP: 1991-92, $25-30
Candy, 9780, Paisley, $25-30
Candle Holder, 9071, $15-20 ea.
Candleholder, 2 way, 9596, YOP: 1991-92, $10-15
Alarm Clock, 8691, $20-25
Clock, 8698, YOP: 1991-92, $20-25
Pitcher, 9666, Sandwich, $25-30
Slipper, 9295, Rose, $10-15
Vase, 5", 7620, Aurora, $10-15
Vase, 8", 9758, Stylized, $20-25
Bud Vase, 8650, Lucille, $10-15

SALEM BLUE SR, YOP: 1990-92: Basket, Footed, 9537, Strawberry, $20-25. *Courtesy of Laurie & Richard Karman.*

SALEM BLUE SR, YOP: 1990-92: Cruet, 7063, Drapery, $75-80. *Courtesy of Donna Hatch.*

Sea Mist Green LE 1991-97

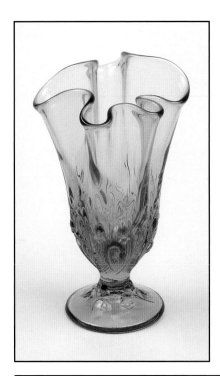

TEAL ROYALE OC, YOP: 1988-89: Basket, Footed, 9537, Strawberry, $30-35; Basket, 8", 1434, Coin Dot, $30-35; Basket, 7.25", 9237, Rose, $25-30; Basket, 8.5", 9732, Caprice, $30-35. *Courtesy of Laurie & Richard Karman.*

SEA MIST GREEN LE, YOP: 1991-97: Vase, 8450, Lily of the Valley, YOP: 1997 only, $20-25.

Teal Royale OC 1988-89

Items Not Pictured:

Basket, 9.5", 9730, Caprice, $35-40
Basket, Footed, 9537, Strawberry, $25-30
Candleholder, 2 way, 9596, $10-15
Hurricane candle, 8376, Valencia, $15-20
Wine, 9244, Empress, $10-15
Goblet, 9245, Empress, $10-$15
Nut Dish, 9532, Strawberry, $15-20
Slipper, 1995, Daisy & Button, $10-15
Vase, 8", 9458, Swan, $35-40
Vase, 4", 3952, $15-20
Vase, 6.5", Urn, 1553, Rib, $15-20

TEAL ROYALE OC, YOP: 1988-89: Bowl, 9627, Beauty, $30-35. *Courtesy of Chuck Bingham.*

TEAL ROYALE OC, YOP: 1988-89: Vase, 4.5", Hobnail, 3854, NIL, $20-25; Vase, 9050, Flute & Dot, $15-20; Pitcher, 32 oz., 1432, Coin Dot, $30-35; Swan, Open, 5127, $20-25; Toothpick, 8294, Paneled Daisy, $10-15; Comport, Open Edge, 8324, $20-25; Vase, 9752, Daffodil, $25-30; Slipper, 9195, Rose, $20-25; Basket, 8", 1434, Coin Dot, $30-35. *Courtesy of Chuck Bingham.*

TEAL ROYALE OC, YOP: 1988-89: Vase, 9752, Daffodil, $25-30. *Courtesy of Donna Hatch.*

TEAL ROYALE OC, YOP: 1988-89: Vase, 9758, Stylized, $40-45; Basket, 7.25", 9237, Rose, $25-30. *Courtesy of Chuck Bingham.*

TEAL ROYALE OC, YOP: 1988-89: Pitcher, 9760, Caprice, YOP: 1988 only, $20-25. *Courtesy of Wiggins Gifts.*

TEAL ROYALE OC, YOP: 1988-89: Pitcher, 9760, Caprice, YOP: 1988 only, $20-25; Rose Bowl, 8", 9751, Caprice, YOP: 1988 only, $20-25; Vase with Bow, 6.5", 9754, Caprice, $25-30; Vase, 4.5", 9753, Caprice, YOP: 1988 only, $20-25; Bowl, 9.5", 9723, Caprice, $20-25. *Courtesy of Chuck Bingham.*

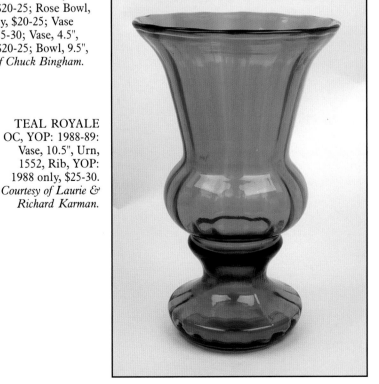

TEAL ROYALE OC, YOP: 1988-89: Vase, 10.5", Urn, 1552, Rib, YOP: 1988 only, $25-30. *Courtesy of Laurie & Richard Karman.*

TEAL ROYALE OC, YOP: 1988-89: Vase, 10.5", 1443, Coin Dot, $30-35; Vase 9458, Swan, $35-40; Vase, 11", Spiral, 3161, $35-40. *Courtesy of Chuck Bingham.*

Twilight Blue TB 1992-94

Items Not Pictured:

Basket, Mini, 6560, Diamond, $10-15
Basket, Mini, 6561, Wild Rose & Bowknot, $10-15
Basket, 9544, Vulcan, $15-20
Basket, 8342, Valencia, $20-25
Rose Bowl, 5", 2789, YOP: 1994 only, $15-20
Rose Bowl, 6", 8623, YOP: 1994 only, $15-20
Candle Holder, 8.5", 9071, $15-20 ea.
Candy, 6780, Paisley, $25-30
Comport, 8397, Valencia, $15-20
Clock, 8698, $20-25
Ring holder, 9144, $5-10
Slipper, 9295, Rose, $10-15
Vase, 5", 2751, YOP: 1993-94, $15-20
Vase, 8", 9758, Stylized, $25-30
Vase, 4655, Daffodil, YOP: 1992 only, $25-30
Votive, 2 way Leaf, 9578,, YOP: 1994 only, $10-15

TWILIGHT BLUE TB, YOP: 1992-94: Perfume, 1970, $30-35. *Courtesy of Laurie & Richard Karman.*

Decorated Patterns

In the late 1960s, when Fenton first offered their decorated line in their catalogs, the majority of the items were either produced in Milk Glass or Custard Satin. In the mid-1980s, it was announced that Fenton would cut back on Milk Glass production due to the fact that the Fluoride in the Milk Glass formula was destroying the Day Tanks as it was being produced. It was then assumed by many at that time that Fenton would continue to produced their decorated patterns on their Custard Satin Glass.

Around the same time, the EPA stepped in, declaring the chemicals that were used by Fenton to "satinize" glass were too difficult to dispose of after their use. They then banned Fenton from using these chemicals, causing Fenton from that time on to use the sandblasting technique of "Satinizing" glass. Due to the time it takes to do this, it was no longer cost effective to have as many "Satin" patterns in their regular line.

Because of this, during the late 1980s, Fenton turned to different glass treatments for their decorators to use. At first decorating was tried on plain Transparent Glass, and also Opal glass (a less corrosive form of Milk Glass). It was later into the 1990s that Fenton discovered that French Opalescent glass, when decorated, especially when a different colored crest would be added, proved to be quite popular with the buying public. It was also during this time that many different treatments were tried with decorations, including Cranberry, Mulberry, and Carnival.

Carnival

It is surprising that, over the years until the 1990s, Fenton had never used Carnival Glass as a base for their decorated lines. Carnival Glass had been used by Fenton in the early 1900s for decorated ware, and these items, though now scarce, are quite beautiful. After Carnival Glass was reintroduced in the early 1970s, it was decorated, from time to time, for samples and special order items, but nothing was ever put into Fenton's regular line until the early 1990s. Since that time, several different patterns have appeared in the Fenton line throughout the 1990s, mostly made to go along with special lines such as the Historic Collection or the Red Carnival issue.

Items Not Pictured:

Floral on Plum Carnival AX 1998: Vase, 6.5", 9252, $75-85

Floral on Plum Carnival AX 1998: Vase, 4.5", 9357, $45-55

Floral on Spruce Carnival US, YOP: 1999: Basket, 8", 5659, $75-85

Floral on Spruce Carnival US, YOP: 1999: Vase, 6", Melon, 7693, $55-65,

Floral on Violet Satin XP 1999: Vase, 11", Tulip, 7255, $75-85

Floral on Violet Satin XP 1999: Basket, 7", 2777, $75-85,

Floral on Violet Satin XP 1999: Covered Box, 7484, George Fenton Signature, $75-80

Floral Interlude on Sea Green Satin GG 1997: Basket, 8", Lily, 5430, $100-125

Vining Hearts on Rose Pearl DW 1993: Basket, 10.5", Footed, 6572, $85-90

Vining Hearts on Rose Pearl DW 1993: Vase, 5", Aurora, 7620, $35-40

Vining Hearts on Rose Pearl DW 1993: Comport, 7", 9229, Empress, $50-55

BUTTER CUPS & BERRIES ON RED CARNIVAL R1, YOP: 1995: Basket, 8.5", 2924, Holly, $150-175. *Courtesy of Laurie & Richard Karman.*

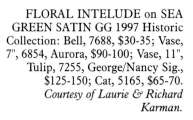

FLORAL INTELUDE on SEA GREEN SATIN GG 1997 Historic Collection: Bell, 7688, $30-35; Vase, 7", 6854, Aurora, $90-100; Vase, 11", Tulip, 7255, George/Nancy Sig., $125-150; Cat, 5165, $65-70. *Courtesy of Laurie & Richard Karman.*

DAMASK ROSE ON RED CARNIVAL RC, YOP: 1996: Basket, 8", 2936, $150-175. *Courtesy of Laurie & Richard Karman.*

DAMASK ROSE ON RED CARNIVAL RC, YOP: 1996: Boots, 9590, $35-45 ea. *Courtesy of Jan Hollingsworth.*

STAR FLOWERS ON GOLD PEARL GF 1992 Historic Collection: Basket, 9", 5481, $55-60. *Courtesy of Laurie & Richard Karman.*

DAMASK ROSE ON RED CARNIVAL RC, YOP: 1996: Vase, 8", 5351, Melon, $100-150. *Courtesy of Laurie & Richard Karman.*

FLORAL ON VIOLET SATIN XP 1999 Historic Collection: Trinket Box, 4106, Heart, $55-65. *Courtesy of Connie & Aaron Patient.*

STAR FLOWERS ON GOLD PEARL GF 1992 Historic Collection: Candleholders. 5526, $25-30 ea.; Basket, 9", 5481, $55-60; Bowl, 9.5", Cupped, 5482, $55-$60; Vase, 12", Swung, 5480, $70-75; Vase, 6", Cupped, 5479, $55-65; Bell, 9667, Aurora, $30-35. Not Pictured: Basket, 10.5", Cupped, 5483, $80-85. *Courtesy of Laurie & Richard Karman.*

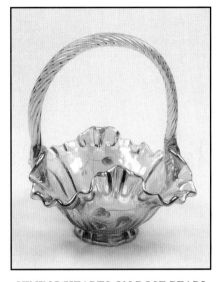

VINING HEARTS ON ROSE PEARL DW, YOP: 1993: Basket, 7", 7630, Aurora, $65-70. *Courtesy of Laurie & Richard Karman.*

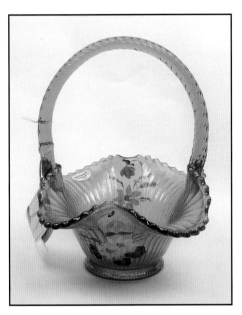

WINDFLOWERS ON STIEGEL GREEN STRETCH SS, YOP: 1994 Historic Collection: Basket, 8", 2787, $80-85. *Courtesy of Myers Mystique.*

WINDFLOWERS ON STIEGEL GREEN STRETCH SS, YOP: 1994 Historic Collection: Rose Bowl, 3.5", 2759, $50-55; Basket, 8", 2787, $80-85; Vase, 8", Handkerchief, 5559, $60-65. Not Pictured: Candy Box, 4381, Lamb's Tongue, $75-80. *Courtesy of Sarah Wells.*

Milk Glass

Only a few patterns have been issued in Decorated Milk Glass since the mid-1980s. These patterns are quite scarce on today's market. Two of these patterns, Lilacs and Pansies, were made with Milk Glass crested with Plum. Elizabeth and Morning Mist were made on a old Fenton favorite, Silver Crest.

"Elizabeth", SILVER CREST WITH BLUE FLORAL ES, YOP: 1989-92: Candy, 6780, Paisley, $70-75. *Courtesy of Norma & Melvin Lampton.*

"Elizabeth", SILVER CREST WITH BLUE FLORAL ES, YOP: 1989-92: Vase, 6", 7693, Beaded Melon, YOP: 1989-90, $45-55; Comport, 9229, Empress, YOP: 1989-92, $55-60; Vase, 7", 7694, Aurora, YOP: 1990-91, $55-60; Vase, 4", 9357, Basket weave, YOP: 1989-92, $40-45; Candy, 6780, Paisley, $70-75; Vase, 6.5", 9252, Rose, YOP: 1989-90, $65-70; Slipper, 9295, Rose, YOP: 1990-92, $30-35; Pitcher, 6", 7692, Beaded Melon, YOP: 1989-90, $65-70. *Courtesy of Laurie & Richard Karman.*

"Elizabeth", SILVER CREST WITH BLUE FLORAL ES, YOP: 1989-92: Basket, 9", 7532; Melon, YOP: 1989-90, $80-85; Vase, 4", 9357, Basket weave, YOP: 1989-92, $40-45; Bell, 6761, Paisley, YOP: 1989-92, $40-45. *Courtesy of Marylin & Dick Treiwelter.*

"Elizabeth", BLUE ROYALE WITH WHITE FLORAL EM, YOP: 1989-92: Basket, Paisley, 6730, $95-100. *Courtesy of Bobbie & Harold Morgan.*

86

"Elizabeth", BLUE ROYALE WITH WHITE FLORAL EM, YOP: 1989-92: Candle Holder, 9071, $40-45 ea.; Comport, 9229, Empress, $40-45; Candy, 6780, very scarce, $95-100. *Courtesy of Laurie & Richard Karman.*

LILACS PJ, YOP: 1993-94: Basket, 8.5", 3539, Spanish Lace, $80-85.

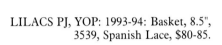

LILACS PJ, YOP: 1993-94: Basket, 7.5", 2738, YOP: 1994 only Shelly Fenton Signature, $80-85, Basket, 8.5", 6730, Paisley, Bill Fenton Signature, $90-100. *Courtesy of Laurie & Richard Karman.*

LILACS PJ, YOP: 1993-94: Vase, 6", 7356, $50-55; Jug, 6", 2765, $65-70; Puff Box, 6750, Paneled Grape, $60-65; Comport, 6", 2739, Empress, YOP: 1994 only, $65-70; Vase, 7", 3559, Spanish Lace, $70-75. Not Pictured: Comport, 7", 9229, Empress, YOP: 1993 only, $55-60; Slipper, 9295, Rose, $30-35. *Courtesy of Laurie & Richard Karman.*

MORNING MIST CG, YOP: 1999: Basket, 8", Ribbed, 6833, $75-80; Box, Covered, 7484, $65-70; Pitcher, 4566, Scott Fenton Signature, $80-85; Basket, 7", 6530, Diamond, $75-80; Vase, 11", 6548, $90-100. *Courtesy of Marylin & Dick Treiwelter.*

MORNING MIST CG, YOP: 1999: Tumble Up with Cover On.

MORNING MIST CG, YOP: 1999: Tumble Up with Cover Off, $100-125. *Courtesy of Marylin & Dick Treiwelter.*

MORNING MIST CG, YOP: 1999: Bell, 4769, $30-35; Box, Covered, 7484, $65-70; Pitcher, 4566, Scott Fenton Signature, $80-85; Slipper, 5290, Beauty, $30-35. *Courtesy of Laurie & Richard Karman.*

PANSIES PF, YOP: 1996: Slipper, 9295, Rose, $30-35; Vase, 8.5", 9450, Melon, $75-80; Pitcher, 5", 5563, $70-75; Basket, 10.5", 6585, $100-125; Bell, 1145, $30-35; Comport, 2739, Empress, $55-60. *Courtesy of Laurie & Richard Karman.*

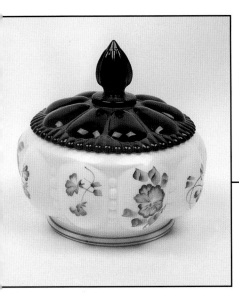

Box, Covered, 5585, Shelly, Signature Series, $90-100. *Courtesy of Laurie & Richard Karman.*

Opaque

In the late 1990s, Fenton (due to the fact that Fenton had curtailed production of most Milk Glass and could no longer "satinize" their Custard Glass with chemicals) turned to Opaque Glass for their decorated ware. Opal, a form of Milk Glass that was less destructive to produce, was used many times for their decorated patterns. Also Ebony Glass, which had been seldom used in the past, was produced in the Copper Rose and the Victorian Bouquet pattern, and proved quite popular at the time of its issue—and also in today's market. Possibly the most unusual and unique decoration made during this time was created by Michael Dickerson and was called Wisteria Lane. Wisteria Lane is a scenic decoration showing an old English manor that is somewhat eerie, reminding a person of an old movie or novel. It almost makes one wonder what is going on inside the Manor!

ANTIQUE ROSE AF, YOP: 6/89-6/90: Basket, 7630, Aurora, $75-80. *Courtesy of Laurie & Richard Karman.*

ANTIQUE ROSE AF, YOP: 6/89-6/90: Heart Box, 5780, Rose, $55-60; Comport, 9229, Empress, $65-70; Vase, 4.5", 7620, Aurora, $55-60; Vase, 6.5", 9252, Rose, $65-70; Votive, 2 Way, 9578, Leaf, $30-35. *Courtesy of Laurie & Richard Karman.*

AUTUMN LEAVES ON BLACK AW, YOP: 1993-94: Clock, 8600, $100-125. *Courtesy of Laurie & Richard Karman.*

AUTUMN LEAVES ON BLACK AW, YOP: 1993-94: Candy, Covered, 7380, Don Signature, $100-125. *Courtesy of Laurie & Richard Karman.*

AUTUMN LEAVES ON BLACK AW, YOP: 1993-94: Basket, Footed, 6572, $100-125; Vase, 5", 2757, $55-60; Vase, 9.5", 2756, $100-125. *Courtesy of Laurie & Richard Karman.*

COPPER ROSES ON BLACK KP, YOP: 1989-93: Basket, 7", 7630, Aurora, $90-100. *Courtesy of Laurie & Richard Karman.*

AUTUMN LEAVES ON BLACK AW, YOP: 1993-94: Rose Bowl, 6", 2759, $55-60; Slipper, 9259, Rose, $40-45; Candle Holders, 8.5", 9071, $40-45 ea.; Vase, 8", 2758, $75-100. *Courtesy of Laurie & Richard Karman.*

COPPER ROSES ON BLACK KP, YOP: 1989-93: Clock, 8600, Not In Line, $100-125; Alarm Clock, 8691, $75-80; Clock, 8698, YOP: 1991-93, $75-80. *Courtesy of Laurie & Richard Karman.*

COPPER ROSES ON BLACK KP, YOP: 1989-93: Trinket Box, 5780, Heart, YOP: 1990-93, $65-70. *Courtesy of Tina & Rick Gaither.*

COPPER ROSES ON BLACK KP, YOP: 1989-93:
Trinket Box, 5780, Heart, YOP: 1990-93, $65-70;
Slipper, 9259, Rose, $40-45; Bud Vase, 7348, $40-45;
Vase, 7.5", 7696, $80-85; Comport, 6322, Flower Band,
YOP: 1989-91, $80-85; Candy, 6080, Wave Crest, YOP:
1990-91, $100-125; Vase, 8.5", 8817, YOP: 1989-91,
$80-85; Candle Holder, 4.5", 9372, YOP: 1990-91, $40-
45 ea.; Bowl, Rolled Rim, 7523, YOP: 1989-91, $90-
100. *Courtesy of Laurie & Richard Karman.*

COPPER ROSES ON BLACK KP, YOP: 1989-93:
Atomizer, 7948, YOP: 1990-91, $90-100; Atomizer,
7948, Crystal with HP Flower (Offered at same
time of Copper Roses Atomizer), $55-60. *Courtesy
of Tina & Rick Gaither.*

HEARTS & FLOWERS FH, YOP: 1988-93: Vase, 4.5", 9357,
Basket weave, $40-45; Comport, 6322, Flower Band, YOP:
1988-92, $50-55. *Courtesy of Melva McGinnis.*

HEARTS & FLOWERS FH, YOP: 1988-93: Basket, 7", 9335, Basket weave,
YOP: 1988-93, $65-70; Basket, Paneled, 9238, YOP: 1989-90, $65-70. *Courtesy of
Laurie & Richard Karman.*

HEARTS & FLOWERS FH, YOP: 1988-93: Comport,
6322, Flower Band, YOP: 1988-92, $50-55; Vase, 4.5", 9357,
Basket weave, $40-45; Vase, 5", 2751, YOP: 1993 only, $50-
55; Heart Box, 5780, Rose, YOP: 1993 only, $40-45; Vase, 8",
7250, Tulip, YOP: 1988-93, $65-70; Vase, 6.5", 9252, Rose,
YOP: 1988-90, $50-55. Not Pictured: Slipper, 9295, Rose,
YOP: 1993 only, $30-35; Bud Vase, 9356, Basket weave,
YOP: 1988-93, $30-35; Jewel Box, Oval, 9589, YOP: 1988-
92, $35-40. *Courtesy of Laurie & Richard Karman.*

TULIPS TL, YOP: 1990-91: Comport, 6322, Flower Band, $65-70. *Courtesy of Williamstown Antique Mall.*

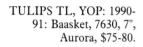

PRIMROSE DS, YOP: 1994: Basket, 7", 2737, $55-60; Basket, 7", 9335, Basket weave, $65-70. *Courtesy of Laurie & Richard Karman.*

TULIPS TL, YOP: 1990-91: Baasket, 7630, 7", Aurora, $75-80.

PRIMROSE DS, YOP: 1994: Vase, 8", Tulip, 7250, $80-85; Slipper, 9295, Rose, $35-40. Not Pictured: Comport, 6.5", 2739, Empress, $60-65; Vase, 5", 2751, $55-60; Comport, 6.5", 2739, Empress, $60-65; Jewel Box, Oval, 9589, $45-50. *Courtesy of Richard & Laurie Karman.*

TULIPS TL, YOP: 1990-91: Alarm Clock, 8691, YOP: 1990 only, $65-70. *Courtesy of Laurie & Richard Karman.*

TULIPS TL, YOP: 1990-91: Vase, 4.5", 9357, Basket weave, $45-55; Comport, 6.5", 2739, Empress, $60-65; Vase, 8", Tulip, 7250, $80-85; Heart Box, 5789, Rose, $55-60. *Courtesy of Laurie & Richard Karman.*

VICTORIAN BOUQUET ON BLACK BT, YOP: 1995: Candy, 7380, $100-125; Vase, 9.5", Feather, 2756, $80-90. *Courtesy of Laurie & Richard Karman.*

VICTORIAN BOUQUET ON BLACK BT, YOP: 1995: Oval Trinket Box, 9589, $45-55. *Courtesy of Bobbie & Harold Morgan.*

VICTORIAN BOUQUET ON BLACK BT, YOP: 1995: Clock, 8600, $65-70. *Courtesy of Laurie & Richard Karman.*

WISTERIA LANE JW, YOP: 1986: Basket, 9", 7439, $200-225. *Courtesy of Norma & Melvin Lampton.*

VICTORIAN BOUQUET ON BLACK BT, YOP: 1995: Bell, 9667, Aurora, $30-35; Vase, 7", 7690, Aurora, $75-80; Slipper, 9295, Rose, $30-35; Oval Trinket Box, 9589, $45-55; Rose Bowl, 3.5", 2759, $45-55; Candlesticks, 8.5", 9071, $30-40 ea.; Vase, 5", 2757, $45-55; Basket, 10.5", 6585, $125-150; Vase, 8.5", JIP, 2985, $80-90. *Courtesy of Laurie & Richard Karman.*

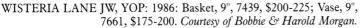

WISTERIA LANE JW, YOP: 1986: Basket, 9", 7439, $200-225; Vase, 9", 7661, $175-200. *Courtesy of Bobbie & Harold Morgan.*

Opalescent/Opaline

Throughout the 1940s and 1950s, Opalescent Glass was a mainstay for Fenton, and a favorite with their buyers. As taste changed in the 1960s and '70s, Fenton turned to Milk Glass, and also different colors of Satin Glass. In the late 1980s, when it proved more difficult and costly to produce both Satin Glass and Milk Glass, Fenton again attempted to reissue Opalescent Glass. The first few attempts, Minted Cream, Peaches 'N' Cream, and French Cream, did not go over well and were quickly discontinued.

In an attempt of making Opalescent glass more attractive to the public, Fenton tried several different hand decorated patterns on it; most notable was Country Garden on French Cream and, even earlier, Strawberries on French Opalescent. Neither hand decorated pattern lasted in the Fenton line for long. In the early 1990s, Fenton introduced several decorated patterns on French Opalescent Glass, usually accented with a different color crest. This type of ware proved quite popular with the public, and led the way for many other decorated Opalescent patterns, including the popular Trellis and Martha's Rose pattern.

Items Not Pictured:

Country Garden on French Cream JF 1986-87: Basket, Wicker, 9939, YOP: 1986 only, $35-40

Country Garden on French Cream JF 1986-87: Heart Candy, 9519, $25-30

Country Garden on French Cream JF 1986-87: Candy, 9551, Vulcan, $30-35

Country Garden on French Cream JF 1986-87: Comport, 7681, Aurora, $25-30

Country Garden on French Cream JF 1986-87: Candleholder/Nut Vase, 9571, $20-25

Country Garden on French Cream JF 1986-87: Vase, 7", 2057, Curtain, $30-35

Country Garden on French Cream JF 1986-87: Bud vase, 7476, $20-25

Country Garden on French Cream JF 1986-87: Votive/Vase, 4", 9555, $20-25

Country Garden on French Cream JF 1986-87: Votive, 6", 9557, $20-25

Country Garden on French Cream JF 1986-87: Votive, 9576, 2.5", $20-24

BLUSH ROSE ON OPALINE TE 1996 Historic Collection: Tumble Up, 1180, $125-150; Pitcher, 6.5", 5367, $80-90; Bell, 4568, $30-35; Vase, 11", 1795, Feather, $125-150; Vase, 8.5", 5357, George Fenton Signature, $100-125; Cruet, 7701, $100-125. Not Pictured: Basket, 8", 1147, $85-90. *Courtesy of Laurie & Richard Karman.*

BLUSH ROSE ON OPALINE TE, YOP: 1996 Historic Collection: Vase, 7", Pinch, 1146, $55-60. *Courtesy of Laurie & Richard Karman.*

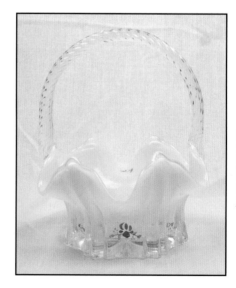

COUNTRY GARDEN ON FRENCH CREAM JF, YOP: 1986-87: Basket, 9544, Vulcan, $30-35. *Courtesy of Laurie & Richard Karman.*

COUNTRY GARDEN ON FRENCH
CREAM JF, YOP: 1986-87: Toothpick, 9572,
YOP: 1986 only, $20-25.

COUNTRY GARDEN ON FRENCH
CREAM JF, YOP: 1986-87: Bell, 9667,
Aurora, $25-30; Candy, 9551, Vulcan, $30-35.

FIELD FLOWERS ON CHAMPAGNE SATIN PI, YOP: 1997:
Basket, 8", 2948, $75-80; Vase, 6", 4751, Shelly Signature, $75-80.
Courtesy of Laurie & Richard Karman.

FIELD FLOWERS ON CHAM-
PAGNE SATIN PI, YOP: 1997:
Vase, 6", 1214, Melon, $65-80. Not
Pictured: Vase, 8.5", 1693, 1998,
$75-80; Pitcher, 9.5", 2796, $65-
70. *Courtesy of Laurie & Richard
Karman.*

GRAPES ON STIEGEL BLUE
OPALESCENT JU, YOP: 1991: Urn,
4602, Diamond, $100-125. Not
Pictured: Bud Vase, 10", 4651,
Colonial, $25-30. *Courtesy of Norma &
Melvin Lampton.*

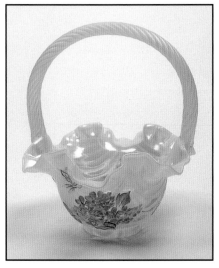

HYDRANGEAS ON TOPAZ
OPALESCENT TP, YOP: 1997:
Basket, 8", 2033, $75-80. *Courtesy of
Bobbie & Harold Morgan.*

HYDRANGEAS ON TOPAZ OPALESCENT TP, YOP: 1997: Fairy Light, 3
piece, 2040, Family Signature, $100-125; Vase, 8", Fan, 9550, Tom Fenton
Signature, $90-100; Pitcher, 6.5", 2072, $70-75; Basket, 8", 2033, $75-80. *Courtesy of
Laurie & Richard Karman.*

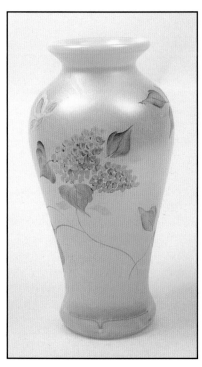

HYDRANGEAS ON TOPAZ
OPALESCENT TP, YOP: 1997:
Vase, 9.5", 2048, $90-100. *Courtesy of
John Tannery.*

IRISES ON MISTY
BLUE SATIN LS,
YOP: 1997: Basket,
6380, Silvertone, $65-
70. *Courtesy of Laurie &
Richard Karman.*

IRISES ON MISTY BLUE SATIN LS, YOP:
1997: Clock, 8691, Lynn Signature, $55-60.
Courtesy of Laurie & Richard Karman.

IRISES ON MISTY BLUE SATIN LS, YOP: 1997: Pitcher, 7.5", 5440, Don Fenton Signature, $75-80. *Courtesy of Laurie & Richard Karman.*

MARTHA'S ROSE AZ, YOP: 1991: Basket, 8.5", 3131, $90-100; Vase, 8.5", JIP, 3070, Shelly Fenton Signature, $80-90; Vase, 5", 3050, $45-50; Vase, 11", 3054, $90-100; Pitcher, 7.25", 3072, $75-80. *Courtesy of Laurie & Richard Karman.*

IRISES ON MISTY BLUE SATIN LS, YOP: 1997: Pitcher, 7.5", 5440, Don Fenton Signature, $75-80; Vase, 11", 2782, Feather, $80-85. *Courtesy of Connie & Aaron Patient.*

MEADOW BEAUTY PD, YOP: 1996: Basket, 7.5", 1219, $65-70; Vase, 6", 3055, $65-70; Vase, 4.5", 1213, $45-50; Pitcher, 7", 1212, $65-70; Bell, 4629, $30-35; Vase, 9", Hex, 3059, $75-80; Vase, 8.5", JIP, 3070, $65-75; Vase, 4.5", Footed, $40-45. *Courtesy of Laurie & Richard Karman.*

IRISES ON MISTY BLUE SATIN LS, YOP: 1997: Vase, 11", 2782, Feather, $80-85; Pitcher, 6.5", 3275, 1998, $65-70. Not Pictured: Basket, 8", 1538, $70-75; Vase, 7", 1683, Aurora, $60-65; Slipper, 9295, Rose, $30-35. *Courtesy of Laurie & Richard Karman.*

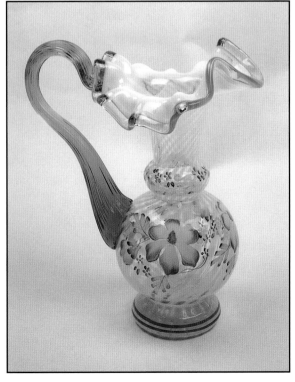

MEADOW BEAUTY PD, YOP: 1996: Pitcher, 8", $75-85. *Courtesy of Laurie & Richard Karman.*

MEADOW BEAUTY PD, YOP: 1996: Vase, 11", 1653, Feather Nancy Fenton Signature, $90-100. *Courtesy of Laurie & Richard Karman.*

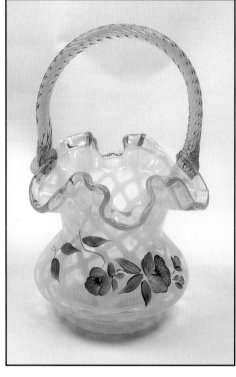

TRELLIS DX, YOP: 1996-99: Basket, 6587, 7", YOP: 1999, $75-80.

TRELLIS DX, YOP: 1996-99: Basket, 8.5", 1131, Lynn Fenton Signature, $85-90. *Courtesy of Laurie & Richard Karman.*

TRELLIS DX, YOP: 1996-99: Pitcher, 7", 1132, $75-80; Pitcher, 7.5", 4767, $65-70; Vase, 4.5", 4755, 1997; Vase, 7", 1129, $65-70; Vase, 7", Pinch 1153, $65-70; Vase, 4", 1143, $45-50. *Courtesy of Laurie & Richard Karman.*

TRELLIS DX, YOP: 1996-99: Basket, 8", Lily, 1144, $75-80; Box, Melon, 5585, $80-90; Hurricane Lamp, 11", 7608, YOP: 1997 only, $100-125; Basket, 4.5", 6585, YOP: 1999, $65-70. Not Pictured: Perfume, 4803, YOP: 1999, $85-90. *Courtesy of Laurie & Richard Karman.*

Overlay

Fenton's decorated Overlay Glass was quite popular during the Second World War and on into the 1950s. This glass, although made by Fenton, was decorated by other companies. These other firms bought the glass, decorated it, and then marketed it themselves. It wasn't until 1993 that Fenton issued any decorated Overlay items. The first issue began innocently enough on Country Cranberry that was decorated with a pale pinkish-purple flower. No name was given to this treatment, except for Decorated Cranberry. The following year, the popular Pansies on Cranberry line were introduced. This line was followed over the next few years by other Overlay treatments that were decorated, including several limited edition lines from the Historic Collection.

ASTERS ON DUSTY ROSE OVERLAY DP, YOP: 1996: Pitcher, 6.5", 3065, Lynn Fenton Signature, $90-100; Basket, 8", 3076, $90-100. Not Pictured: Vase, 9", Hexagonal, 1648, $90-100; Pitcher, 7.5", 1562, YOP: 1997, $90-100. *Courtesy of Phyllis & Terry Sterett.*

COLONIAL SCROLL ON ROYAL PURPLE N4, YOP: 1998: Basket, 8", 1617, Limited to 2,950, $175-200; Vase, 9.25", 1689, Limited to 2,950, $125-150. *Courtesy of Bobbie & Harold Morgan.*

ASTERS ON DUSTY ROSE OVERLAY DP, YOP: 1996: Vase, 7", 1683, Aurora, $80-90. *Courtesy of Vickie Ticen.*

COLONIAL SCROLL ON ROYAL PURPLE N4, YOP: 1998: Basket, 8", 1617, Limited to 2,950, $175-200; Vase, 9.25", 1689, Limited to 2,950, $125-150; Bell, Blown, 3271, $60-65; Pitcher, 6.5", 3265, Limited to 2,950, $75-200; Perfume, 3290, Limited to 2,950, YOP: 1998 only, $150-175; Fairy Light, 3 piece, 1610, Limited to 2,950, YOP: 1998, $150-175. *Courtesy of Laurie & Richard Karman.*

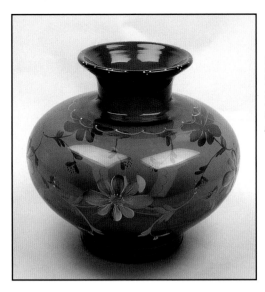

COLONIAL SCROLL ON ROYAL PURPLE N4, YOP: 1998: Vase, 6.5", 6470, Limited to 2,950, $175-200. *Courtesy of Laurie & Richard Karman.*

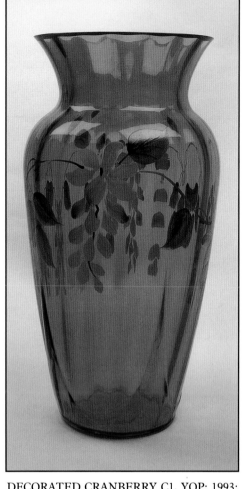

DECORATED CRANBERRY C1, YOP: 1993: Basket, 1748, Beaded Melon, $125-150. *Courtesy of Laurie & Richard Karman.*

DECORATED CRANBERRY C1, YOP: 1993: Vase, 11", 1640, Rib, George Signature, $125-150. *Courtesy of Laurie & Richard Karman.*

DECORATED CRANBERRY C1, YOP: 1993: Vase, 9", Pinch, 1749, Diamond Optic, $100-125. *Courtesy of Laurie & Richard Karman.*

DRAGONFLY & FLOWER ON RUBINA VERDE BW 1997 Historic Collection: Box, 1581, Melon, Limited to 1,750, $150-175; Vase, 11", 7458, Melon, Limited to 1,750, $150-175; Basket, 7.5", 7139, Melon, Limited to 1,750, $150-175; Vase, 8", 7565, Reverse Melon, Limited to 1,750, $125-150; Pitcher, 6", 3066, Limited to 1,750, $150-175. *Courtesy of Tina & Joe Boris.*

EVENING BLOS-
SOMS & LADYBUGS
ON MULBERRY MD,
YOP: 1996: Pitcher,
7.5", 1671, Limited to
1,250, $150-175.
*Courtesy of Laurie &
Richard Karman.*

FLORAL ON GOLD
AMBERINA AV, YOP: 1999
AV: Vase, 6.5", 3047, Limited
to 2500 pieces, $100-125; Vase,
11", 3240, Limited to 2500
pieces, $150-175; Cruet, 3075,
Limited to 2500 pieces, $150-
175; Basket, 11", Hexagonal,
1533, Limited to 2500 pieces,
$150-175; Pitcher, 9.5", 1211,
Limited to 2500 pieces, $150-
175. *Courtesy of Laurie &
Richard Karman.*

HUMMINGBIRD & WILD ROSES ON
MULBERRY MS, YOP: 1996: Vase, 8", 2750,
Limited to 1,250, $125-150; Vase, 9.5", 1689,
Limited to 1,250, $150-175. *Courtesy of Laurie &
Richard Karman.*

HUMMINGBIRD & WILD ROSES
ON MULBERRY MS, YOP: 1996:
Basket, 8", 1531, Limited to 1,250,
$150-175. *Courtesy of Laurie & Richard
Karman.*

MOUNTIAN BERRY
ON GOLD OVERLAY
KT, YOP: 1996: Vase, 7",
1683, Aurora, $65-70;
Pitcher, 6.5", 3065, $65-
70. *Courtesy of Laurie &
Richard Karman.*

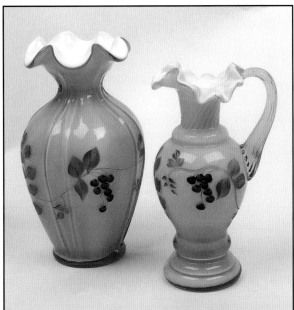

MOUNTIAN BERRY ON GOLD OVERLAY
KT, YOP: 1996: Basket, 7.5", 3127, $65-70;
Basket, 8", 3076, Don Fenton Signature, $65-70.
Courtesy of Laurie & Richard Karman.

PANSIES ON CRANBERRY CW, YOP: 1994-99: Vase, 9", Rib, 1554, $80-85; Pitcher, 6", 3068, YOP: 1998, $90-100; Pitcher, 11", Ribbed, 1672, YOP: 1997, $100-125; Basket, 8", 1639, $100-125. *Courtesy of Laurie & Richard Karman.*

PANSIES ON CRAN-BERRY CW, YOP: 1994-99: Basket, 6", Hat, 3239, $90-100. *Courtesy of Bobbie & Harold Morgan.*

PANSIES ON CRANBERRY CW, YOP: 1994-99: Pitcher, 6.5", 1568, $85-90; Vase, 9.5", Fine Rib, 1559, Bill Fenton Signature, YOP: 1994, $95-100; Vase, 7", 1567, Aurora, Don Fenton Signature, YOP: 1995, $75-90. *Courtesy of Laurie & Richard Karman.*

STARFLOWERS ON CRANBERRY NG, YOP: 1996: Basket, 7.5", 3127, $100-125. *Courtesy of Bobbie & Harold Morgan.*

PANSIES ON CRANBERRY CW, YOP: 1994-99: Vase, 8", Square, 1643, YOP: 1998, $90-100; Fairy Light, 1700, YOP: 1998, $75-80; Vase, 9", 3244, YOP: 1999, $100-125; Basket, 6", Hat, 3239, $90-100; Vase, 7.5", Tulip, 1685, $100-125; Vase, 4", 1557, $75-80. *Courtesy of Laurie & Richard Karman.*

SWEETBRIAR ON PLUM OVERLAY P9, YOP: 1997: Basket, 9", 4648, Melon, Lynn Signature, $100-125; Pitcher, 7.5", 1562, $85-90. *Courtesy of Phyllis & Terry Sterett.*

SWEETBRIAR ON PLUM OVERLAY P9, YOP: 1997: Vase, 9", 1648, Hexagonal, $95-100; Pitcher, 7.5", 1562, $85-90; Vase, 7", 1560, $85-90. *Courtesy of Laurie & Richard Karman.*

THISTLE FS, YOP: 1995: Vase, 9", Hexagonal, 1554, $100-125. Not Pictured: Vase, 11", 1561, $125-150; Basket, 8", 2766, $125-$150; Candle Holder, 9578, $30-35 ea. *Courtesy of Laurie & Richard Karman.*

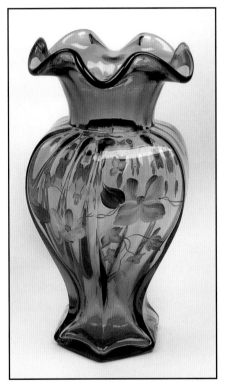

THISTLE FS, YOP: 1995: Pitcher, 9", 1566, Don Fenton Signature, $150-175. *Courtesy of Laurie & Richard Karman.*

TRANQUILITY AK, YOP: 1999: Vase, 5", 1689, Bill/Don Signature, $125-150.

Satin/Opal

Over the past thirty years of Fenton production, the most popular items have to be the Decorated items in either Custard Satin or Opal Satin. When I wrote the *Fenton Glass Compendium 1970-85*, it was surprising to me that so many people had already caught on to such a recently issued glass. (It is recently issued too! I'm not admitting to getting older, so it can't either!) Since the issue of that book, I have noticed that more people have caught onto all the decorated patterns from that time period and now collect them with a furious fervor!

In spite of the curtailed production of Satin Glass (due to the restrictions of the EPA in the late 1980s that resulted in Fenton having to sandblast all the items to achieve the satin finish), the company still produced a certain number of decorated patterns in Satin Glass.

Probably the two patterns that are the most desired by both collectors of Decorated Satin and collectors of decorated Scenic items are Cottage and Country Scene, both on Opal Satin.

Possibly the most collected floral pattern is Rose Garden. When it was discontinued in the latter part of 2001, the news was met with howls of anguish from certain dealers and collectors.

Items Not Pictured:

Kristen Floral YB 1995: Basket, 7.5", 2788, $60-65
Kristen Floral YB 1995: Basket, 7", 3535, $60-65
Kristen Floral YB 1995: Slipper, 9295, Rose, $30-35
Kristen Floral YB 1995: Vase, 4", 7241, $35-40
Pastel Violets on Custard VC 1987: Comport, 1628, $45-50
Pastel Violets on Custard VC 1987: Vase, 4.5", 7254, $30-35
Pastel Violets on Custard VC 1987: Vase, 7.5", Ribbed, 7660, $65-70
Pastel Violets on Custard VC 1987: Bud Vase, 9056, $25-30

COTTAGE ON OPAL SATIN ZB, YOP: 1993-6/94: Basket, 7.75", 2735, $85-70. *Courtesy of Laurie & Richard Karman.*

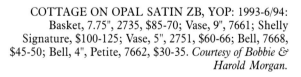

COTTAGE ON OPAL SATIN ZB, YOP: 1993-6/94: Basket, 7.75", 2735, $85-70; Vase, 9", 7661; Shelly Signature, $100-125; Vase, 5", 2751, $60-66; Bell, 7668, $45-50; Bell, 4", Petite, 7662, $30-35. *Courtesy of Bobbie & Harold Morgan.*

COTTAGE ON OPAL SATIN ZB, YOP: 1993-6/94: Vase, 9", 7661, Shelly Signature, $100-125. *Courtesy of Norma & Melvin Lampton.*

COUNTRY SCENE ON IVORY SATIN LT, YOP: 1990-91: Basket, 7", 7237, $80-85. *Courtesy of Laurie & Richard Karman.*

COUNTRY SCENE ON IVORY SATIN LT, YOP: 1990-91: Basket, 7", 7237, $80-85; Plate, 8", 7418, $70-75; Bell, 7668, $40-45; Vase, 7", 7252, $75-80; Clock, 8600, $100-125. Not Pictured: Vase, 4.5", 7254, $55-60. *Courtesy of Bobbie & Harold Morgan.*

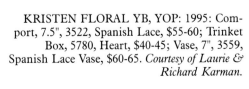

KRISTEN FLORAL YB, YOP: 1995: Comport, 7.5", 3522, Spanish Lace, $55-60; Trinket Box, 5780, Heart, $40-45; Vase, 7", 3559, Spanish Lace Vase, $60-65. *Courtesy of Laurie & Richard Karman.*

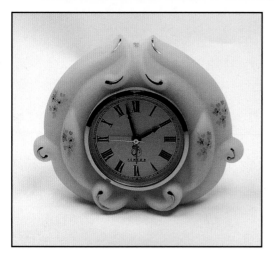

KRISTEN FLORAL YB, YOP: 1995:
Perfume, 2785, Limited to 2,500, YOP:
1995, $70-75. *Courtesy of Myers Mystique.*

KRISTEN FLORAL YB, YOP: 1995: Clock,
8691, $50-55. *Courtesy of Laurie & Richard Karman.*

MEADOW BLOSSOMS ON
OPAL SATIN SF, YOP: 1991-93:
Basket, 6.5", Paneled, 9238, $65-70.
Courtesy of Laurie & Richard Karman.

MEADOW BLOSSOMS ON OPAL
SATIN SF, YOP: 1991-93: Clock,
4638, Victorian, $55-60. *Courtesy of
Laurie & Richard Karman.*

MEADOW BLOSSOMS ON
OPAL SATIN SF, YOP: 1991-93:
Vase, 8", Tulip, 7250, $65-70;
Slipper, 9295, Rose, $30-35; Jewel
Box, Oval, 9589, 1991-92, $40-45.
Not Pictured: Comport, 1628, $50-
55. *Courtesy of Laurie & Richard
Karman.*

PASTEL VIOLETS ON CUSTARD
VC, YOP: 1987: Basket, 7.5", Square,
7635, $65-70. *Courtesy of Laurie &
Richard Karman.*

PROVINICIAL BOUQUET FS, YOP: 1987-88: Vase, 11", Spiral, 3161, $100-125; Vase, 4.5", 7254, $45-50; Basket, 7.5", Square, 7635, $75-80; Bud Vase, 9056, $30-35; Vase, 13", 3196, $125-150. *Courtesy of Bobbie & Harold Morgan.*

PROVINICIAL BOUQUET FS, YOP: 1987-88: Vase, 7", 3195, $90-100. Not Pictured: Comport, 1628, $55-60. *Courtesy of Wiggins Gifts.*

ROSE GARDEN EG, YOP: 1994-99: Basket, 7", Footed, 3535, $55-65; Basket, 4.5", Mini, 6560, Diamond, $65-70. *Courtesy of Laurie & Richard Karman.*

ROSE GARDEN EG, YOP: 1994-99: Basket, 7", Footed, 3535, $55-65; Comport, 7429, 1997, $75-80; Basket, 7", 2737, $70-75. *Courtesy of Connie & Aaron Patient.*

ROSE GARDEN EG, YOP: 1994-99: Box, Heart, 5789, $55-60.

ROSE GARDEN EG, YOP: 1994-99: Box, 9685, Teardrop, $45-50; Vase, 11", Spiral, 3161, $100-125; Vase, 7", 7315, 1999, $65-70; Box, Heart, 5789, $55-60. *Courtesy of Laurie & Richard Karman.*

ROSE GARDEN EG, YOP: 1994-99: Vase, 4.5", 7254, 1997, $45-50; Comport, 7429, 1997, $75-80; Vase, 11", Tulip, 1556, $80-90; Candy Box, 7484, $55-60; Vase, 8.5", 6859, 1997, $60-65; Slipper, Stylized, 2931, $30-35; Pitcher, 5.5", Melon, 6464, 1997, $65-70. *Courtesy of Laurie & Richard Karman.*

ROSE GARDEN EG, YOP: 1994-99: Slipper, 9295, Rose, $35-40; Bell, 1773, $35-40; Heart Box, 5780, $55-60; Vase, 6", 7451, Rose, $55-60; Doll, Bridesmaid, $90-100; Basket, 10.5", Footed, 6585, $75-80. *Courtesy of Myers Mystique.*

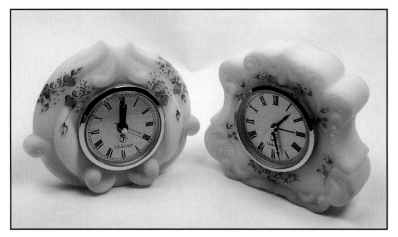

ROSE GARDEN EG, YOP: 1994-99: Clock, 4.5", 8691, 1999, $75-80; Clock, 4638, Victorian, $75-80. Not Pictured: Basket, 8", 2913, YOP: 1999, $75-80; Comport, 6322, Flower Band, $65-70. *Courtesy of Laurie & Richard Karman.*

THISTLE & BOWS EW, YOP: 1986: Basket, 7.5", Square, 7635, $65-70; Bell, 7668, $30-35; Comport, 1628, $50-55. Not Pictured: Votive, Footed, 7275, $25-30; Bud Vase, 9056, $25-30.

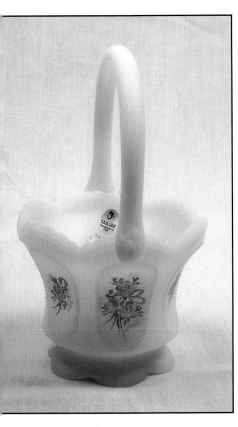

VICTORIAN ROSES VJ, YOP: 1987-89: Alarm Clock, 8691, $90-100; Jewel Box, Oval, 9589, $45-50; Vase, 6", 7451, $40-45; Clock, 8691, $55-60. Not Pictured: Comport, 1628, YOP: 1987-88, $45-50; Candy Box, 8288, Medallion, $65-70; Bud Vase, 9056, $25-30. *Courtesy of Bobbie & Harold Morgan.*

YOP: 1987-89: Basket, 8", Paneled, 9639, $65-70. *Courtesy of Laurie & Richard Karman.*

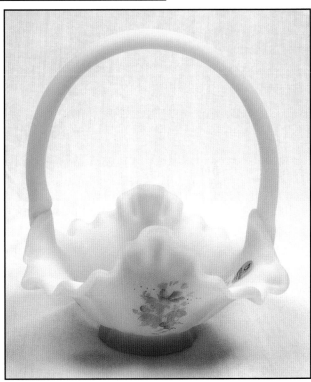

VICTORIAN ROSES VJ, YOP: 1987-89: Vase, 7", 3195, YOP: 1987-88, $60-65; Vase, 13", 3196, YOP: 1987-88, $80-100. Both of these vases were produced on Opaline, rather than White Satin. *Courtesy of Bobbie & Harold Morgan.*

WATER COLORS PF, YOP: 1990: Basket, 7", 7630, Aurora, $70-75. *Courtesy of Laurie & Richard Karman.*

WATER COLORS PF, YOP: 1990: Vase, 8", Tulip, 7250, $65-70; Jewel Box, Oval, 9589, $45-55; Vase, 4.5", 7620, $40-45; Comport, 9229, Empress, $55-60. *Courtesy of Laurie & Richard Karman.*

WATER COLORS PF, YOP: 1990: Alarm Clock, 8691, $55-60. *Courtesy of Laurie & Richard Karman.*

Transparent

It was in the 1990s that Fenton marketed plain Transparent colors with decorations on them. Throughout that time period, several of these patterns became quite popular and were in the line for several years.

Items Not Pictured:

Vining Garden on Sea Mist Green FP 1991-94: Vase, 8", Feather Rib, 1218, YOP: 1994 only, $40-45

Vining Garden on Sea Mist Green FP 1991-94: Vase, 10", Tulip, 1556, YOP: 1991-94, $40-45

Vining Garden on Sea Mist Green FP 1991-94: Vase, 9.5", 1689, $45-50

Vining Garden on Sea Mist Green FP 1991-94: Vase, 10.5", Wide Rib, 3260, YOP: 1991-93, $45-50

Vining Garden on Sea Mist Green FP 1991-94: Vase, 5", 7620, Aurora, YOP: 1993-94, $30-35

Vining Garden on Sea Mist Green FP 1991-94: Votive, 2 Way Leaf, 9578, YOP: 1993-94, $20-25

ARBOR BLOSSOMS ON PETAL PINK JY, YOP: 1991-93: Vase, 6", Wide Rib, 3263, YOP: 1991-92, $35-40; Pitcher, 32 oz., 3265, $40-45; Slipper, 9295, Rose, YOP: 1992-93, $20-25; Vase, 10", Tulip, 1556, $50-55. Not Pictured: Vase, 5", 7620, Aurora, YOP: 1993 only, $25-30. *Courtesy of Laurie & Richard Karman.*

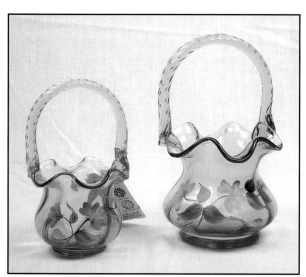

ARBOR BLOSSOMS ON PETAL PINK JY 1991-93: Basket, 6", Wide Rib, 3231, $40-45; Basket, 7.75", 3234, $40-45. *Courtesy of Laurie & Richard Karman.*

ICE BLUE WITH BELL FLOWERS LH, YOP: 1999: Bell, Aurora, 9674, $35-40; Pitcher, 5.5", 272, Melon, $55-60; Vase, 8", Reverse Melon, 7565, $60-65; Vase, 11", 7682, $70-75; Basket, 7", 2777, $65-70. *Courtesy of Laurie & Richard Karman.*

ICE BLUE WITH BELL FLOWERS LH, YOP: 1999: Pitcher, 5.5", 272, Melon, $55-60; Vase, 8", Reverse Melon, 7565, $60-65; Vase, 11", 7682, $70-75; Basket, 7", 2777, $65-70; Pitcher, 32 oz., 3265, $45-55. *Courtesy of Connie & Aaron Patient.*

GOLDEN FLAX ON COBALT KG, YOP: 1993: Basket, 7", 1153, $65-70; Basket, 8", 2766, $70-75. *Courtesy of Laurie & Richard Karman.*

GOLDEN FLAX ON COBALT KG, YOP: 1993: Bell, Aurora, 9674, $35-40; Basket, 7", 1153, $65-70. *Courtesy of Bobbie & Harold Morgan.*

GOLDEN FLAX ON COBALT KG, YOP: 1993: Pitcher, 32 oz., 3265, $70-75; Candy, Footed, 7380, $75-80; Vase, 9", Hexagonal, 2953, $65-70. *Courtesy of Laurie & Richard Karman.*

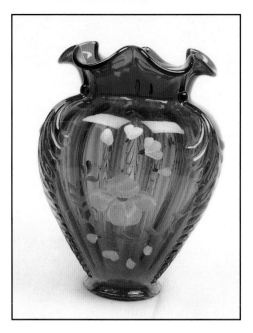

MORNING GLORIES ON SEA MIST GREEN L3, YOP: 1997: Vase, 9", 1693, $40-45; Pitcher, 6.5", 325, $40-45. Not Pictured: Basket, 8", 2766, $40-45. *Courtesy of Laurie & Richard Karman.*

GOLDEN FLAX ON COBALT KG, YOP: 1993: Vase, 1649, Feather, Shelly Signature, $65-70. Not Pictured: Candy, Footed, 7380, $75-80; Vase, 9", Hexagonal, 2953, $65-70; Comport, 9229, Empress, $65-70. *Courtesy of Laurie & Richard Karman.*

TWILIGHT TULIPS TT, YOP: 1992-93: Pitcher, 32 oz., 3265, $65-70; Vase, 14.5", Wide Ribbed, 3237, YOP: 1992 only, $75-80; Slipper, 9295, Rose, $25-30; Vase, 5", 2751, YOP: 1993-94, $55-60; Vase, 10.5", Wide Ribbed, 3260, $75-80. Not Pictured: Vase, 10", 1556, Tulip, $65-70; Vase, 8", Ribbed, 3236, $55-60; Vase, 5", 7620, Aurora, $35-40. *Courtesy of Laurie & Richard Karman.*

VINING GARDEN ON SEA MIST GREEN FP, YOP: 1991-94: Basket, 6", Wide Rib, 3231, YOP: 1991-94, $40-45; Basket, 5", 2751, YOP: 1993-94, $30-35; Basket, 8", 3233, YOP: 1991-93, $35-40; Basket, 8", 2766, YOP: 1994 only, $40-45. *Courtesy of Laurie & Richard Karman.*

TWILIGHT TULIPS TT, YOP: 1992-93: Basket, 10.5", Footed, 6572, $65-70. *Courtesy of Laurie & Richard Karman.*

VINING GARDEN ON SEA MIST GREEN FP, YOP: 1991-94: Basket, 8", 2766, YOP: 1994 only, $40-45; Vase, 8.5", Wide Rib, 3259, YOP: 1991 only, $35-40. *Courtesy of Wiggins Gifts.*

VINING GARDEN ON SEA MIST
GREEN FP, YOP: 1991-94: Shakers,
6006, Wavecrest, $30-35. *Courtesy of
Shelia & Pete McMillian.*

VINING GARDEN ON SEA MIST GREEN FP, YOP:
1991-94: Slipper, 9295, Rose, YOP: 1992-94, $20-25; Vase,
11", Wide Rib, 3254, YOP: 1991-93, $45-50; Vase, 5",
2751, Pitcher, 32 oz., 3265, YOP: 1991-94, $40-45; Bowl,
9.5", 3221, YOP: 1991-92, $35-40. *Courtesy of Laurie &
Richard Karman.*

VINING GARDEN ON SEA MIST
GREEN FP, YOP: 1991-94: Vase, 6",
Wide Rib, 3263, YOP: 1991-93, $35-40.

VINTAGE ON
PLUM PV, YOP:
1993-94: Basket, 7",
7630, Aurora, $45-
50. *Courtesy of Laurie
& Richard Karman.*

VINTAGE ON PLUM
PV, YOP: 1993-94: Vase,
8", 1785, Diamond, $40-
45; Slipper, 9295, Rose,
$20-25. Not Pictured:
Vase, 10", Melon, 1786,
Don Fenton Signature,
$45-50; Comport, 9229,
$35-40.

VIOLAS ON PETAL PINK PU 1994: Basket, 10.5",
Footed, 6572, $35-40. *Courtesy of Laurie & Richard Karman.*

VIOLAS ON PETAL PINK PU 1994: Vase, 8", 1218, Feather Rib, $40-45; Pitcher, 32 oz., 3265, $40-45. Not Pictured: Vase, 4", 2767, $25-30; Slipper, 9295, Rose, $25-30. *Courtesy of Laurie & Richard Karman.*

WILDFLOWERS ON CRYSTAL F5, YOP: 1991: Basket, 8", 3233, $35-40. *Courtesy of Laurie & Richard Karman.*

WILDFLOWERS ON CRYSTAL F5, YOP: 1991: Basket, 8", 3233, $35-40; Candlesticks, 9071, $20-25 ea.; Bowl, 9.5", 3221, $35-40; Vase, 8.5", Wide Rib, 3259, $30-35; Bell, Aurora, 9667, $25-30. Not Pictured: Pitcher, 70 oz., 1660, $55-60; Wine, 8 oz., 4941, $15-20; Water Glass, 12 oz., 4942, $15-20; Vase, 10.5", Wide Rib, 3260, $45-50. *Courtesy of Bobbie & Harold Morgan.*

Special Series

Throughout the late 1980s, and on into the 1990s, Fenton continued to issue special series. Most of these series were limited as to the time that they would be out. Several were issued, for Easter, and many were from the popular Designer series. Fenton designers Michael Dickinson and Beverly Cumberledge designed many of these special series.

American Classics

"Studebaker" SU 1986-87: Designed by Michael Dickinson: Clock, 8600, $150-200; Plate, 8", 7418, $125-150; Bell, 7668, $65-70; Desk Plaque, 7698, Mounted on a Wooden Plaque, not originally sold this way, $55-60 (for Glass Plaque only). Not Pictured: Lamp, 7204, 16", Hammered Colonial, $350-400. *Courtesy of Bobbie & Harold Morgan.*

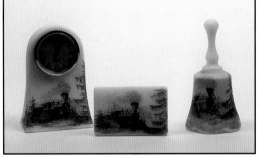

"Juptier" TP 198-87: Designed by Michael Dickinson: Clock, 8600, $150-200; Desk Plaque, 7698, $55-60; Bell, 7668, $65-70. *Courtesy of Bobbie & Harold Morgan.*

"Juptier" TP 198-87: Designed by Michael Dickinson: Lamp, 23", Student, 7514, $650-700. *Courtesy of Audrey & Joe Elsinger.*

"Juptier" TP 198-87: Designed by Michael Dickinson: Plate, 8", 7418, $175-200. *Courtesy of Sharon & Alan Fenner.*

Deer Scene PG 1988-89: Bell, 7668, $45-50; Plate, 7186, $55-60; Fairy Light, 7300, $75-80; Clock, 8600, $125-150. *Courtesy of Bobbie & Harold Morgan.*

Deer Scene PG 1988-89: Bell, 7668, $45-50.

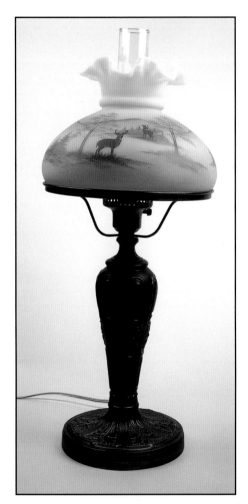

Deer Scene PG 1988-89: Lamp, Student, 7209, $450-500. *Courtesy of Bobbie & Harold Morgan.*

Artist Series: A Gift to Nature AC 1989-6/89: Bell, Petite, 1760, $20-25; Cup Plate, 7615, $20-25. The Hummingbird HW 1986: Bell, Petite, 1760, $20-25; Cup Plate, 7615, $20-25. *Courtesy of Sharon & Alan Fenner.*

Artist Series: Serenity AT 1988: Bell, Petite, 1760, $20-25; Cup Plate, 7615, $20-25. Childhood Treasures: Teddy Bear 1986: Bell, Petite, 1760, $20-25; Cup Plate, 7615, $20-25. *Courtesy of Sharon & Alan Fenner.*

Artist Series: Wild Geese: Bell, Petite, 1760, $20-25; Cup Plate, 7615, $20-25. Out in the Country SF 1986: Bell, Petite, 1760, $20-25; Cup Plate, 7615, $20-25. *Courtesy of Sharon & Alan Fenner.*

Artist Series: House hunting AC 1989: Bell, Petite, 1760, $20-25; Cup Plate, 7615, $20-25. Childhood Treasures: The Clown: Bell, Petite, 1760, $20-25; Cup Plate, 7615, $20-25. *Courtesy of Sharon & Alan Fenner.*

Childhood Treasures: Dream Castles 1989: Bell, Petite, 1760, $20-25; Cup Plate, 7615, $20-25. Childhood Treasures: Rocking Horse: Bell, Petite, 1760, $20-25; Cup Plate, 7615, $20-25. *Courtesy of Sharon & Alan Fenner.*

Childhood Treasures: Caught In the Act 1987: Bell, Petite, 1760, $20-25; Cup Plate, 7615, $20-25. Childhood Treasures: The Kitten: Bell, Petite, 1760, $20-25; Cup Plate, 7615, $20-25. *Courtesy of Sharon & Alan Fenner.*

Childhood Treasures: Cuddly Friend CX 1989: Bell, Petite, 1760, $20-25; Cup Plate, 7615, $20-25. Artist Series: Homestead SF 1987: Bell, Petite, 1760, $20-25; Cup Plate, 7615, $20-25. *Courtesy of Sharon & Alan Fenner.*

Mother's Day Series

Mother Day Series: Deer & Fawn X7 1993: Plate, 8", 7418, $40-45; Bell, 7668, $35-40. Not Pictured: Clock, 8600, $100-125. *Courtesy of Sharon & Alan Fenner.*

Mother's Day Series: Mother's Watchful Eye MS 1991: Plate, 8", 7418, $40-45; Bell, 7668, $35-40. Not Pictured: Clock, 8600, $100-125. *Courtesy of Sharon & Alan Fenner.*

Left: Mother Day Series: Let's Play with Mom 1992 X5: Plate, 8", 7418, $40-45; Bell, 7668, $35-40. Not Pictured: Clock, 8600, $100-125. *Courtesy of Sharon & Alan Fenner.*

Right: Mother's Day Series: Loving Puppy XS 1994: Plate, 8", 7418, $40-45; Bell, 7668, $35-40. Not Pictured: Clock, 8600, $100-125. *Courtesy of Sharon & Alan Fenner.*

Special Issues

After Rosalene was discontinued in the early 1980s due to the problems in making this treatment, it sometimes would be resurrected, either in limited edition items or for the Connoisseur Series. In the late 1990s, several decorated series in Rosalene were issued which proved quite popular with collectors. Also during this same time, Blue Burmese, which also was difficult to produced, appeared for the first time in many years in the Honor Series in 1999. This series was used to call attention to different designers, chemists, and glassmakers who had worked at Fenton over the years. It recognized the items and treatments that they had developed.

Periwinkle on Blue Burmese UQ 1999

Periwinkle on Blue Burmese UQ, YOP: 1999: Basket, 5.5", 6330, $125-150; Guest Set, 8100, $250; Vase, 11", 6548, $150-200. *Courtesy of Anne Musser.*

Rosebuds on Rosalene WA 1998

Rosebuds on Rosalene WA, YOP: 1998: Cologne, 7000, $100-125; Puff Box, 7009, $100-125; Ballerina, 5270; Natalie, $100-125; Vase, 6", 7051, $100-125. *Courtesy of Laurie & Richard Karman.*

Rosebuds on Rosalene WA, YOP: 1998: Ballerina, 5270, Natalie, $100-125. *Courtesy of Phyllis & Terry Sterett.*

Violets on Rosalene NX 1999

Violets on Rosalene NX, YOP: 1999: Butterfly, 5271, $75-80. *Courtesy of Bev & Jon Spencer.*

Violets on Rosalene NX, YOP: 1999: Perfume, 2785, Heart, $125-150; Trinket Box, 4105, Heart, $125-150; Bridesmaid Doll, 7", 5228, $100-125; Praying Children, 5203, $90-100 pair; Butterfly, 5271, $75-80. *Courtesy of Laurie & Richard Karman.*

Mary Gregory

The first item that Fenton produced in Mary Gregory was an Egg in 1991. Several years later, in 1994, the Mary Gregory was issued on Ruby Glass. Several years later, it was announced that the Mary Gregory pattern would be made in Cranberry Glass. At that time, Fenton was unaware of the fervor that this pattern would cause with collectors. Each item was made in limited numbers and only issued for one year. But one of the main reasons for its appeal to collectors is the extraordinary detail given to the decoration, even down to the buttons on the cuffs of the character's outfits and their ruffles. Each year several different pieces are issued. On each piece is a different scene of a young child, either at work or play.

Basket, Oval, 8673 RY, YOP: 1994, "He Loves Me, He Love Me Not", $150-175. *Courtesy of Jan Hollingsworth.*

Bell, 7463, YOP: 1994, $100-125. *Courtesy of Laurie & Richard Karman.*

Basket, 1593 DQ: Girl Swimming Basket, Limited to 1,500, YOP: 1997, $225-250; Basket, 8", 1613 R8, Boy Fishing, Limited to 1,250, YOP: 1999, $150-175. *Courtesy of Laurie & Richard Karman.*

Fairy Light, 1505 DW, Meadow Flowers, Limited to 1,500, YOP: 1997, $150-200.

Bell, 6590 RK, YOP: 2,000, $90-100; Perfume, 2906 RK, Swan, Limited to 1,950, YOP: 1998, $150-175; Guest Set, 1500 DI, Breezy Day, Limited to 1,500, $300+; Fairy Light, YOP: 1997, 1505 DW, Meadow Flowers, Limited to 1,500, YOP: 1997, $150-200.

Vase, 5", 3248 R8, Boy Fishing, Limited to 1,250, YOP: 1999, $100-125; Pitcher, 12", 3275 DM, Girl, Limited to 1,950, $150-175; Basket, 1533 DI, Breezy Day, Limited to 1,950, YOP: 1998, $250-275; Hat Basket, 1532 RK, Swan, Limited to 2,000, YOP: 1996, $150-175; Vase, 9", 1554 RP, Day Dreaming, Limited to 1,500, YOP: 1996, $175-200. Not Picture: Pitcher, 1671 RD, Girl/Butterfly, Limited to 1,250, YOP: 1999, $200-225. *Courtesy of Laurie & Richard Karman.*

Lamp, 3201 RK, Swan, Limited to 1,250, YOP: 1999, $350+. *Courtesy of Laurie & Richard Karman.*

Sentiments Collections

First issued in 1992 as part of the Sentiments collection for Valentines Day, the Heart Optic pattern in Cranberry has become a favorite of Fenton Collectors. Each piece was issued for that year only, and was only available for several months at the beginning of each year. Those pieces quickly were snatched up by collectors and are now quite scarce today. Earlier items in the Sentiments Collections include several Southern Bell dolls

Southern Girl Figural, 5141 NI, White Opal Decorated, Sentiments Collection, $70-80. *Courtesy of Laurie & Richard Karman.*

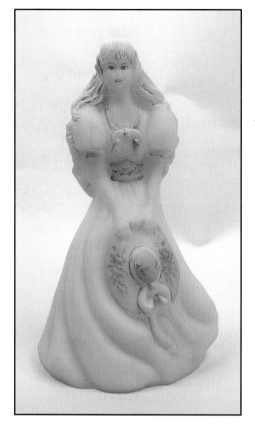

Southern Girl Figural, 5141 NX, Rose Pearl, Sentiments Collection, $70-80. *Courtesy of Laurie & Richard Karman.*

Basket, 7", Hat, 4965, YOP: 1997, $150-175. *Courtesy of Laurie & Richard Karman.*

Fairy Light, 4905, YOP: 1998 only, $125-150; Fairy Light, 3 piece, 2903, YOP: 1996, $250+. *Courtesy of Laurie & Richard Karman.*

Trinket Box, 2740, YOP: 1993 only, $150-175;
Perfume with Oval Stopper, 6580, YOP: 1992
only, $150-175; Box, 4.5", Covered, 4990, YOP:
1998 only, $175-200; Puff Box, 4950, YOP:
1997, $150-175; Perfume with Heart Stopper, 5",
2760, YOP: 1994 only, $150-175; Perfume, 5",
7100, Beaded Melon, YOP: 1996, $150-175.
Courtesy of Laurie & Richard Karman.

Basket, 7", 2736, YOP: 1994 only, $125-150;
Basket, 2732, 7", Caprice, YOP: 1993 only, $150-
175; Basket, 8", 2745, YOP: 1995 only, $175-200;
Basket, 8", 7122, Beaded Melon, YOP: 1996,
$175-200; Basket, 5", 2740, YOP: 1993 only,
$125-150. Not Pictured: Basket, 6", 6567, YOP:
1992 only, $175-200. *Courtesy of Laurie &
Richard Karman.*

Vase, 4", 6568, YOP: 1992 only, $150-175; Vase,
5.5", 2755, Ribbed, YOP: 1994 only, $125-150;
Vase, 5.5", Melon Rib, 2749, YOP: 1993 only, $125-150;
Vase, 5", 4955, YOP: 1998 only, $75-80; Pitcher,
6.5", 2169, YOP: 1997, $175-200; Pitcher, 5.5",
Melon, 2774, YOP: 1995 only, $150-175. *Courtesy of
Laurie & Richard Karman.*

Romance Collection CK ON 1997-99 Issues

First issued in 1998, the Romance collection was originally intended to be a series of items that could be used as gifts for weddings or anniversaries. The first issue, in 1997, was Iridescent Ivory with Gold Specks, and White Roses. In the following years, it was issued in decorated Iridescent French Opalescent.

Candy Box, 8288, Medallion, YOP: 1997, $55-60; Box, Heart Trinket, 5780, YOP: 1997, $35-40; Basket, 7.5", 4639, YOP: 1997, $45-50; Bird, Happiness, 5197, YOP: 1997, $35-40. *Courtesy of Laurie & Richard Karman.*

Bird, Happiness, 5197, 1997, $35-40.

Doll, 5228, $75-85. *Courtesy of Fran & Bill Ersham.*

Bell, 1127, $35-40. *Courtesy of Laurie & Richard Karman.*

Egg on stand, 5146, $45-50; Vase, 6", Fan, 1136, $65-70; Doll, 5228 Bridesmaid, $90-100; Bird, Small, 5163, $40-45; Basket, 8", 2918, $75-80. Not Pictured: Bell, 8267, Medallion, 1997, $30-35; Vase, 4.5", 9357, 1997, $35-40; Vase, 6.5", 9252, Rose, YOP: 1999, $55-60. *Courtesy of Laurie & Richard Karman.*

Millennium Collection JE 1999

To celebrate the end of the twentieth century, and to herald in the coming of the twenty-first, Fenton issued the Millennium Collection. With the rolled edge bowl, whose mould dates from the 1920s, and Fenton's happiness bird, it aptly deciphers the past, and the treatment of Iridescent French Opalescent gives it a metallic shine that looks eerily futuristic.

Millennium Collection JE 1999: Vase, 7", 6470, $100-125; Bowl, 10", Rolled Rim, 2747, $80-100; Happiness Bird, 5197, $45-55. *Courtesy of Tina & Joe Boris.*

Proud To Be An American Issue 1981

The Proud To Be An American series, first issued during Desert Storm, has gained new appeal since 9-11 and Fenton's issue of The Stars & Stripes series. This series, which had been always quite desirable with Fenton collectors, quickly took on new meaning in the later part of 2001. Difficult to find are the bear figural, especially the Schwartz Bear.

Flying Ace Bear, 5151 TA, $65-70. *Courtesy of Bobbie & Harold Morgan.*

Schwartz Bear, 5151 NC, $85-90; Red/White/ Blue Bear, 5151 RA, $85-90. *Courtesy of Bev & Jon Spencer.*

Yellow Ribbon Bell, 7668 YQ, $45-55; Christmas Yellow Ribbon Bell, 7668, $65-70. *Courtesy of Jan Hollingsworth.*

Limited Editions

Throughout the 1990s Fenton would issue different limited edition items, either for special series, such as the Sentiments Collection, or just as special offerings in their catalogs. Usually they would be only offered for a single year, making these items especially difficult to find. Possibly the most difficult are the Bridesmaids Dolls and Southern Girl Figural, which have almost developed a cult following.

Epergne, Mini, 4807 PT, Champagne Satin with Plum Ring, YOP: 1998, $45-50. *Courtesy of Bobbie & Harold Morgan.*

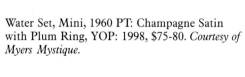

Mini Punch Bowl Set, 6801 PT: Champagne Satin with Plum Ring, 1998; Mini Punch Bowl Set, 6800 EZ, $55-60; Spruce Green Hobstar & Feather, YOP: 1997, $55-60. *Courtesy of Bobbie & Harold Morgan.*

Water Set, Mini, 1960 PT: Champagne Satin with Plum Ring, YOP: 1998, $75-80. *Courtesy of Myers Mystique.*

Mini Punch Bowl Set 6800 DZ: Dusty Rose Iridescent, YOP: 1996, $45-50. *Courtesy of Laurie & Richard Karman.*

Mini Table Set on Tray 8901 N9: HP English Daisy on Iridescent Crystal, 1999, $75-80. *Courtesy of Laurie & Richard Karman.*

Doll Figurine 5228 YB: Kristen's Floral, Limited to 2,500, YOP: 1995, $80-90. *Courtesy of Fran & Bill Ersham.*

Doll Figurine 5228 WB: Limited to 2,500, YOP: 1996, $85-95. *Courtesy of Fran & Bill Ersham.*

Vanity Set, 3 piece on Crystal Tray 7199 WB: HP Milk Glass Sentiments Collection, Limited to 1,500, YOP: 1996, $300+. *Courtesy of Bobbie & Harold Morgan.*

Vanity Set 2905 BG Burmese HP, Limited to 2,000, YOP: 1997, $350+; Southern Girl Figurine, 8", 5141 BG Burmese HP, Limited to 2,000, YOP: 1997, $100-125. *Courtesy of Laurie & Richard Karman.*

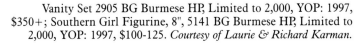

Geometrics EP 1986

In a new marketing strategy during the 1980s Fenton developed the Artisan series, which would be sold at larger department stores and cater to a non-traditional and more influential market. One of the lines developed for the Artisan Series was Geometrics, which took various shapes in both Transparent Rose and Gray and sandblasted them with an Art Deco design. This pattern, although very striking, did not go over well with the regular Fenton buyers and was soon discontinued. It's quite scarce to find on today's market.

Bowl, 9", Shallow, 8810, $60-70. *Courtesy of Melvin & Norma Lampton*

Items Not Pictured:

Bowl, 9", Shallow, 8810, $90-100
Bowl, 18", Deep, 8811, $100-125
Vase, 7", 8806, $80-90
Vase, 12", Wide Oval, 8801, $100-125
Vase, 12", Tall Oval, 8802, $100-125

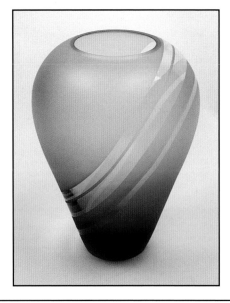

Vase, 9", 8807, $90-100.
Courtesy of Roserita Ziegler.

Vase, 6", 8805, $60-70. *Courtesy of Linda & John Flippen.*

Lifestyles 1998

In the late 1990s Fenton again attempted to secure a place in the decorator's and home interior market, this time with the Lifestyles collection. A large, full color catalog featured large, unusual, and striking items intended for interior decorators and their clients. Ironically, it was the long-time Fenton collectors who bought this line, due to many of the pieces being made off popular Verlys moulds from the 1930s.

Several different colors and lines were developed for this series including Royal Purple, Sea Green Satin, and a French Opalescent Iridescent Treatment which had a fine Pin Stripe Optic. Shown below are just a few of the items produced for this series.

Bowl, Leaf, 10", 8722 FZ on Brass Stand, $100-125; Pinstripe Collection (French Opalescent). *Courtesy of Bev & Jon Spencer.*

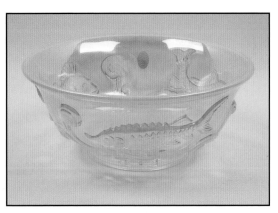

Bowl, 9", 9529 FZ, Fish, $55-60; Pinstripe Collection (French Opalescent). *Courtesy of Bev & Jon Spencer.*

Vase, 10", 9446 FZ, Thistle, $100-125; Pinstripe Collection (French Opalescent). *Courtesy of Bev & Jon Spencer.*

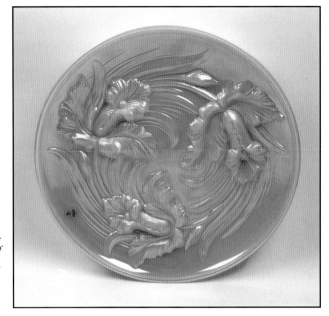

Platter, 14", 2974 GE, Orchid, $65-75; Sea Green Iridescent. *Courtesy of Bev & Jon Spencer.*

Vase, 6.5", 5150 XG, Atlantis, $65-70; Sea Green Satin; Box, 4.5", 9477 XG, Swallows, $55-60; Sea Green Satin. *Courtesy of Connie & Aaron Patient.*

Bowl, 9", 9529 XG, Fish, $45-50; Sea Green Satin; Bowl, 9", 9529 FZ, Fish, $55-60; Pinstripe Collection (French Opalescent).

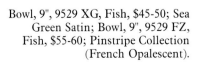

Connoisseur Collection

Throughout the 1980s and '90s, perhaps the most popular of Fenton's Special Series is the Connoisseur Collection. These items were always limited in number and were only offered in their catalogs throughout the latter part of each year. Many collectors eagerly anticipate the issue of each June Fenton Catalog supplement, so they can add to their collection of Connoisseur items.

The Connoisseur Collection was first establish in 1983 with the idea to create unique items and treatments in glass that required special skills; items that would showcase Fenton glassmakers' and decorators' talents.

It is in this series that Fenton has continued to produced its popular Burmese treatment, and also Rosalene, besides many other innovative treatments including Faverene, a treatment that is reminiscent of Stueban's Aureane.

Items Not Pictured:

Owl Figural, 5258 FN, Favrene Limited to 1500, YOP: 1993, $250+

Amphora with Stand, 2748 FW, HP Favrene Limited to 850, YOP: 1993, $500+

Lamp, 2760 CX, Spring Woods Reverse HP Limited to 500, YOP: 1993, $1000+

Lamp, 7939 BJ, Scenic Floral Reverse Pained Limited to 550, YOP: 1997, $800+

Vase, 8", 8817 DJ, French Opalescent After the Rain Limited to 2250, YOP: 1998, $250-275

Lamp, 6250 DR, Tulips Reverse Painted Limited to 750, YOP: 1999, $800+

Bell, 7666 SB, Burmese with HP Shells, Limited to 500, $100+. *Courtesy of Chuck Bingham.*

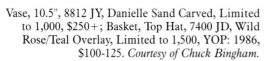

Vase, 10.5", 8812 JY, Danielle Sand Carved, Limited to 1,000, $250+; Basket, Top Hat, 7400 JD, Wild Rose/Teal Overlay, Limited to 1,500, YOP: 1986, $100-125. *Courtesy of Chuck Bingham.*

Vase, Handled, 3190 KF, French Royale, Limited to 1,000, YOP: 1986, $200-225. *Courtesy of Bobbie & Harold Morgan.*

Fairy Light, 7300, $65-75; Iceberg, 3" x 4", 8741, $25-30; Vase, 10.5", 8812 ET, Misty Morn, Limited to 1,000, YOP: 1986, $175-200. The Ice Berg & Fairy Light were not part of the Connoisseur Collection and were continued in the Fenton Line until 1989. *Courtesy of Bobbie & Harold Morgan.*

Cruet, 7863 CZ, Cranberry Pearl, Limited to 1,000, YOP: 1986, $250-300. *Courtesy of Linda & John Flippen.*

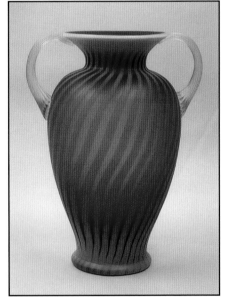

Vanity Set, 3104 BI, Blue Ridge, Limited to 1,000, YOP: 1986, $400+. *Courtesy of Linda & John Flippen.*

Urn, 13", Handled, 3194 ZS, Cranberry Satin, Limited to 1,000, YOP: 1986, $500+. *Courtesy of Bobbie & Harold Morgan.*

Lamp, Boudoir, 7802 CZ, Cranberry Pearl, Limited to 750, YOP: 1986, $250-300. *Courtesy of Bobbie & Harold Morgan.*

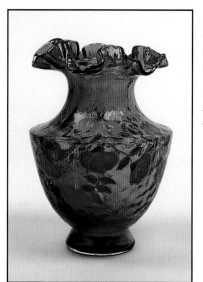

Vase, 7.25", 1796 BY, HP Cranberry Blossoms/Bows, Limited to 950, YOP: 1987, $175-200. *Courtesy of Bobbie & Harold Morgan.*

Pitcher, 8", 9468 QY, HP Enameled Azure, Limited to 950, YOP: 1987, $125-150. *Courtesy of Norma & Melvin Lampton.*

Vase, 10.5", 8812 ET, Misty Morn, Limited to 1,000, YOP: 1986, $175-200. *Courtesy of Trudy & Dick Green.*

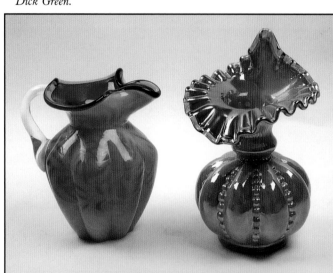

Pitcher, 2065 ZC, Cased Cranberry Opal/ Teal Ring, Limited to 2,500, $150-175; Vase, 6", 2556 ZI, Cased Cranberry Opal/ Teal Iridescent, Limited to 3500, YOP: 1988, $150-175. *Courtesy of Bev & Jon Spencer.*

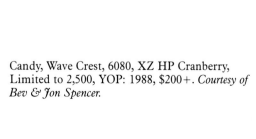

Basket, 3132 OT, Iridescent Teal Case Vasa Murrhina, Limited to 2,500, YOP: 1988, $150-175. *Courtesy of Bev & Jon Spencer.*

Candy, Wave Crest, 6080, XZ HP Cranberry, Limited to 2,500, YOP: 1988, $200+. *Courtesy of Bev & Jon Spencer.*

Bell, 7666, ZW Wisteria HP,
YOP: 1988, $55-65. *Courtesy of
Chuck Bingham.*

Epergne, 7605 RE, Rosalene, Limited to 2,000,
YOP: 1989, $1,000+. *Courtesy of Chuck
Bingham.*

Pitcher, 7060 RE, Rosalene Diamond Optic,
Limited to 2,500, YOP: 1989, $100-125. *Courtesy
of Bev & Jon Spencer.*

Bell, 9967 KT, Rosalene Satin HP, Limited
to ??, YOP: 1989. *Courtesy of Bev & Jon
Spencer.*

Lamp, 21", 9308 TT, Rosalene Satin HP,
Limited to 1,000, YOP: 1989, $750+.
Courtesy of Bev & Jon Spencer.

Vase, Basket weave, 8354 RE,
Rosalene, Limited to 2,500, YOP:
1989, $125-150. *Courtesy of Bev & Jon
Spencer.*

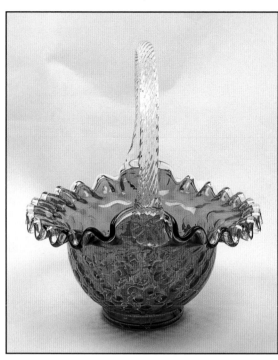

Basket, 7", 1330 TE, Cranberry with Crystal Ring HP, Limited to 2,500, YOP: 1989, $200+. *Courtesy of Laurie & Richard Karman.*

Candy Box, Ogee, 9394 FN, Favrene, Limited to 1,000, YOP: 1991, $350+. *Courtesy of Kansas City Fenton Finders.*

Candy Box, 2085 TM, Cranberry HP, Limited to 2,500, YOP: 1989, $200+. *Courtesy of Laurie & Richard Karman.*

Vase, 8812 G1, Fruit on Favrene HP, Limited to 850, $500+; Vase, 8812 FQ, Floral on Favrene HP, Limited to 850, YOP: 1991, $500+. *Courtesy of Norma & Melvin Lampton.*

Paperweight, 5193 RE, Rosalene, Limited to 2,000, YOP: 1991, $80-100; Basket, 4647 MD, HP Floral on Rosalene, Limited to 1,500, YOP: 1991, $150-200. *Courtesy of Bev & Jon Spencer.* Bell, 6761 UZ, HP Roses on Rosalene, Limited to 2,000, YOP: 1991, $75-80. *Courtesy of Laurie & Richard Karman.*

Vase, 8", Pinch, 6453 RG, Vasa Murrhina, Limited to 2,000, YOP: 1989, $150-175. *Courtesy of Laurie & Richard Karman.*

Vase, 7.5", 7572 QH, HP Raspberries on Burmese, Limited to 1,500, YOP: 1992, $125-150; Vase, 6.5", 5541 QH, HP Raspberries on Burmese, Limited to 1,500, YOP: 1991, $125-150. *Courtesy of Laurie & Richard Karman.*

Lamp, 20", 6701 RB, HP Roses on Burmese, Limited to 500, YOP: 1991, $750+. *Courtesy of Norma & Melvin Lampton.*

Vase, 8", 8817 QZ, HP Seascape, Limited to 750, YOP: 1992, $175-200. *Courtesy of Chuck Bingham.*

Box, Covered, 6080 RH, Poppy/Daisy HP, Limited to 1,250, YOP: 1992, $150-175. *Courtesy of Bev & Jon Spencer.*

Vase, 1684 RP, Twining Floral Rosalene Satin, Limited to 950, YOP: 1992, $200-250. *Courtesy of Bev & Jon Spencer.*

Pitcher, 4.5", 5531 QP, HP Berries on Burmese, Limited to 1,500, YOP: 1992, $150-175. *Courtesy of Linda & John Flippen.*

Vase, 8805 X3, Victorian Rose Persian Blue Opal HP, Limited to 950, YOP: 1993, $125-159. *Courtesy of Norma & Melvin Lampton.*

Pitcher, 9", 1211 RW, Empire On Cranberry HP, Limited to 950, YOP: 1992, $200-225. *Courtesy of Laurie & Richard Karman.*

Perfume, 1710 R5, Rose Trellis Rosalene, Limited to 1,250, YOP: 1993, $150-175. *Courtesy of Laurie & Richard Karman.*

Vase, 9", 7661 P4, Gold Leaves Sand Carved on Plum Iridescent, Limited to 950, YOP: 1993, $200-250. *Courtesy of Bev & Jon Spencer.*

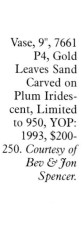

Bowl, 2747 RX, Ruby Stretch with Gold Scrolls HP, Limited to 1,250, YOP: 1993, $225-250. *Courtesy of Laurie & Richard Karman.*

Bowl, 14", 7727, Cranberry Cameo Sand Carved, Limited to 500, YOP: 1994, $500+. *Courtesy of Lori & Michael Palmer.*

Vase, 8", 2744 JK, Plum Opal HP, Limited to 750, YOP: 1994, $250-275. *Courtesy of Bev & Jon Spencer.*

Lamp, 5580 JB, Hummingbird Reverse HP, Limited to 300, YOP: 1994, $100+. *Courtesy of LuAnn & Atlee Beene.*

Clock, 8691 JV, Favrene HP, Limited to 850, YOP: 1994, $300+; Candy Box, Ogee, 9394 FN, Favrene, Limited to 1,000, YOP: 1991, $350+; Vase, 7", 2743 JP, Favrene HP, Limited to 850, YOP: 1994, $350+; Ginger Jar, 2950 VN, Favrene HP, Limited to 790, YOP: 1995, $750+. *Courtesy of Bev & Jon Spencer.*

Vase, 11", 3161 JQ, Gold Amberina HP, Limited to 750, YOP: 1994, $450+. *Courtesy of Bev & Jon Spencer.*

Clock, 8691 JV, Favrene HP, Limited to 850, YOP: 1994, $300+. *Courtesy of Laurie & Richard Karman.*

Pitcher, 10", 2729 JI, HP
Lattice on Burmese,
Limited to 750, YOP: 1994,
$300+. *Courtesy of Laurie &
Richard Karman.*

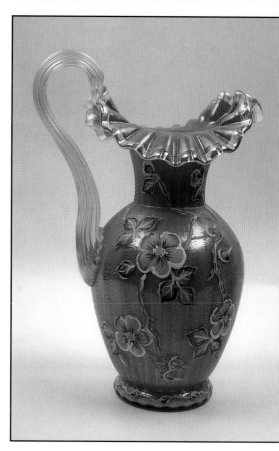

Pitcher, 9.5", 2796 ZM,
Victorian Art Glass HP,
Limited to 490, YOP:
1995, $175-200. *Courtesy of
Bev & Jon Spencer.*

Vase, 7", 7691 WF, Aurora Wild Rose
HP, Limited to 890, YOP: 1995, $200-
225. *Courtesy of Norma & Melvin
Lampton.*

Amphora with Stand, 10.25", 2947
US, Royal Purple HP, Limited to
890, YOP: 1995, $450+. *Courtesy of
Bobbie & Harold Morgan.*

Lamp, 21", 5468 VU, Butterfly/Floral Reverse
HP, Limited to 300, YOP: 1995, $1,000+.
Courtesy of Laurie & Richard Karman.

Vase, 11", 2782 OD, Berries on Wild Rose HP, Limited to 1,250, YOP: 1996, $300+. *Courtesy of Phyllis & Terry Sterett.*

Vase, 2961 BY, Burmese Trillium, Limited to 1,750, YOP: 1997, $200-225; Pitcher, 8", 2960 WQ, Dragon Fly on Burmese HP, Limited to 1450, YOP: 1996, $200-225. *Courtesy of Laurie & Richard Karman.*

Vase, 8", 9866 TR, HP Trout on Burmese, Limited to 1450, YOP: 1996, $200+. *Courtesy of Linda & John Flippen.*

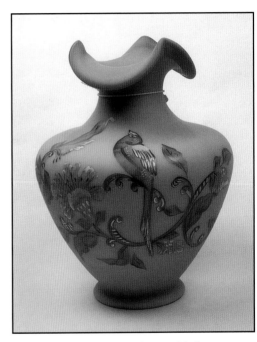

Vase, 11", 3254 QJ, HP Queens Bird on Burmese, Limited to 1350, YOP: 1996, $350+. *Courtesy of Williamstown Antique Mall.*

Vase, 7.5", 9855 EV, Favrene Cut Back Sand Carved, Limited to 1,250, YOP 1996, $400+; Daisy Vase with Metal Lid, 8807 FR, Favrene Sand Carved, Limited to 1350, $500+, YOP: 1997: *Courtesy of Bev & Jon Spencer.*

Box, Covered, 6584 CD, Mandarin Red HP, Limited to 1,250, YOP: 1996, $150-175. *Courtesy of Bobbie & Harold Morgan.*

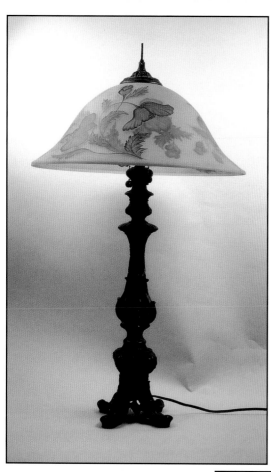

Lamp, 33", 6805 EA,
Reverse Painted Poppies
HP, Limited to 400, YOP:
1996, $1,000+. *Courtesy of
Linda & Dennis Sowers.*

Pitcher, 7", 2998 YZ,
Burmese Bountiful
Harvest, Limited to 2,250,
YOP: 1998, $200-$225;
Basket, 11.5", 7632 BQ,
Burmese Fenced Garden,
Limited to 1,750, $225-
250. *Courtesy of Laurie &
Richard Karman.*

Vase, 2965 UD, Opaline
Floral, Limited to 1,500,
$125-150. *Courtesy of
Laurie & Richard
Karman.*

Pitcher, 8966 ZJ, Wild Rose with
Rose Decoration, Limited to 1350,
YOP: 1997, $200+. *Courtesy of
Phyllis & Terry Sterett.*

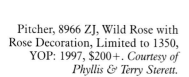

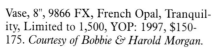

Vase, 8", 9866 FX, French Opal, Tranquility, Limited to 1,500, YOP: 1997, $150-
175. *Courtesy of Bobbie & Harold Morgan.*

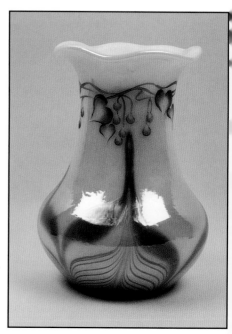

Vase, 9", 5359 WP, Leaves & Vines,
Limited to 950, YOP: 1998, $250-
300. *Courtesy of Bev & Jon Spencer.*

Basket, 7.5", 7139 NP, Burmese Blackberry Bouquet, Limited to 2,250, YOP: 1998, $150-175; Vase, 10", 7557 UW, Burmese Papillion, Limited to 2,500, $250+; Pitcher, 7", 2998 YZ, Burmese Bountiful Harvest, Limited to 2,250, YOP: 1998, $200-$225. *Courtesy of Norma & Melvin Lampton.*

Vase, 6", 4604 BZ, Wild Rose Alhambra, Limited to 1,500, $125-150. *Courtesy of Connie & Aaron Patient.*

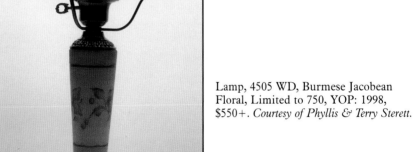

Lamp, 4505 WD, Burmese Jacobean Floral, Limited to 750, YOP: 1998, $550+. *Courtesy of Phyllis & Terry Sterett.*

Vase, 9", 9259 FY, Favrene Seasons Spring Side, Limited to 1350, YOP: 1998, $400+. *Courtesy of Chuck Bingham.*

Vase, 9", 9259 FY, Favrene Seasons, Fall Side.

Lamp, 6802 SV, Trysting Place, Reverse Painted, Limited to 750, YOP: 1998, $1,000+. *Courtesy of Chuck Bingham.*

141

Basket, 7139 YC, Peach Crest HP with Roses decoration, Limited to 1,750, YOP: 1999, $150-175. *Courtesy of Bev & Jon Spencer.*

Ginger Jar, 7488 FH, Favrene with Orchid Decoration, Limited to 1,750, YOP: 1999, $425+. *Courtesy of Chuck Bingham.*

Basket, 7.5", 7139 NP, Burmese Blackberry Bouquet, Limited to 2,250, YOP: 1998, $150-175; Basket, 9.5", 6831 U5, Burmese Blue Bird, Limited to 2,950, $250+; Ewer, 1862 VV, Burmese Golden Gourds, Limited to 2,500, $200+. *Courtesy of Laurie & Richard Karman.*

Amphora with Metal Stand, 3090 ZF, Mulberry Mystical Bird Limited to 1,250, $350+. *Courtesy of Donna Hatch.*

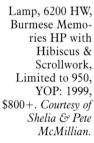

Vase, 13", 6395 WS, Burmese Poppies, Limited to 2,500, YOP: 1999, $250+. *Courtesy of Phyllis & Terry Sterett.*

Lamp, 6200 HW, Burmese Memories HP with Hibiscus & Scrollwork, Limited to 950, YOP: 1999, $800+. *Courtesy of Shelia & Pete McMillian.*

Anniversary Series

Beginning in 1980, for each anniversary, Fenton would issue special anniversary treatments. For their 75th Anniversary, in 1980, it was Velva Rose Stretch Glass. In 1985, Blue Ride (French Opalescent crested with a cobalt edge) was made. It was in 1985 that Burmese, for the first time in several years, was issued. Many pieces were made in this issue that would complement the patterns that Fenton had produced earlier in their regular line. In 1995, Stretch Glass was again issued for their Anniversary, this time in Celeste Blue, another color that had been produced in the 1920s. Also in 1995, in the Historic collection, Burmese again was issued in a line of limited edition pieces.

85th Anniversary Issue Burmese 1989

85TH ANNIVERSARY ISSUE, YOP: 1990: Basket, 7", 7731QH, Raspberries, $150-175. *Courtesy of Linda & John Flippen.*

85TH ANNIVERSARY ISSUE, YOP: 1990: Water Set, 7 piece, 7700 QH, Raspberries Pitcher, $500+; Tumblers, $45-55 ea. *Courtesy of Norma & Melvin Lampton.*

85TH ANNIVERSARY ISSUE, YOP: 1990: Lamp, 21", Student, 7412QH, Raspberries, $750+. *Courtesy of Bobbie & Harold Morgan.*

85TH ANNIVERSARY ISSUE, YOP: 1990: Water Set Sample, NIL, UND. *Courtesy of Tina & Rick Gaither.*

85TH ANNIVERSARY ISSUE, YOP: 1990: Epergne, 2 piece, 7202QJ, Petite Floral, $350+; Cruet, 7701QJ, Petite Floral, $300+. *Courtesy of Noralee Rogers.*

85TH ANNIVERSARY ISSUE, YOP: 1990: Vase, 9", 7792QD, Trees Scene, $250+. *Courtesy of Phyllis & Terry Sterett.*

85TH ANNIVERSARY ISSUE, YOP: 1990: Epergne, 2 piece, 7202QJ, Petite Floral, $350+. *Courtesy of Kansas City Fenton Finders.*

85TH ANNIVERSARY ISSUE, YOP: 1990: Lamp, 20", Classic, 9308RB, Roses, $800+. *Courtesy of Shelia & Pete McMillian.*

85TH ANNIVERSARY ISSUE, YOP: 1990: Vase, 6.5", 5541 QH, HP Raspberries on Burmese, Limited to 1,500, YOP: 1991 (From Connoisseur Series), $125-150; Basket, 7732QD, Tree Scene, $150-175; Vase, 6.5", 7791RB, Roses, $150-$175; Vase, 6", Fan, 7790RB, Roses, $150-$175. *Courtesy of Doris & Junior Devall.*

90th ANNIVERSARY ISSUE: CELESTE BLUE STRETCH KA, YOP: 1995: Epergne, 7601, $400+. *Courtesy of Bobbie Morgan.*

90th ANNIVERSARY ISSUE: CELESTE BLUE STRETCH KA, YOP: 1995:Comport, 1134, $55-60.

90th ANNIVERSARY ISSUE: CELESTE BLUE STRETCH KA, YOP: 1995: Bell, 9667, Aurora, $35-40; Vase, 7.5", with Cobalt Base, 1140, $75-80; Water Set, 9001, Lincoln Inn Pitcher, $150+; Tumblers, $30-35 ea.; Vase, 4.5", 2767, $35-40; Basket, 7", Footed, 1142, $55-60; Logo, 9499, $45-50. *Courtesy of Laurie & Richard Karman.*

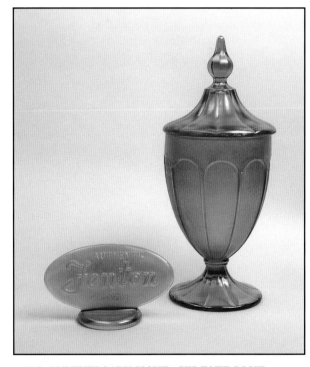

90th ANNIVERSARY ISSUE: CELESTE BLUE STRETCH KA, YOP: 1995: Logo, 9499, $45-50; Candy Box, 10.5", 9488, $65-70. *Courtesy of Chuck Bingham.*

90th ANNIVERSARY ISSUE: CELESTE BLUE STRETCH KA, YOP: 1995: Basket, 9", 1135, $75-80; Vase, 6", Fan, 1136, $65-75; Vase, 4.5", 2767, $35-40; Centerpiece with Nymph on Stand, 2990, $100-125; Top Hat, 4.5", 1137, $65-70. Not Pictured: Candlesticks, 2911, $25-30 ea. *Courtesy of Laurie & Richard Karman.*

90th ANNIVERSARY ISSUE: BURMESE, YOP: 1995: Pitcher, 10", 2968 UN, Cherry Blossom, Designed by Martha Reynolds, Limited to 790, $300+; Basket, 8", 2932 UL, Butterfly, Limited to 790, Martha Reynolds Designed, $225-250; Vase, 9", 2955 UU, Humming Bird, Designed By Martha Reynolds, Limited to 790, $250-275. *Courtesy of Laurie & Richard Karman.*

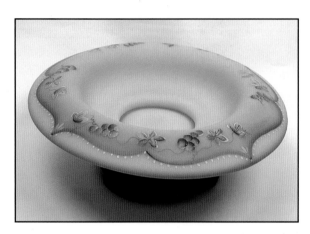

90th ANNIVERSARY ISSUE: BURMESE, YOP: 1995:Vintage Bowl, 10.25", with Base, 2909 UK, Designed by Martha Reynolds, Limited to 790, $225-250. *Courtesy of Laurie & Richard Karman.*

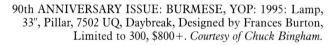

90th ANNIVERSARY ISSUE: BURMESE, YOP: 1995: Lamp, 33", Pillar, 7502 UQ, Daybreak, Designed by Frances Burton, Limited to 300, $800+. *Courtesy of Chuck Bingham.*

Christmas Items

Throughout the 1970s, Fenton begin to produced special items and patterns for the Christmas holidays. Beginning slowly at first, and then adding more items each year as their popularity grew, this has become one of Fenton's largest productions each year.

Over the course of the past twenty years, Fenton has begun each year to produce special decorated Christmas patterns, which have proved quite popular with both Fenton collector's and Christmas Collectors. Also, the miniature Christmas trees issued each year in different treatments and decorations have proven to be one of the most popular collections that Fenton has produced.

Other popular series include Fenton's Nativity series, where a different grouping of figures depicting a portion of the Nativity would be issued each year until the whole set would be completed. Also, over latter part of the 1990s, the Enchanted Santas, that were made each year in limited numbers and in different treatments, have become quite popular.

Special Series

Possibly the most popular item issued throughout the 1985-2000 time period was Fenton's Christmas Series "the Birds of Winter," which was produced from 1987-91. Both Fenton collectors and bird lovers have swooped on these items, making them extremely difficult to find now.

The Christmas at Home series debuted in 1991. It was a beautiful series that lasted over four years, depicting Norman Rockwell types of Christmas scenes. This series is extremely difficult to find now. The Christmas Star series and the Birth of a Savior series came out in the mid- and late 1990s respectively; both series were decorated on different colors of Satin Glass. This type of glass is unique in itself, as Fenton advised the buyer to use Amour-all, to clean the pieces!

Birds of Winter

BIRDS OF WINTER: THE CARDNIAL BC: Clock, 8600, YOP: 6/87-1988, $125-150; Fairy Light, 7300, YOP: 6/87-1988, $85-90; Bell, 7667, YOP: 6/87-1988, $40-45. *Courtesy of Bobbie & Harold Morgan.*

BIRDS OF WINTER: THE CARDNIAL BC: Lamp, 9702, YOP: 6/87-1988, $300-350. Not Pictured: Plate, 7418, YOP: 6/87-1988, $55-60. *Courtesy of Bobbie & Harold Morgan.*

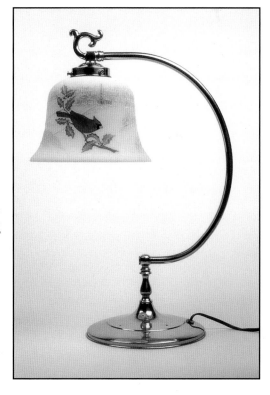

BIRDS OF WINTER: A CHICKADEE BALLET:
Fairy Light, 7300, YOP: 6/88-1989, $85-90; Clock,
8600, YOP: 6/88-1989, $125-150; Bell, 7667, YOP: 6/
88-1989, $40-45; Plate, 7418, YOP: 6/88-1989, $55-60.
Not Pictured: Lamp, 7209, YOP: 6/88-1989, $300-350.
Courtesy of Bobbie & Harold Morgan.

BIRDS OF WINTER: DOWNY WOODPECKER: Fairy
Light, 7300, YOP: 6/89-1990, $85-90; Clock, 8600, YOP: 6/
89-1990, $125-150; Bell, 7667, YOP: 6/89-1990, $40-45;
Plate, 7418, YOP: 6/89-1990, $55-60. Not Pictured: Lamp,
7204, YOP: 6/89-1909, $300-350. *Courtesy of Bobbie & Harold
Morgan.*

BIRDS OF WINTER: BLUE BIRD IN SNOWFALL
NB: Clock, 8600, YOP: 6/91-1991, $125-150; Fairy Light,
7300, YOP: 6/90-1991, $85-90; Bell, 7667, YOP: 6/90-
1991, $40-45; Plate, 7418, YOP: 6/90-1991, $55-60.
Courtesy of Bobbie & Harold Morgan.

BIRDS OF WINTER: THE CARDNIAL BC: Clock, 8600, YOP: 6/
87-1988, $125-150. BLUE BIRD IN SNOWFALL NB: Clock, 8600,
YOP: 6/91-1991, $125-150. Not Pictured: Lamp, 7209, YOP: 6/90-
1991, $300-350. Not Pictured: Lamp, 16", Hammered Colonial, 7204,
$350+; Clock, 8600, $150-200. *Courtesy of Laurie & Richard Karman.*

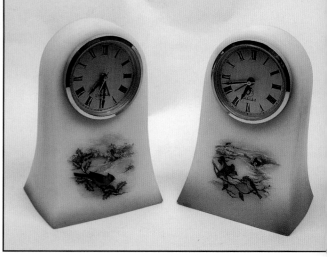

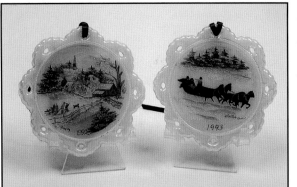

CHRISTMAS AT HOME
Series Ornaments: Family
Tradition: Sleigh Ride, $20-
25 ea. *Courtesy of Jan
Hollingsworth.*

CHRISTMAS AT HOME: 1990, No. 1: SLEIGH
RIDE HD, 1990, Fairy Light, 7300, $80-90; Plate,
8", 7418, $65-70; Bell, 7668, YOP: 1990, $45-50.
Courtesy of Bobbie & Harold Morgan.

CHRISTMAS AT
HOME: 1991, No.
2: CHRISTMAS
EVE HJ 1991:
Lamp, 16",
Hammered
Colonial, 7204,
$350+; Fairy
Light, 7300, $80-
90; Plate, 8", 7418,
$65-70. Not
Pictured: Bell,
7668, $45-50.
*Courtesy of Laurie
& Richard
Karman.*

CHRISTMAS AT HOME: 1992, No. 3: FAMILY TRADI-
TION HQ 1992: Bell, 7668, $45-50; Plate, 8", 7418, $65-70;
Fairy Light, 7300, $80-90. Not Pictured: Lamp, 16", Ham-
mered Colonial, 7204, $350+. *Courtesy of Laurie & Richard
Karman.*

CHRISTMAS AT HOME: Clocks, 8600, $150-200 ea. CHRIST-
MAS EVE HJ 1991; SLEIGH RIDE HD 1990; FAMILY TRADI-
TION HQ 1992; FAMILY HOLIDAY 1994. *Courtesy of Laurie &
Richard Karman.*

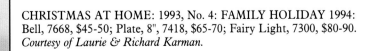

CHRISTMAS AT HOME: 1993, No. 4: FAMILY HOLIDAY 1994:
Bell, 7668, $45-50; Plate, 8", 7418, $65-70; Fairy Light, 7300, $80-90.
Courtesy of Laurie & Richard Karman.

Christmas Star Series

CHRISTMAS STAR SERIES: No. 1: SILENT NIGHT 1994: Blue Satin Glass VS: Lamp, 14", Hammered Colonial, 7204, $250-300. *Courtesy of Tina & Rick Gaither.*

CHRISTMAS STAR: No. 3: STAR OF WONDER 1996: Gold Satin Glass SN: Fairy Light, 7300, $55-65; Plate, 8", 7418, $45-55; Egg on Leaf Base, 5145, $55-65; Bell, 7463, $30-35. Not Pictured: Lamp, 16", Hammered Colonial, 7204, $250-300. *Courtesy of Laurie & Richard Karman.*

CHISTMAS STAR: No. 2: OUR HOME IS BLESSED 1995 Green Satin Glass VT: Fairy Light, 7300, $55-65; Plate, 8", 7418, $45-55; Egg on Leaf Base, 5145, $55-65; Bell, 7463, $30-35. Not Pictured: Lamp, 16", Hammered Colonial, 7204, $250-300. *Courtesy of Laurie & Richard Karman.*

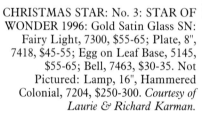

CHRISTMAS STAR SERIES: No. 1: SILENT NIGHT 1994: Blue Satin Glass VS: Fairy Light, 7300, $55-65; Plate, 8", 7418, $45-55; Egg on Leaf Base, 5145, $55-65; Bell, 7463, $30-35.

CHRISTMAS STAR - THE WAY HOME 1997: Ruby Satin Glass: Fairy Light, 7300, $55-65; Plate, 8", 7418, $45-55; Egg on Leaf Base, 5145, $55-65; Bell, 7463, $30-35. Not Pictured: Lamp, 16", Hammered Colonial, 7204, $250-300. *Courtesy of Laurie & Richard Karman.*

Birth of a Savior

THE ARRIVAL: Spruce Green Satin XS: Fairy Light, 7300, YOP: 1998, $45-50. *Courtesy of Bobbie & Harold Morgan.*

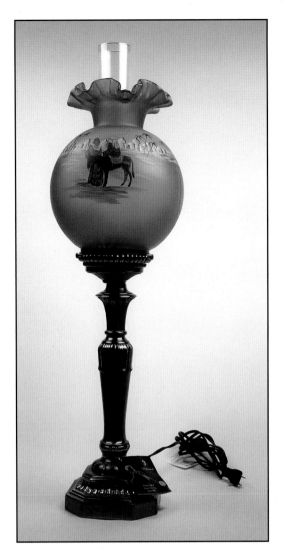

THE ANNOUNCEMENT: Cobalt Satin KP: Egg, 5146, $35-40; Fairy Light, 7300, YOP: 1999, $45-50. Not Pictured: Lamp, 26", 7678, $250-300; Plate, 7610, $35-40; Bell, 7566, $30-45. *Courtesy of Bobbie & Harold Morgan.*

THE ARRIVAL: Spruce Green Satin XS: Lamp, 26", 7678, YOP: 1998, $250-300. Not Pictured: Egg, 5146, $35-40; Plate, 7610, $35-40; Bell, 7566, $30-45. *Courtesy of Bobbie & Harold Morgan.*

Christmas Colors

Throughout the late 1980s and all through the 1990s Fenton produced several colors that were special to Christmas. Two of these were Holiday Green and Spruce Green. Ruby was also a featured color in Fenton's Christmas Catalogs, although items in this color were also in Fenton's regular line. Many entertaining items in these colors were made, especially large bowls and platters.

Holiday Green GH 1991

HOLIDAY GREEN GH, YOP: 1991-94: Boot, 1975, Daisy & Button, YOP: 1991-1993, $25-30. *Courtesy of Bobbie & Harold Morgan.*

HOLIDAY GREEN GH, YOP: 1991-94: Basket, 8", 9544, Vulcan, $20-25; Basket, Footed Mini, 6563, $15-20; Basket, 7.5", 9164, Fine Cut & Block, YOP: 1993 only, $35-40. *Courtesy of Laurie & Richard Karman.*

HOLIDAY GREEN GH, YOP: 1991-94: Happiness Bird, 5197, YOP: 1991-93, $25-30. *Courtesy of Jan Hollingsworth.*

HOLIDAY GREEN GH, YOP: 1991-94: Fairy Light, Mini Footed, 7600, $30-35.

HOLIDAY GREEN GH, YOP: 1991-94: Boy Angel, 5113, $40-45; Girl Angel, 5114, $40-45; Cake Plate, 12", 1975, Button & Daisy, $20-25; Candlesticks, 4.5", 9372, $20-25. *Courtesy of Laurie & Richard Karman.*

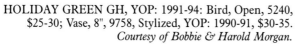

HOLIDAY GREEN GH, YOP: 1991-94: Bird, Open, 5240, $25-30; Vase, 8", 9758, Stylized, YOP: 1990-91, $30-35. *Courtesy of Bobbie & Harold Morgan.*

RUBY RU, YOP: 1985-2000:
Basket, 4.5", 8638, Regency,
$20-25. *Courtesy of Laurie &
Richard Karman.*

RUBY RU, YOP: 1985-
2000: Votive, 9673, Santa,
$20-25.

RUBY RU, YOP: 1985-2000: Fairy Light, Mini
Footed, 7600, $45-50; Sleigh, 4695, $40-45. *Courtesy
of Laurie & Richard Karman.*

RUBY RU, YOP: 1985-2000: Bird, 5115, $20-25; Angel Boy, 5113,
$20-25; Angel Girl, 5114, $20-25; Tree, 5556, $20-25; Vase, with
Bow, 9754, 6.25", Caprice, YOP: 1989-91, $25-30; Cat, 5165, $30-35;
Bear, Reclining, 5233, $30-35; Bell, 4560, Strawberry, $20-25; Bell,
7463, Paisley, $25-30; Candy, 6780, Paisley, $30-35. *Courtesy of
Laurie & Richard Karman.*

Spruce Green SO 1998-99

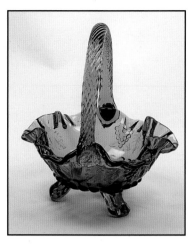

SPRUCE GREEN SO, YOP: 1998-99: Basket, 3-toed, 5738, Panel Grape, $25-30. *Courtesy of Laurie & Richard Karman.*

SPRUCE GREEN SO, YOP: 1998-99: Sleigh, 4695, $45-50; Santa, 5249, Spruce Green Carnival, $55-60. *Courtesy of Bobbie & Harold Morgan.*

SPRUCE GREEN SO, YOP: 1998-99: Bell, 9065, Sable Arch, $30-35. *Courtesy of Bobbie & Harold Morgan.*

SPRUCE GREEN SO, YOP: 1998-99: Sleigh, 4695, $45-50; Vase, 8", 5751, Paneled Grape, $25-30; Votive, 2 way, 9596, $15-20. *Courtesy of Myers Mystique.*

Decorated Christmas Patterns

Beginning in the mid-1980s with Holly Berry, Fenton issued a special Decorated Christmas pattern every year. Sometimes a pattern would be so successful that it would be issued for two consecutive years. Over the past several years, these patterns have caught the attention of both Christmas collectors and Fenton collectors, and pieces in them have become quite difficult to locate.

GOLDEN PINE CONES VC, YOP: 1994: Pitcher, $55-60. *Courtesy of Laurie & Richard Karman.*

CHRISTMAS ROSE TR, YOP: 6/89-12/89: Votives, 2 way, 9578, Leaf, $25-30 ea.; Comport, 9229, Empress, $45-55; Happiness Bird, 5197, $40-45; Basket, 7", 7630, Aurora, $55-65. *Courtesy of Bobbie & Harold Morgan.*

GILDED STAR FLOWERS HV, YOP: 1993: Cat, 5165, $50-55; Small Bird, 5163, $40-45; Comport, 7623, $45-55; Vase, 4.5", 7241, $40-45; Candleholders, 6", 7475, $35-40 ea.; Bowl, 8.5", Flared, 7326, $55-65; Boy Angel, 5113, $40-45; Girl Angel, 5114, $40-45; Basket, 7", 7534, $65-70; Fairy Light, Mini Footed, 7600, $45-50; Deer, 5160, $45-50; Bell, 1127, $30-35. *Courtesy of Laurie & Richard Karman.*

GOLDEN PINE CONES VC 1994: Lamp, 16", Hammered Colonial, 7204, $200-250. *Courtesy of Bobbie & Harold Morgan.*

GOLDEN PINE CONES VC 1994: Tree, 5535, $35-40; Small Bird, 5163, $35-40; Fawn, 5160, $40-45; Candy, Covered, 7380, $65-70; Candlestick, 6", 5277, $30-35 ea.; Slipper, 2931, $25-30; Polar Bear, 5109, $40-45; Comport, 7431, $50-55; Bell, 7768, $30-35. *Courtesy of Laurie & Richard Karman.*

GOLDEN PINE CONES VC 1994: Basket, 10.5", Footed, 585, $90-100; Fairy Lamp, 7300, $45-50; Girl Angel, 5114, $45-50; Candle Holders, 4.5", Ram's Head, 9372, $35-40; Bowl, 10", Rolled Rim, 2747, $55-60; Boy Angel, 5113, $45-50. *Courtesy of Laurie & Richard Karman.*

GOLDEN PINE CONES VC 1994: Basket, 7", 2737, $60-65; Slipper, 9295, Rose, $30-35; Vase, 4", 7241, $30-35; Basket, 7.5", 2788, $60-65. *Courtesy of Laurie & Richard Karman.*

ICED POINSETTAS ON IRIDESCENT OPAL CV, YOP: 1991: Bear, 5151, $40-45. *Courtesy of Diane & Tom Rohow.*

HOLLY BERRY HL, YOP: 1988: Vase, 4.5", 7254, $45-50; Hurricane Lamp, 11", 3761, Valencia, $65-70; Bell, Petite, 7662, $30-35; Comport, 9229, Empress, $70-75; Fairy Light, 5106, Santa, $80-90; Basket, 9235, Paneled, $75-80. *Courtesy of Bobbie & Harold Morgan.*

HOLLY BERRY HL, YOP: 1988: Cat, 5165, $75-80; Bird, 5115, $55-60; Bear, Reclining, 5233, $80-90. Not Pictured: Bear, 5151, $80-90; Hurricane Candle, 8376, $80-85. *Courtesy of Bobbie & Harold Morgan.*

ICED POINSETTAS ON IRIDESCENT OPAL CV, YOP: 1991: Bell, 7668, $35-40; Boy Angel, 5113, $40-45; Girl Angel, 5114, $40-45; Candle Holders, 9372, Ram's Head, $25-30 ea.; Vase, 4.5", 9257, $30-35; Fairy Light, Mini Footed, 7600, $45-50; Basket, 7", 7237, $55-65; Bell, Mini, 7662, $25-30; Bird, 5163, $35-40; Bear, 5151, $40-45; Comport, 6322, Flower Band, $40-45. Not Pictured: Cat, 5165, Vase, 4", 9357, Basket weave. *Courtesy of Laurie & Richard Karman.*

MAGNOLIA & BERRY ON SPRUCE GREEN SE, YOP: 1996-97: Basket, 10.5", Footed, 6839, Paneled, $90-100. *Courtesy of Laurie & Richard Karman.*

MAGNOLIA & BERRY ON SPRUCE GREEN SE, YOP: 1996-97: Bear Cub, 5151, $45-50; Bell, 1127, $35-40; Fawn, 5160, $45-50; Vase, 9.5", 1896, $65-70; Pitcher, 8.5", 3269, $65-70; Cat, 5165, $55-60; Pitcher, 7.5", 265, $60-65; Mouse, 5148, $45-55. *Courtesy of Laurie & Richard Karman.*

MAGNOLIA & BERRY ON SPRUCE GREEN SE, YOP: 1996-97: Covered Urn, 4602, George Signature, $80-90; Pitcher, 8.5", 3269, $65-70; Vase, 9.5", 1896, $65-70. *Courtesy of Shelia & Pete McMillian.*

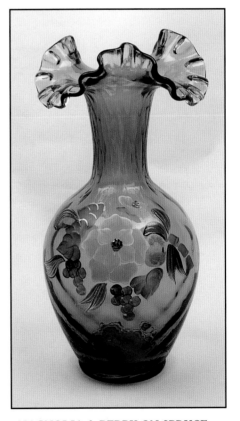

MAGNOLIA & BERRY ON SPRUCE GREEN SE, YOP: 1996-97: Vase, 10", 4759, Signature Tom Fenton, $65-70.

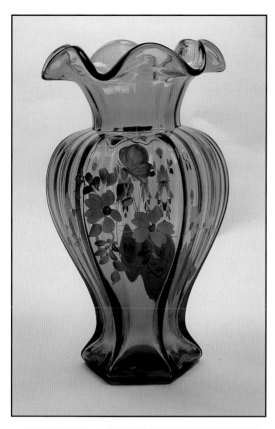

MAGNOLIA & BERRY ON SPRUCE GREEN
SE, YOP: 1996-97: Vase, 9", 1554, $55-60.
Courtesy of Laurie & Richard Karman.

POINSETTIA GLOW P7, YOP: 1997:
Lamp, 5576, 13", $90-100. *Courtesy of
Bobbie & Harold Morgan.*

POINSETTIA GLOW P7, YOP: 1997: Pitcher, 9", 6865, $80-85;
Mallard, 5147, $35-30; Cat, 5165, $55-65; Sleigh, 3695, $60-56; Boot,
9590, $20-25; Fawn, 510, $40-45; Comport, 7431, $45-55; Mouse,
5148, $45-55. *Courtesy of Laurie & Richard Karman.*

POINSETTIA GLOW P7, YOP: 1997: Bell, 1127, $30-35; Basket, 8", 2975, Lily,
$70-75; Hurricane Lamp, 11", 7520, $100-125; Bell, Girl Angel, 5144, $40-45;
Candlesticks, 8.5", 9071, $35-40 ea.; Tree, 6.25", 5535, $35-40; Bell, Boy Angel, 5143,
$40-45; Basket, 8", 5460, Lily, $70-75; Bell, 7463, $30-35. Not Pictured: Santa, 5299,
$70-75; Radiant Angel, 5542, $65-70. *Courtesy of Laurie & Richard Karman.*

POINSETTIA ON MILK GLASS NP, YOP: 6/90-12/90: Cat, 5165, $50-55;
Fawn, 5160, $40-45; Basket, 9335, Basket weave, $45-50; Bear, 5151, $50-55;
Bell, 9268, Bow & Drape, $25-30; Bear, Reclining, 5233, $50-55; Comport,
9229, 7", Empress, $40-45; Vase, 7", 7694, Aurora, $40-45; Votive, 9578, 2 Way
Leaf, $20-25. *Courtesy of Laurie & Richard Karman.*

SNOWBERRY SB, YOP: 1992-93: Bird, 5163, $40-45; Fawn, 5160, $40-45; Basket, 7", 9335, Basket weave, $65-70; Bell, Petite, 9266, Bow & Drape, $25-30; Bell, 8267, Medallion, $30-65; Candleholder, 5.5", Column, 9079, $35-40 ea.; Vase, 4", 9357, Basket weave, $45-50; Boy Angel, 5113, $45-55; Girl Angel, 5114, $45-55; Fairy Light, 8405, Beaded, $55-60. *Courtesy of Laurie & Richard Karman.*

STAR OF BETHLEHEM ON GREEN GB, YOP: 1992: Fairy Light, 8405, Beaded, $65-70.

STAR OF BETHLEHEM ON GREEN GB, YOP: 1992: Basket, 10.5", Footed, 6572, $75-80; Bell, 6761, Paisley, $30-35; Fairy Light, 8405, Beaded, $65-75; Candleholder, 9072, $35-40 ea.; Comport, 9229, Empress, $45-50. *Courtesy of Laurie & Richard Karman.*

TWINING BERRIES JX, YOP: 1999: Santa, 5299, $75-80; Reindeer, 5261, $45-50; Sleigh, 4695, Mike Fenton Signature, YOP: 1998, $55-60; Cat, 5065, $45-50; Mouse, 5148, $55-60; Bell, Angel Girl, 5144, $45-55; Bell, Angel Boy, 5143, $45-55. *Courtesy of Laurie & Richard Karman.*

TWINING BERRIES JX, YOP: 1999: Fawn, 5140, $45-50; Comport, 7431, $55-60; Basket, 8", 5969, $75-80; Hurricane Lamp, 7520, $100-125; Bell, 1127, $30-35; Candlestick, 8.5", 9071, $35-40; Basket, 8", 2975, $70-75. Not Pictured: Box, Covered, 6833, Tom Fenton signature, YOP: 1999, $70-75; Candy Box, 9333, Tom Fenton signature, $80-85. *Courtesy of Laurie & Richard Karman.*

159

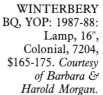

WINTERBERY
BQ, YOP: 1987-88:
Lamp, 16",
Colonial, 7204,
$165-175. *Courtesy
of Barbara &
Harold Morgan.*

WINTERBERY BQ, YOP: 1987-88: Bud Vase, 9056, YOP: 1987 only, $25-30; Candy Box, 8288, Medallion, YOP: 1987 only, $65-70; Bell, 4", Petite, 7662, $25-30; Basket, 8", Paneled, 9639, $65-70; Fairy Light, 7300, YOP: 1988 only, $55-60; Jewel Box, Oval, 9589, YOP: 1987 only, $45-50; Hurricane Candle, 8376, Valencia, $40-45; Vase, 4.5", 7254, YOP: 1987 only, $40-45. *Courtesy of Bobbie & Harold Morgan.*

WINTERBERY BQ, YOP: 1987-88: Comport, 6322, Flower Band, YOP: 1988 only, $55-60; Bell, 8267, Medallion, $30-35. *Courtesy of Jan Hollingsworth.*

WINTER ROSE ON IRIDESCENT OPAL TS, YOP: 1989: Fawn h/p, 5160, $50-55; Bear, 5151, $50-55; Bear, 5233, Reclining, $50-55; Bird, 5163, $40-45.

WOODLAND FROST FE, YOP: 1999: Sleigh, 4965, $55-60; Bell, 7768, $40-45; Reindeer, 5261, $45-50; Bell, Angel Girl, 5144, $40-45; Candy/Cover, 7380, $55-60; Polar Bear, 5109, $40-45; Basket, 8", 2787, $65-70; Vase, 5", 9869, $30-35. Not Pictured: Lamp, 6500, $100-125. *Courtesy of Laurie & Richard Karman.*

WINTERBERY BQ, YOP: 1987-88: Fawn, 5160, $40-45; Cat, 5165, $50-55; Happiness Bird, 5197, $40-45; Bear Cub, 5151, $50-44. *Courtesy of Bobbie & Harold Morgan.*

WOODLAND FROST FE, YOP: 1999: Bell, 9474, Aurora, $25-30. *Courtesy of Laurie & Richard Karman.*

Cat, 5065 SB, $20-25; Fawn, 5160 SB, $25-30; Mouse, 5148 SB, $25-30, YOP: 1999. *Courtesy of Richard & Laurie Karman.*

Bells & Eggs

Possibly one of the most collected series that Fenton has produced for the Christmas season is their limited edition of Bells and Eggs. Some years these items would be a limited time offer, and other years they would be limited by how many were produced.

Eggs/Bells

Magnolia on Golden Glow, YOP: 1994: Egg, 5145 VG, $40-45; Bell, 7463 VG, YOP: 1994, $30-35. Golden Partridge, YOP: 1994: Egg, 5145 VK, Limited to 1,500, $40-45; Bell, Musical, 7465 VK, $30-35. Manger Scene, YOP: 1994: Egg, 5140 SD, $40-45; Bell, 7463 SD, $30-35. Chickadee on Golden Glow, YOP: 1995: Egg, 5145 TP, $40-45; Bell, 7463 TP, $30-35. *Courtesy of Laurie & Richard Karman.*

ANGEL BELLS: 7668 QY Horn/Lamb, $30-35; 7668 QQ, Harp/Puppy, $30-35; 7668 QR, Flute/Fawn, $30-35. *Courtesy of Bobbie & Harold Morgan.*

Poinsettias & Snowflakes on Golden Glow, YOP: 1997: Bell, 7463 GB, $30-35; Egg, 5145 GB, $40-45; Fairy Light, 7300 GB, $45-50. Poinsettias on Ruby, YOP: 1999: Bell, 7668 RH, $30-35; Fairy Light, 5405 RH, $55-60; Egg, 5146 RH, $40-45. Iced Pinecones on Gold, YOP: 1999: Bell, 6864 GM, $30-35; Egg, 5146 GM, $40-45; Fairy Light, 7300, $45-50. *Courtesy of Laurie & Richard Karman.*

Holly Berries, YOP: 1996: Bell, 6662 CH, Limited to 1,500, $30-35; Egg, 5145 CH, $40-45. Poinsettias on Ruby, Limited to 900 ea., YOP: 1995: Bell, 7667 TQ, $30-35; Egg, 5145 TQ, $40-45. Golden Poinsettias on Ivory, YOP: 1995: Bell, 2967 TH, Limited to 900, $30-35; Egg, 5145 TH, Limited to 900, $40-45. Moon Lit Meadow, YOP: 1996: Bell, 7768 QV, Limited to 1,500, $30-35. Golden Partridge: Bell, 7668 QP, $30-35; Egg, 5145 QP, Limited to 1,500, $40-45. *Courtesy of Laurie & Richard Karman.*

Magnolias on Ruby, YOP: 1997: Bell, 9667 R2, $30-35; Fairy Light, 5405 R2, $50-60; Egg, 5145 R2, $40-45; Golden Winged Angel EA, Limited to 1,500, YOP 1996, $40-45; Bell, 2967 AV, $35-40; Egg, 5145 AV, $40-45; Fairy Light, 7300 AV, $40-45. Nativity EA, Limited to 1,500, YOP: 1996: Bell, 9463, $30-35; Fairy Light, 9401 N7, $40-45. Ornamental Magic, YOP: 1998: Melon Bell, 6854 RY, $30-35; Fairy Light, 5405 RY, $55-60; Egg, 5146 RY, $40-45. *Courtesy of Laurie & Richard Karman.*

Lenton Rose, YOP: 1998: Egg, 5146 GV, $40-45; Bell, 1145 GV, $30-35; Fairy Light, 7300 GV, $45-55. Woodland Frost, YOP: 1998: Bell, 7768 FE, $30-35; Egg, 5145 FE, $40-45; Fairy Light, 7300 FE, $50-55. Berries on French Opalescent, YOP: 1998: Bell, 7768 FU, $30-35; Egg, 5145 FU, $40-45; Fairy Light, 7300 FU, $50-55. Jolly Snowman, YOP: 1999: Fairy Light, 7300 KE, $55-65; Egg, 5146 KE, $40-45; Bell, 7768 KE, $40-45. *Courtesy of Laurie & Richard Karman.*

Bell, Musical, 7465 GQ, Green, YOP: 1993, $30-35; Bell, 7463, Christmas Rose, $30-35; Bell, 7463 VP, Angel, $30-35; Bell, 7463 TV, YOP: 1993, $30-35. *Courtesy of Laurie & Richard Karman.*

Flowers of Christmas: Bell, 7664 XQ, Star of Bethlehem, $30-35; Bell, 7664 XA, Christmas Cactus, $30-35; Bell, 7669 ZX, Christmas Rose, $30-35; Bell, 7664 XG, Winter Berry, $30-35 *Courtesy of Laurie & Richard Karman.*

Bell, Musical, 1775, White Christmas, $35-40; Bell, 7463 ZW, Winter TWILIGHT, $30-35; Bell, 7668 SW, The Angel, $40-45. *Courtesy of Laurie & Richard Karman.*

Egg, 5140 SV, Woods; Egg, 5140 __, Currier & Ives; Egg, 5145__; Egg, 5145 QP, Golden Partridge; Egg, 5145 SW, The Angel; Egg, 5145 VK, Golden Partridge Egg, Limited to 1,500. All: $40-45 ea. *Courtesy of Laurie & Richard Karman.*

Bell, Musical, 1775, White Christmas, $35-40; Bell, Musical, 1776, $35-40.

Egg, 5145 VG; Egg, 5145 SD, Manger Scene; Egg, 5146 RH, Iced Poinsettias on Opal; Egg, 5145 CV; Egg, 5145 SW, Mary Gregory; Egg, 5145 SU, Poinsettia; Egg, 5145 __, Snowflakes. All: $40-45 ea. *Courtesy of Laurie & Richard Karman.*

Bell, Musical, 7669 ND, YOP: 1991, $30-35; Bell, Musical, 7696 DB, French Horn on Opal Satin, YOP: 1989-92, $30-35. *Courtesy of Bobbie & Harold Morgan.*

Angel Boy, 5113, $45-55; Radiant Angel, 5542, $75-80; Guardian Angel, 5533, $30-35; Angel Girl, 5114 PU, $45-55; YOP: All 1999. *Courtesy of Laurie & Richard Karman.*

Heavenly Angel: Angel Bell, 5144 IJ, $40-45.

Heavenly Angel: Guardian Angel, 5533 IJ, $30-35. *Courtesy of Laurie & Richard Karman.*

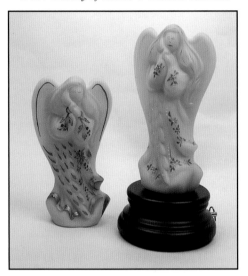

Radiant Angel, 5542QB, Limited to 1,000, YOP: 1996, $75-80; Radiant Angel on Wooden Stand, 5542TA, Limited to 900, YOP: 1995, $75-80. *Courtesy of Laurie & Richard Karman.*

Santa, 5237, Musical, $60-65. *Courtesy of Bobbie & Harold Morgan.*

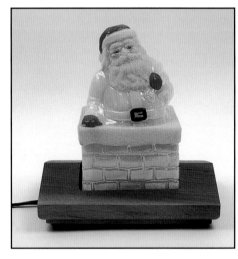

Santa, 5236, Electric with Wooden Rooftop, $75-80. *Courtesy of Bev & Jon Spencer.*

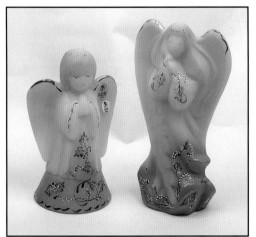

Angels Aglow, YOP: 1999, Angel Bell, 5144 PU, $65-70; Radiant Angel, 5542 PU, $75-80. *Courtesy of Laurie & Richard Karman.*

HAPPY SANTAS ON OPAL SATIN NS 6/90-12/90: Pig, 5220, $55-65; Bear Cub, 5151, $55-65; Bear, Daydreaming, 5239, $65-70; Mouse, 5148, $55-65; Bear Cub, Reclining, 5233, $65-70. *Courtesy of Claire and Alan Kauffng.*

Heaven & Nature Sing: YOP 1986: Squirrel, $55-65; Mouse, 5148, $55-65. *Courtesy of Jan Hollingsworth.*

Icicle Kingdom VI: Bear Cub, 5151, $45-50. Not Pictured: Polar Bear, 5109, $45-50; Fawn, 5160, $45-50; Cardinal, 5245, $45-50. *Courtesy of Bobbie & Harold Morgan.*

Bejeweled Santa, 5299 JO, YOP: 1999, $80-90; Golden Age Santa, 5249 JN, YOP: 1999, $80-90; Enchantment Santa, 5279 JM, YOP: 1999, Limited to 4750, $80-90.

Nativity Set 1997-2000, 1st edition, Gloria Angel Set, 5050 NA: Angel, $35-40; Camel, $25-30; Donkey, $25-30, YOP: 1999. Shepherd Set 5500 NS: Standing Shepherd, $30-35; Kneeling Shepherd, $30-35; Lamb, $25-30, YOP: 2000. Holy Family, 5280: Mary, $45-50; Joseph, $45-50; Baby Jesus, $45-50, YOP: 1997. Wise Men, 5289 WM: Melchior, $30-35; Gaspar, $30-35; Balthazar, $30-35, YOP: 1998. *Courtesy of Laurie & Richard Karman.*

Northen Lights Santa, 5299 VL, YOP: 1998, $80-90; Patriotic Santa, 5249 VP, YOP: 1998, Limited to 4750, $80-90; Old Worlde Santa, 5299, YOP: 1997, Limited to 3750, $80-90.

Santa, 5249 JX, YOP: 1999, $80-90.

Tree, 3", 5556 ZN; Tree, 4", 5556 ZN; Tree, 6", 5556 ZN; Misty Blue Iridescent with Gold Squirrel, YOP: 1998, $25-30 ea. *Courtesy of Laurie & Richard Karman.*

Tree, 4.5", 5536 R9; Tree, 6.5", 5535 R9; Tree, 3", 5537 R9; Tree Ornament, 3", 5537 R9; Iced Ruby, $25-30 ea. *Courtesy of Laurie & Richard Karman.*

Golden Glow GL: Girl Angel GL, $40-45; Radiant Angel GL, $60-65; Boy Angel GL, $40-45; Tree, 3", 5537 GL; Tree, 6.5", 5535 GL; Tree, 4.5", 5536 GL; All, $25-30 ea. Crystal Satin WH: Tree, 6.5", 5535 WH; Tree, 4.5", 5536 WH; Tree, 3", 5537 WH; All, $25-30 ea. Radiant Angel WH, $60-65. *Courtesy of Laurie & Richard Karman.*

Tree, 4.5", 5536 XW; Tree, 6.5", 5535 XW; Tree, 3", 5537 XW; Small Spruce Green. Tree, 4.5", 5536 GT; Tree, 6.5", 5535 GT; Tree, 3", 5537 GT; Holiday Green. $25-30 ea. *Courtesy of Laurie & Richard Karman.*

Angel Bell, 5144 VL, $45-55; Radiant Angel, 5542 VL, $60-65; Guardian Angel, 5333 VL, $30-35. *Courtesy of Laurie & Richard Karman.*

Cats, 5165: Winter Rose On Iridescent Opal; Holly Berry; Iced Poinsettia on Iridescent Opal, $50-55 ea.

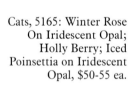

Rose Pearl Angel Bell, 5144 XI, $40-45; Tree, 4.5", 5536 XI; Tree, 6.5", 5535 XI; Tree, 3", 5537 XI, All: $25-30 ea. Radiant Angel, 5542 XI, $60-65; Guardian Angel, 5333 XI, $30-35. *Courtesy of Laurie & Richard Karman.*

Hobby Horse, 5135 JW, Baby's First Christmas, YOP: 1991, $45-50.

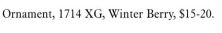

Ornament, 1714 XG, Winter Berry, $15-20.

Easter Collections

Beginning in the early 1990s, due to the success of their Christmas line, Fenton began to produce items for Easter. In the early 1990s a series of Limited Edition decorated Large Eggs were produced that are now very scarce and quite desirable.

During this same time period, Fenton started to issue covered Animal Dishes in different treatments each year. Many of these animals were made off old Westmoreland Moulds, which Fenton was leasing off of Levay. It was during this time also that Fenton, each year, would produce a special grouping of Baskets in different pastel colors and treatments.

The most popular of the Easter items was the Folk Art series, which was first produced in 1986.

Limited Large Eggs 5031

Blown Eggs: Cobalt HP, 5031 FV, YOP: 1994, $80-90; Cranberry HP, 1642 JM, YOP: 1996, $90-100; French Opalescent Rib Optic HP, 1642 JM, YOP: 1996, $80-90; Plum HP, 5031 WE, YOP: 1993, $70-75; Opal Iridescent HP, 5031 WD, YOP: 1991, $70-80; Ocean Blue HP, 5031 WJ, YOP: 1993, $80-90; Front: Iridescent Opal HP, 5030 QB, YOP: 1991, $65-70. *Courtesy of Laurie & Richard Karman.*

Blown Eggs: Dusty Rose Carnival HP, 5031, YOP: 1992, $70-80; Sea Mist Green HP, 5031 YW, YOP: 1995, $70-80; Dusty Rose Overlay HP, 5031 FU, YOP: 1994, $80-90; Sea Mist Green Carnival, 5031 Q3, YOP: 1992, $70-80; Yellow Carnival, 5031 HP YX, YOP: 1995, $70-80. *Courtesy of Laurie & Richard Karman.*

Blown Egg: Cranberry HP, 1642 JM, YOP: 1996, $90-100. *Courtesy of Kelly Meyer.*

167

Assortment of Mini Baskets. Note: Various shapes of these baskets were issued throughout the 1990s as part of the Fenton Easter Series. Many of the colors that these baskets were issued in were colors that were in Fenton's regular line at the time. $15-20 ea. *Courtesy of Laurie & Richard Karman.*

Assortment of Mini Baskets, $15-20 ea. *Courtesy of Laurie & Richard Karman.*

Basket, 4.5", 3834, Iridescent French Opalescent with Sea Green Mist Crest FR, YOP: 1994, $40-45. *Courtesy of Kathy & Ernie Mathus.*

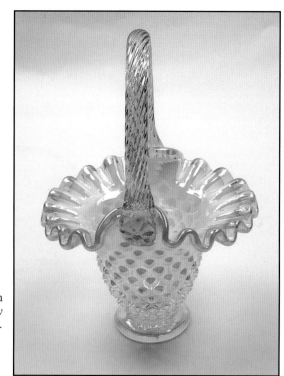

Basket, 4.5", 3834, Iridescent French Opalescent with Yellow Crest FT, YOP: 1994, $40-45. *Courtesy of Kathy & Ernie Mathus.*

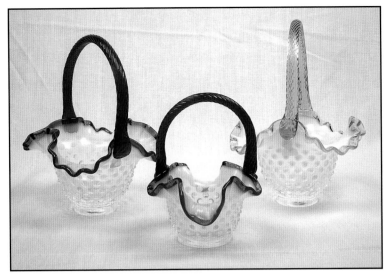

Basket, 6.5", 3767 F3, Hobnail, YOP: 1993, $45-50; Basket, 4.5", 3834 F3, Hobnail, YOP: 1994, $40-45; Basket, 6.5", 3767 FD, Hobnail, YOP: 1993, $45-50. *Courtesy of Laurie & Richard Karman.*

Basket, 7", 1158 FT, Hobnail, YOP: 1994, $45-50; Basket, 8.5", FT 3638, Hobnail, YOP: 1994, $50-55; Basket, 4.5", FT 3834, Hobnail, YOP: 1994, $40-45. *Courtesy of Laurie & Richard Karman.*

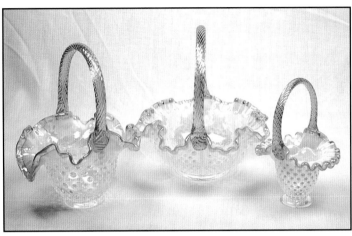

Basket, 8.5", 1160 FO with Cobalt IQ/ Handle & Crest, YOP: 1985, $55-60; Basket, 10.5", 3830 FO with Dusty Rose IH Handle & Crest, $65-70. *Courtesy of Wiggins Gifts.*

Basket, 4.5", 3834 FR, Hobnail, YOP: 1994, $40-45; Basket, 8.5", 3638 FR, Hobnail, YOP: 1994, $50-55; Basket, 7", 1158 FR, Hobnail, YOP: 1994, $50-55. *Courtesy of Laurie & Richard Karman.*

Basket, 4.5", 3834 FD, Hobnail, YOP: 1994; Basket, 8.5", 3638 FD, Hobnail, YOP: 1994 only, $50-55; Basket, 9", 1156 FD, Hobnail, YOP: 1994 only, $50-55; Basket, 7", 1158 FD, Hobnail, YOP: 1994 only, $50-55; *Courtesy of Laurie & Richard Karman.*

Basket, Mini, 6563 TG, Opaline, $20-25. *Courtesy of Jan Hollingsworth.*

Basket, 7", 1158 FR, Hobnail, YOP: 1994 only, $50-55; Basket, 4.5", 3834 FR, Hobnail, YOP: 1994, $40-45; Basket, 10.5", 3830 FR, Hobnail, YOP: 1994 only, $55-65. *Courtesy of Laurie & Richard Karman.*

Basket, 7", 4632 TG, Wildflower, $40-45; Basket, 7", 4632 PM, Wildflower, $40-45. *Courtesy of Jan Hollingsworth.*

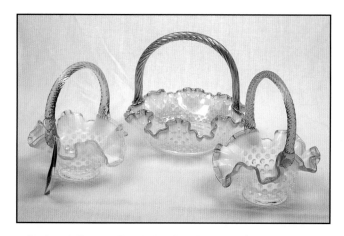

Basket, 4.5", 3834 FD, Hobnail, YOP: 1994, $40-45; Basket, 8.5", 1160 FR, Hobnail, YOP: 1994, $40-45; Basket, 4.5", 3834 FR, Hobnail, YOP: 1994, $40-45. *Courtesy of Laurie & Richard Karman.*

Basket, Mini, 6563 TG, Opaline, $20-25; Basket, 7", 2778 TG, Strawberry, $35-40, YOP: 1996. *Courtesy of Laurie & Richard Karman.*

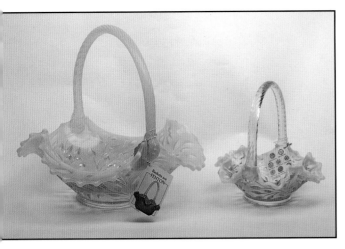

Basket, 11", 2935 PM, Wildflower, $65-70; Basket, 2946 PM, Wildflower, $25-30. *Courtesy of Laurie & Richard Karman.*

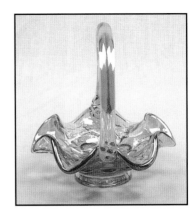

Basket, 5.5", 2919 PY, Paneled Grape Champagne Stain, $45-55. *Courtesy of Laurie & Richard Karman.*

Basket, Mini, 6556 PM, Champagne Opalescent, $15-20; Basket, 7", 2778 PM, Strawberry, $35-40. *Courtesy of Laurie & Richard Karman.*

Basket, 6", 2731 PY, Lamb's Tongue, $75-80.

Basket, 5.5", 2919 LK, Paneled Grape Misty Blue, $45-55. *Courtesy of Laurie & Richard Karman.*

Basket, 2778, Strawberry Footed, $25-30.

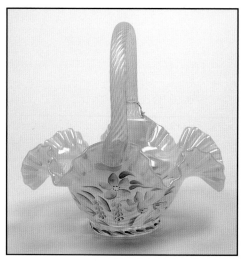

Basket, 10.5", 2039SF, Topaz Opal Decorated, Shelly Signature, $150-175. *Courtesy of Bobbie & Harold Morgan.*

Basket, 8.5", 2912 LC, Diamond Flute Ice Blue, $45-50; Basket, 11.5", 2917 LC, Diamond Flute Ice Blue, $55-60. *Courtesy of Wiggins Gifts.*

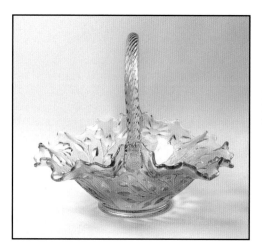

Basket, 10.5", 2836AA, Wild Flower Aquamarine, $45-55. *Courtesy of Wiggins Gifts.*

Basket, 8", 6833 HH, Rosalene HP, Lynn Signature, $90-100. *Courtesy of Bobbie & Harold Morgan.*

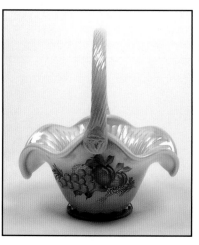

Basket, 11.5", 2917 PY, Diamond Flute Champagne Satin, $55-60; Basket, 11.5", 2917 AI, Diamond Flute, Aquamarine, $55-60. *Courtesy of Connie & Aaron Patient.*

Easter Series

Chick Out of Egg, 4685, Jade Opaline EZ, YOP: 1991, $30-35.

Small Hen on Nest, 5186, $35-40; Rooster Box, 4680, $45-50; Ducklings, Mini, 5212, $10-15 ea., Iridescent Jade Opaline EZ, YOP: 1991-92. *Courtesy of Bobbie & Harold Morgan.*

Small Hen on Nest, 5186, $35-40; Rooster Box, 4680, $45-50; Duckling, Mini, 5212, $10-15, Shell Pink PE, YOP: 1991. *Courtesy of Bobbie & Harold Morgan.*

Chick on Nest, 5185, $30-35; Bunny Box, 4683, $40-45, Ocean Blue OB, YOP: 1993. *Courtesy of Bobbie & Harold Morgan.*

Bunny Covered Box, 4683, Iridescent Jade Opaline EZ, YOP: 1992, $45-50. *Courtesy of Bobbie & Harold Morgan.*

Bunny Box, 4683, Hand Painted Iridescent Opal CD, 1993, $50-55. *Courtesy of Bobbie & Harold Morgan.*

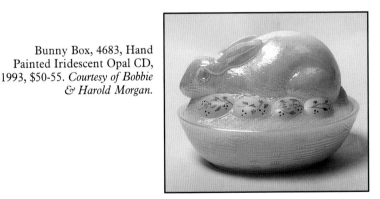

Small Hen on Nest, 5186, $40-45; Rooster Covered Box, 4680, $55-60; Bunny Box, 4683, $55-60, White "Pearlized" BT, YOP: 1992. *Courtesy of Bobbie & Harold Morgan.*

Rooster Covered Box, 4680, $50-55; Small Hen on Nest, 5186, $40-45, White Pearlized BT, YOP: 1993. *Courtesy of Bobbie & Harold Morgan.*

173

Bunny, Mini, 5209; Duckling, Mini, 5212; Hen, Mini, 5211, $20-25 ea., Plum Slag 8A, YOP: 1/94-5/94. *Courtesy of Bobbie & Harold Morgan.*

Assortment of Easter Minis in Pink Pearl, Rose Pearl, Iridescent Jade Opaline, Sea Mist Green Slag, Salem Blue, and Aquamarine, $20-25 ea. *Courtesy of Sharon & Alan Fenner.*

Bunny Box, 4863 BT, YOP: 1991, $50-55; Egg, 5140 PM, YOP: 1991, $30-35. *Courtesy of Jan Hollingsworth.*

HP Iridescent Opal, YOP: 1991: Bird, 5163 PM, $30-35; Bunny, 5162, YOP: 1991, $30-35; Duckling, PM 5169, $30-35. HP Iridescent Opal, YOP: 1993: Bird, 5163 CD, $30-35; Bunny, 5162 CD, $30-35; Duckling, 5169 CD, $30-35. Violets on Iridescent Opal, YOP: 1992: Bird, 5163, $30-35; Duckling, 5169, $30-35; Bunny, 5162, $30-35. *Courtesy of Laurie & Richard Karman.*

Bunny Box, 4683, Plum Slag 8A, YOP: 1/94-5/94, $65-70; Duckling, Mini, 5212, Sea Mist Slag 2A, 1999-5/94, $20-25.

Hen Egg Plate, 5188 YZ, YOP: 1996, $100-125. *Courtesy of Bobbie & Harold Morgan.*

Fairy Light, 8405, Egg YZ, YOP: 1996, $75-85. *Courtesy of Bobbie & Harold Morgan.*

174

Rooster, 5292 PQ, $45-50; Rooster, 5292 LR, $45-50.

Hen Egg Plate, 5188 TJ, Limited to 950, $100-125. *Courtesy of Bobbie & Harold Morgan.*

Bunny Box, 4863 LR, $45-55; Bunny Box, 4863 PQ, $45-55; Rooster, Mini, 5265 PQ, $10-15; Bunny, Mini, 5275 PQ, $10-15.

Folk Art

Rooster Box, 4680NA, $100-125; Hen on Nest, 5168NH, $75-80; Bunny Box, 4683NB, $90-95, Folk Art Collection, 1996. *Courtesy of Wiggins Gifts.*

Rooster, 5292 FV, $150+, Folk Art Collection, 1998. *Courtesy of Wiggins Gifts.*

Bunny Box, 4683 NU, $90-95, Folk Art Collection, 1997. *Courtesy of Bobbie & Harold Morgan.*

Hen on Nest, 5186 FK, $70-75, Folk Art Collection, 1998. *Courtesy of Bobbie & Harold Morgan.*

Bunny Box, 4680 FG, $90-100, Folk Art Collection, 1998. *Courtesy of Bobbie & Harold Morgan.*

Rooster, 8.5", 5257 NV, $150+. *Courtesy of Linda & Dennis Sowers.*

Rooster, Standing, 5257 FV, $65-70, Folk Art Collection, 1998. *Courtesy of Bobbie & Harold Morgan.*

Mini Rooster, 5265 CE, $35-40, Folk Art Collection, 1999. *Courtesy of Bobbie & Harold Morgan.*

Rooster, 8.5", 5257 NV, $150+; Rooster, 5292 CB, $65-80, Folk Art Collection, 1999. *Courtesy of Wiggins Gifts.*

Butterfly, 5271 AA, $45-50; Butterfly, 5271 PQ, $45-50; Butterfly, 5271 CP, $45-50; Butterfly, 5271 LR, $45-50; Butterfly, 5271 FZ, $45-50, Issued in 1999 as part of the Easter Series. *Courtesy of Laurie & Richard Karman.*

Showcase Dealers' Exclusives/Catalog Exclusive/Glass Messenger Items/Family Signing Events Items

In 1995, Fenton began to offer many of its top dealers items that were known as Showcase Dealers' Exclusives. These dealers, whose sales totaled a certain mark, would be eligible to buy these pieces to offer to their customers. These pieces were issued two per year, one would be limited in the time that it was offered, and one would be limited in the numbers made.

Several years prior to that, Fenton had offered many of its dealers small versions of their catalogs that could be mailed easily. Starting in the mid-1990s, Fenton would include what would be known as Catalog Exclusives. These items would be offered only through these small mail order catalogs and not in the dealers' stores, or through the regular Fenton catalogs.

Also, in 1995, the first issue of the *Glass Messenger* premiered. This magazine, published four times a year by Fenton, would detail new lines, treatments, and also go into the history of the Fenton Company, and the process of making various treatments of glass. Each year, a different item would be offered through the *Glass Messenger* to its subscribers.

Beginning in 1993, different members of the Fenton family would visit at different Fenton dealers throughout the U.S. and Canada to meet customers and sign their various pieces of glass. Also, each year a different piece of glass would be offered only at these signings. Many of these pieces are quite scarce today.

Showcase Dealers' Exclusives

Vase, 3558 CR, Buttons & Braids in Cranberry Opalescent, YOP: Spring 1995, $150-175.

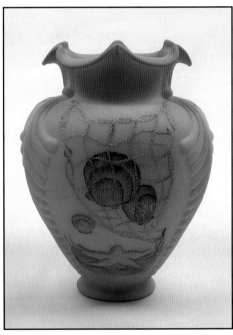

Vase, 1649 UY, Burmese Sea Dreams, YOP: Fall 1995, Limited to 790, $250+.

Fan Vase, 9550 DC, Champagne Satin with HP Hummingbird, YOP: Spring 1996, $100-125.
Courtesy of Laurie & Richard Karman.

Fairy Light, 3 Piece, 7501 TA, Periwinkle on Blue Burmese, Fall 1999, Limited to 1,950, $125-150.

Covered Box, 7603 MD, Mulberry with HP Evening Blossom Fall, Limited to 1,250, YOP: 1996, $150-175; Vase, 1649 MZ, Mulberry with HP Wisteria Fall, Limited to 1,750, YOP: 1997, $125-150. *Courtesy of Laurie & Richard Karman.*

Vase, 9.5", 1559 HC, Rubina Verde Field Of Gold Fall, Limited to 1,950, YOP: 1998, $150-175. *Courtesy of Laurie & Richard Karman.*

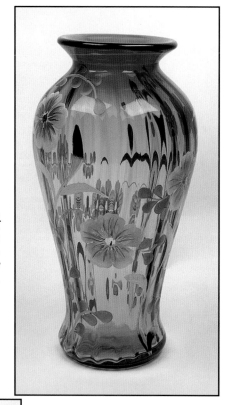

Basket, 1531 P6, HP Plum Overlay, YOP: 1995, $100-125. *Courtesy of Phyllis & Terry Sterrett.*

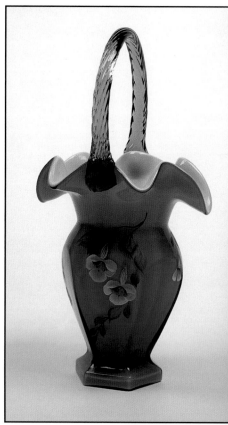

Little Sister Doll, 5328 XP, Violet Satin, Spring 1999, $45-50. *Courtesy of Fran & Bill Ersham.*

Vase, 8", 2965 WC, French Opalescent Satin HP with Fuchsia, YOP: 1998, $75-80. *Courtesy of Bobbie & Harold Morgan.*

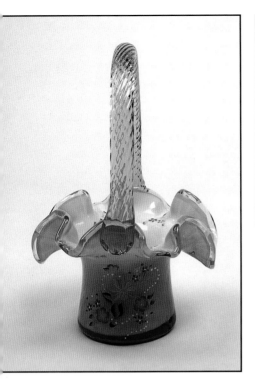

Cat, 5065 S3, Burmese, $70-75; Basket, 2915 S3, Burmese, YOP: 1999, $90-100. *Courtesy of Bobbie & Harold Morgan.*

Butterfly, Stylized, 5271 WE, French Opalescent Satin HP, YOP: 1998, $65-70.

Basket, 3144 QM, Dusty Rose with Floral Decoration, YOP: 1996, $100-125. *Courtesy of Phyllis & Terry Sterrett.*

Butterfly on Stand, 5171 XU, Champagne Satin, YOP: 1997, $65-70. *Courtesy of Bobbie & Harold Morgan.*

Glass Messenger Items

Basket, 8", 1533 JN, Roselle On Cranberry, YOP: 1996, $150-175. *Courtesy of Phyllis & Terry Sterrett.*

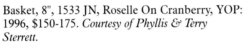

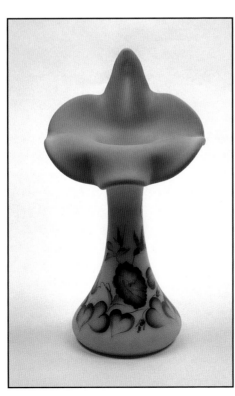

Vase, Melon, 9475 R6, French Rose on Rosalene, YOP: 1997, $100-125. *Courtesy of Laurie & Richard Karman.*

Tulip Vase, 7255 UZ; Morning Glory on Burmese, YOP: 1998, $150-175. *Courtesy of Bobbie & Harold Morgan.*

Vase, 4026 VQ, Blue Harmony, YOP: 1999, $150-175. *Courtesy of Laurie & Richard Karman.*

Family Signing Event Items

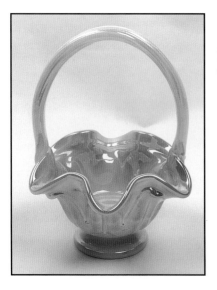

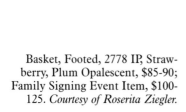

Basket, 2731 RJ, Lamb's Tongue, Rosalene, YOP: 1993, $75-80. *Courtesy of Laurie & Richard Karman.*

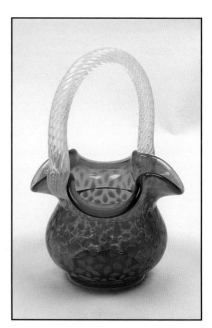

Basket, 2786 KO, Cobalt Opalescent, Snowflake Optic, Family Signing Event Item, YOP: 1995, $100-125. *Courtesy of Jan Hollingsworth.*

Basket, Footed, 2778 IP, Strawberry, Plum Opalescent, $85-90; Family Signing Event Item, $100-125. *Courtesy of Roserita Ziegler.*

Vase, S6858 3H, Sea Green Satin HP, Rep. Event Item, YOP: 1998, $80-90. *Courtesy of Anne Musser.*

Basket, 4637 IP, Button Arches, Plum Opalescent, Family Signing Event Item, YOP: 1997, $75-80. *Courtesy of Connie & Aaron Patient.*

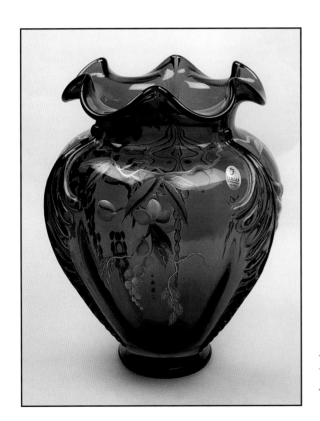

Vase, 7793, Daffodil, Blue Burmese, Rep. Event Item, YOP: 1999, $90-100. *Courtesy of Donna Hatch.*

Vase, S1577MD, HP Mulberry, Rep. Event Item, YOP: 1997, $85-90 *Courtesy of Laurie & Richard Karman.*

Animals, Bells, & More

Animals

Since the early 1970s, Fenton has produced many Animal Figures to go with their decorated patterns. These early figural items have become highly collectible. So collectible in fact that some have surpassed the value of some of the other items in the patterns they were produced in. Throughout the 1980s and into the 1990s, many other Animals were produced, either for Fenton's regular lines or for sale in the gift shop.

Throughout this time period, several of these moulds have become highly collectible, including the Fenton Alley Cat and the Bridesmaid doll. Also highly collectible are any of the Cats or Bear figures.

Items Not Pictured:

Aquamarine AA: Dolphin, 5137, YOP: 1999, $45-50

Arbor Blossoms on Petal Pink JY 1991-93: Bear Cub, 5151, YOP: 1993 only, $45-50

Arbor Blossoms on Petal Pink JY 1991-93: Cat, 5165, YOP: 1993 only, $45-50

Autumn Gold AM 6/93-12/93: Cat, 5165, $35-40

Bell Flowers LH 1999 MM: Elephant, 5136, $30-35

Bell Flowers LH 1999 MM: Bear Cub, 5151, $40-45

Blue Royale KK 1988-90: Happiness Bird, 5197, $30-35

Blue Royale KK 1988-90: Lion, 5241, YOP: 1990 only, $30-35

Buttercups & Berries on Red Carnival R1 1995: Polar Bear, 5109, $45-50

Champagne Satin PQ 1997: Butterfly with stand, 5170, $55-60

Champagne Satin PQ 1997: Butterfly on Stand, 5151, $50-55

Champagne Satin PQ 1997: Ballerina, 5270, 1999, $75-80

Cobalt Marigold NK 1985-87: Kitten, 5119, YOP: 1986, $55-60

Cobalt Marigold NK 1985-87: Mouse, 5148, YOP: 1986, $55-60

Cobalt Marigold NK 1985-87: Praying Boy/Girl, 5200, YOP: 1987, $55-60 PR

Cobalt Marigold NK 1985-87: Pig, 5220, YOP: 1987, $70-75

Cobalt Marigold NK 1985-87: Puppy, 5225, YOP: 1987, $50-55

Cobalt Marigold NK 1985-87: Fox, 5226, YOP: 1987, $65-70

Cobalt Blue Jay: 5245, 1999, $25-30

Copper Roses on Black KP 1989-93: Cat, 5165, $60-65

Dusty Rose DK 1984-94: Swan, 5127, YOP: 1987-92, $35-40

Dusty Rose DK 1984-94: Small Bird, 5163, YOP: 1992-94, $35-40

Dusty Rose DK 1984-94: Reclining Bear Cub, 5233, YOP: 1992-94, $55-60

Field Flowers on Champagne Satin PI Mouse: 5148, $65-70

Field Flowers on Champagne Satin PI Bear: 5151, $65-70

Floral on Spruce Carnival US 1999: Cat set, 3 piece, 5000, $75-80 ea.

Gold Pearl GP 1992: Owl, 7", 5252, $150-200

Golden Flax on Cobalt KG 1995: Rearing Elephant, 5136, $40-45

Hearts & Flowers FH 1988-93: Clown with Top Hat, 5217, YOP: 1988-89, $55-60

Hearts & Flowers FH 1988-93: Clown with Jester Hat, 5219, YOP: 1988-89, $55-60

Jade Opaline AP 1990: Bear, 5151, $50-55

Jade Opaline AP 1990: Happiness Bird, 5197, $35-40

Medallion Collection 1996-97: Elephant, 5136 X8, $60-65

Medallion Collection 1996-97: Small Bird, 5163 Y4, $65-70

Morning Mist GG 1999: Bird, 5163, $40-45

Pansies PF 1996: Mouse, 5148, $55-60

Pansies PF 1996: Cat, 5165, $50-55

Petal Pink PN: Bear Cub, 5151, YOP: 1990-93, $40-45

Petal Pink PN: Cat, 5165, YOP: 1991-94, $40-45

Petal Pink PN: Reclining Bear Cub, 5233, YOP: 1990-92, $40-45

Pink Pearl HZ 1991-94: Swan, 5127, YOP: 1991 only, $30-35

Provincial Blue OO 1987-89: Swan, 5127, $30-35

Provincial Blue OO 1987-89: Happiness Bird, 5197, $45-50

Red Carnival RN 1990-94: Sunfish, 5167, YOP: 1992-1993, $25-30

Red Carnival RN 1990-94: Butterfly on stand, 5171, YOP: 1992 only, $50-55

Rose Pearl DN 1992-94: Sunfish, 5167, YOP: 1992-93, $25-30

Rose Pearl DN 1992-94: Cat, 5243, YOP: 1993 only, $45-50

Ruby RU 1985-2000: Angel Boy, 5113, YOP: 1991 only, $30-35

Ruby RU 1985-2000: Angel Girl, 5114, YOP: 1991 only, $30-35

Ruby RU 1985-2000: Bird, 5115, YOP: 1991 only, $25-30

Ruby RU 1985-2000: Swan, 5127, YOP: 1987-90, $25-30

Ruby RU 1985-2000: Cat, 5165, YOP: 1990-91, $45-50

Ruby RU 1985-2000: Cardinal, 5245, YOP: 1991-94, $30-35

Salem Blue SR 1990-92: Cat, 5243, $30-35

Salem Blue SR 1990-92: Butterfly on Stand, 5171, YOP: 1991-92, $40-45

Salem Blue SR 1990-92: Open Bird, 5240, $25-30

Salem Blue SR 1990-92: Cardinal, 5245, YOP: 1991-92, $25-30

Sea Mist Green LE 1991-94: Elephant, 5136, $30-35

Sea Mist Green LE 1991-94: Mouse, 5148, $40-45
Sea Mist Green LE 1991-94: Small Bird, 5163, $30-35
Sea Mist Green LE 1991-94: Butterfly on stand, 5170, $40-45
Sea Mist Green LE 1991-94: Pig, 5220, 1997, $40-45, $40-45
Sea Mist Green LE 1991-94: Reclining Bear Cub, 5233, YOP: 1992-94, $40-45
Sea Mist Green LE 1991-94: Unicorn, 5253, $40-45
Spruce Carnival SI 1999: Scottie, 5214, $45-50
Teal Marigold OI 1988-89: Swan, 5127, YOP: 1989 only, $30-35
Teal Royale OC 1988-89: Swan, 5127, $30-35
Tulips TL Clown with Head on Hand: 5216, YOP: 1990 only,

$60-65
Tulips TL Clown with Top Hat: 5217, YOP: 1990 only, $60-65
Tulips TL Clown with Hands Up: 5218, YOP: 1990 only, $60-65
Tulips TL Clown with Jester Hat: 5219, YOP: 1990 only, $60-65
Twilight Blue TB 1992-94: Bear Cub, 5151, $40-45
Twilight Blue TB 1992-94: Small Bird, 5163, $30-35
Twilight Blue TB 1992-94: Whale, 5152, $30-35
Victorian Bouquet on Black BT 1995: Cat, 5165, $60-65
Victorian Roses VJ 1987-89: Small Bird, 5163, $40-45
Violas on Petal Pink PU 1994: Bear Cub, 5151, $45-50

Antique Rose AF, YOP: 6/89-690: Bird, 5115, $35-40; Cat, 5165, $50-55. *Courtesy of Laurie & Richard Karman.*

Autumn Leaves on Black AW, YOP: 1994: Fox, 5226, $55-60; Unicorn, 5253, $55-60. *Courtesy of Laurie & Richard Karman.*

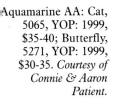

Aquamarine AA: Cat, 5065, YOP: 1999, $35-40; Butterfly, 5271, YOP: 1999, $30-35. *Courtesy of Connie & Aaron Patient.*

Black BK: Unicorn, 5253, YOP: 1994, $40-45. *Courtesy of Bobbie & Harold Morgan.*

Autumn Gold AM: Small Bird, 5163, YOP: 6/93-12/93, $25-30.

Blue Royale KK: YOP: 1998-99, Whale, 5152, $30-35; Cat, 5165, $35-40; Bear, 5151, $35-40. *Courtesy of Laurie & Richard Karman.*

Blue Royale with White Floral EM: Happiness bird, 5197, YOP: 1989-90, $45-50. *Courtesy of Bobbie & Harold Morgan.*

Boutonniere Buddie, 5248 W1 Jan, $40-45. *Courtesy of Tina & Rick Gaither.*

Calendar Cats: PK: All 5165: Made as birthday gifts with a different rhinestone necklace fixed to cat's neck for each month of the year. They are as follows: Cat, W1, Jan.; Cat, W2, Feb; Cat, W3, Mar.; Cat, W4, Apr.; Cat, W5, May; Cat, W6, Jun; Cat, W7, Jul; Cat, W8, Aug.; Cat, W9, Sep.; Cat, W10, Oct; Cat, W11, Nov; Cat, W12, Dec., $40-45 ea. *Courtesy of Myers Mystique.*

Calender Cat, 5165 PK: Cat W1, $40-45. *Courtesy of Tina & Rick Gaither.*

Children Gifts: Baby Shoe, 4610 BP, $30-35; Rocking Horses, 5135 BP, $40-45 ea.; Ball Cap, 5040 BP, $40-45; Bear, 5151 BP, $55-60; Kitten, 5119 BP, $35-40; Kitten, 5119 GU, $35-40; Bear, 5151 GU, $55-60; Rocking Horses, 5135 GU, $40-45 ea.; Ball Cap, 5040 GU, $40-45; Baby Shoe, 4610 GU, $30-35. *Courtesy of Donna Hatch.*

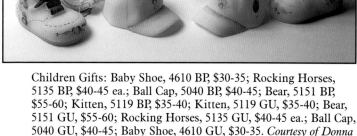

Children Gifts: Praying Boy, 5273 BP; Praying Girl, 5272 GU, $40-45 ea. *Courtesy of Bobbie & Harold Morgan.*

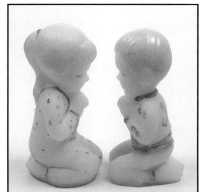

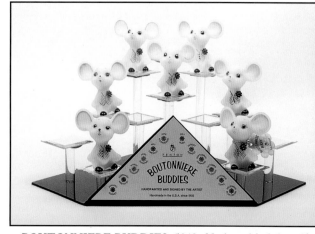

BOUTONNIERE BUDDIES, 5248: Made as birthday gifts, with rhinestone attached next to a HP flower for each month of the year, they are as follows: Mouse, W1, Jan.; Mouse, W2, Feb.; Mouse, W3, Mar.; Mouse, W4, Apr.; Mouse, W5, May; Mouse W6, Jun.; Mouse, W7, Jul.; Mouse, W8, Aug.; Mouse, W9, Sep.; Mouse, W10, Oct.; Mouse, W11, Nov.; Mouse, W12, Dec., $40-45 ea. *Courtesy of Shelia & Pete McMillian.*

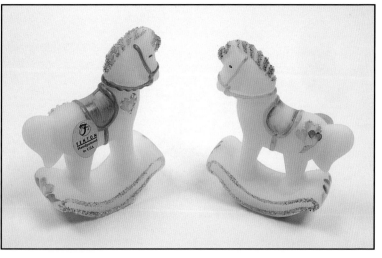

Children Gifts: Rocking Horse, 5135 BP; Rocking Horse, 5135 GU, $40-45 ea. *Courtesy of Bev & Jon Spencer.*

Cobalt KN: Cat, 5065, YOP: 1999, $40-45; Butterfly, 5271, 1999, $35-40. *Courtesy of Myers Mystique.*

Copper Roses on Black KP: Cat, 5165, $65-70. *Courtesy of Laurie & Richard Karman.*

Country Cranberry CC: Bear Cub, 5151, YOP: 1994 only, $100-125. *Courtesy of Laurie & Richard Karman.*

Colonial Amber CA: Happiness Bird, 5197, YOP: 1987, $25-30.

Dusty Rose DK: Unicorn, 5253, YOP: 1993-94, $50-55.

Dusty Rose DK: Bear Cub, 5151, $50-55.

Copper Roses on Black KP: Bear Cub, 5151, YOP: 1990-93, $60-65; Happiness Bird, 5197, YOP: 1989-93, $45-50. *Courtesy of Laurie & Richard Karman.*

Dusty Rose DK: Mouse, 5148, YOP: 1997, $65-70.

Dusty Rose DK: Butterfly on Stand, 5171, YOP: 1984-87, $40-45. *Courtesy of Diane Rohow.*

"Elizabeth" Silver Crest with Blue Floral ES: Cat, 5165, YOP: 1990-92, $65-70; Bear Cub, 5151, YOP: 1990-92, $65-70. Blue Royale with White Floral EM: Happiness Bird, 5197, YOP: 1989-90, $45-50. *Courtesy of Laurie & Richard Karman.*

Dusty Rose DK: Open Bird, 5240, YOP: 1990-91, $20-25. *Courtesy of Diane Rohow.*

Empress Rose CP: Bear, 5151, YOP: 1998, $35-40.

Empress Rose CP: Elephant, 5136, YOP: 1998, $25-30; Small Bird, 5163, YOP: 1998, $25-30; Bear, 5151, YOP: 1998, $35-40; Cat, 5165, YOP: 1998, $25-30. *Courtesy of Myers Mystique.*

Dusty Rose DK: Happiness Bird, 5197, YOP: 1987-92, $30-35; Cat, 5065, $55-60.

Empress Rose CP: Cat, 5065, YOP: 1999, $35-40. *Courtesy of Judy Henselman.*

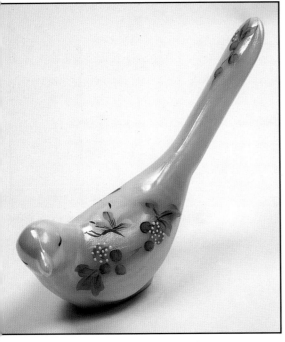

Floral on Plum Carnival AZ: Bear Set, 3 pieces, 5207 AZ, Limited to 1,250 Set, YOP: 1998, $65-70 ea. *Courtesy of Bev & Jon Spencer.*

Floral Interlude on Sea Green Satin GG: Happiness Bird, 5197, YOP: 1998, $45-50. *Courtesy of Jan Hollingsworth.*

Floral Interlude on Sea Green Satin GG: Cat, 5165, $65-70. *Courtesy of Laurie & Richard Karman.*

Floral on Spruce Carnival US: Bridesmaid Doll, 5228, YOP: 1999, $40-45. *Courtesy of Fran & Bill Ersham.*

Floral on Plum Carnival P2: Clown Set, 4 pieces, 5205 P2, Limited to 970 sets, YOP: 1997, $55-60 ea. *Courtesy of Bev & Jon Spencer.*

Floral on Violet Satin XP: Bear, 5151, $65-70; Cat, 5065, $65-70, YOP: 1999. *Courtesy of Bobbie & Harold Morgan.*

Fools in Love on Iridescent Opal CW: Clown with Hands Up, 5218; Clown with Jester's Hat, 5219; Sitting Clown, 5111; Clown with Head on Hand, 5216; Clown with Top Hat, 5217, $80-90 ea., YOP: 1991. *Courtesy of Bobbie & Harold Morgan.*

French Cream FO: Mouse, 5148, YOP: 1986 only, $50-55; Basket, Rose Mini, $15-20; Bear Cub, 5151, YOP: 1986 only, $45-50.

Golden Flax on Cobalt KG: Polar Bear, 5109, $40-45; Cat, 5165, $50-55. *Courtesy of Laurie & Richard Karman.*

Hearts & Flowers FH: Cat, 5165, YOP: 1988-93, $55-60; Reclining Bear Cub, 5233, YOP: 1988-93, $55-60; Mouse, 5148, YOP: 1989-92, $55-60; Small Bird, 5163, YOP: 1993 only, $45-50; Fawn, 5160, YOP: 1988-90, $50-55; Bear Cub, 5151, YOP: 1988-90, $55-60; Raccoon, 5142, YOP: 1993 only, $55-60; Happiness Bird, 5197, YOP: 1988-92, $45-50. *Courtesy of Laurie & Richard Karman.*

Hearts & Flowers FH: Clown with Hands Up, 5218, YOP: 1988-89, $55-60; Clown with Head on Hand, 5216, YOP: 1988-89, $55-60. *Courtesy of Bobbie Morgan.*

Irises on Misty Blue Satin LS, YOP: 1997: Bear Cub, 5151, $50-55; Bird, 5163, $40-45. *Courtesy of Laurie & Richard Karman.*

Jade Opaline AP, YOP: 1990: Cat, 5165, $50-55. *Courtesy of Judy Henselman.*

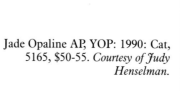

Kristen's Floral, YOP: 1995: Bear Cub, 5151, $60-65. *Courtesy of Myers Mystique.*

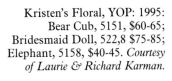

Kristen's Floral, YOP: 1995: Bear Cub, 5151, $60-65; Bridesmaid Doll, 522,8 $75-85; Elephant, 5158, $40-45. *Courtesy of Laurie & Richard Karman.*

Lilac LX: Cat, 5243, Side View.

Last of the Red Hot Lovers Series: YOP: 1989: Reclining Bear, 5233, Heart Beat, $55-60; Daydreaming Bear, 5239BY, Heart Fanny, $55-60; Daydreaming Bear, 5239EW, Heart Eyes, $55-60; Sitting Bear Cub, 5151FX, Heart Foot, $55-60; Reclining Bear, 5233, Heart on Ear, $55-60; Heart Throb Bear Cub, 5151 HC, YOP: 1987-92, $60-65; Heart Throb Kitten, 5119 HC, Heart Fanny, YOP: 1989-92, $50-55; Reclining Bear, 5233, Heart on Knee, $55-60. Not Pictured: Heart Throb Mouse, 5148 HC, YOP: 1989-90, $60-65. *Courtesy of Donna Hatch.*

Light Amethyst Carnival DT, YOP: 1991: Owl Figural, 5.5", 5254, $65-70. *Courtesy of Bobbie & Harold Morgan.*

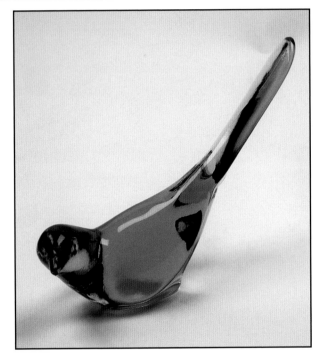

Lilac LX: Happiness Bird, 5197, YOP: 6/90-12/90, $35-40. *Courtesy of Jan Hollingsworth.*

Lilac LX: Cat, 5243, YOP: 6/90-12/90, $40-45.

Lilacs PJ, YOP: 1993-94: Cat, 5165, $60-65; Mouse, 5148, $40-45. *Courtesy of Laurie & Richard Karman.*

Lilacs PJ, YOP 1993-94: Bear Cub, 5151, $60-65; Small Bird, 5163, $40-45. *Courtesy of Laurie & Richard Karman.*

Meadow Blossoms on Opal Satin SF, YOP: 1991-93: Cat, 5165, $45-50; Kitten, 5119, $50-55. *Courtesy of Judy Henselman.*

Martha's Rose AZ, YOP: 1999: Fawn, 5160, $40-45; Cat, 5165, $50-55; Elephant, 5158, $35-40; Mallard, 5147, $35-40. *Courtesy of Laurie & Richard Karman.*

Meadow Beauty PD, YOP: 1997: Bunny, 5162, YOP: 1997, $50-45; Bird, 5163, YOP: 1997, $40-45; Squirrel, 5215, $40-45; Bear, 5151, $50-55; Cat, 5165, $50-55. *Courtesy of Sharon & Alan Fenner.*

Medallion Collection, YOP: 1996-97: Happiness Bird, 5197 Y5, $60-65; Cat, 5243 Y7, $75-80; Fox, 5226 Y6, $80-90; Mallard, 5147 Y9, YOP: 1997, $65-70; Owl, 5258 Y8, $100+; Cat, 5165 X7, YOP: 1997, $80-90. *Courtesy of Bobbie & Harold Morgan.*

Meadow Blossoms on Opal Satin SF, YOP: 1991-93: Reclining Bear Cub, 5233, $50-55; Pig 5220, $45-50; Small Bird, 5163, $40-45; Happiness Bird, 5197, $40-45. *Courtesy of Laurie & Richard Karman.*

Medallion Collection, YOP: 1996-97: Happiness Bird, 5197 Y5, $60-65; Fawn, 5160 Y3, $70-75; Mallard, 5147 Y9, YOP: 1997, $65-70. *Courtesy of Jan Hollingsworth.*

Medallion Collection: Mallard, 5147 X9, $65-70. *Courtesy of Jan Hollingsworth.*

Medallion Collection, YOP: 1996-97: Vase, 7", 7565 X5, sold to go along with Medallion Collection, $65-70. *Courtesy of Laurie & Richard Karman.*

Misty Blue Satin LR: Blue Jay, 5245, 1998, $30-35; Cat, 5165, $45-50; Butterfly, 5271, 1999, $35-40. *Courtesy of Myers Mystique.*

Millinium JE, YOP: 1999: Happiness Bird, 5197, $40-45.

Misty Blue Satin LR: Cat, 5165, $45-50.

Minted Cream EO: Happiness Bird, 5197, YOP: 1987 only, $30-35.

Misty Blue Satin LR: Butterfly, 5170, $45-50.

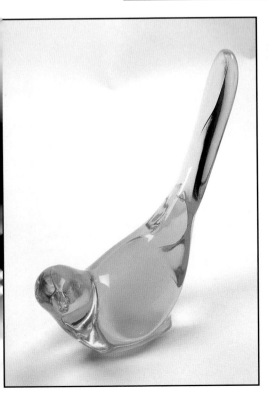

Morning Mist GG: Bear Cub, 5151, YOP: 1999, $60-65.

Pastel Violets on Custard VC, YOP: 1987: Bear Cub, 5151, YOP: 1987, $60-65. *Courtesy of Bobbie & Harold Morgan.*

Pearly Sentiments PT: Bear Cub, 5151, YOP: 1988-93, $45-50; Heart Paperweight, $20-25.

Pastel Violets on Custard VC, YOP: 1987: Kitten, 5119, $50-55. *Courtesy of Judy Henselman.*

Pearly Sentiments PT: Elephant, 5158, YOP: 1992-93, $30-35; Fawn, 5160, YOP: 1988-93, $30-35; Cat, 5165, YOP: 1988-93, $40-45; Whale, 5152, YOP: 1992 only, $30-35; Small Bird, 5163, YOP: 1988-93, $30-35; Kitten, 5119, YOP: 1988-93, $35-40; Bear Cub, 5151, YOP: 1988-93, $45-50; Happiness Bird, 5197, YOP: 1989-94, $40-45; Reclining Bear Cub, 5233, YOP: 1989-93, $45-50. *Courtesy of Marilyn Bingham.*

Pastel Violets on Custard VC, YOP: 1987: Mouse, 5148, YOP: 1987, $65-70.

Pastel Violets on Custard VC, YOP: 1987: Puppy, 5225, YOP: 1987, $50-55. *Courtesy of Bobbie & Harold Morgan.*

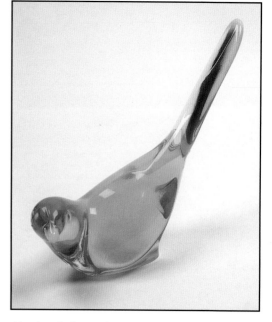

Peaches & Cream UO: Happiness Bird, 5197, YOP: 1987-89, $35-50.

Pearly Sentiments PT: Whale, 5152, YOP: 1992 only, $30-35.

Petal Pink PN: Day-dreaming Bear, 5239, YOP: 1990-94, $40-45.

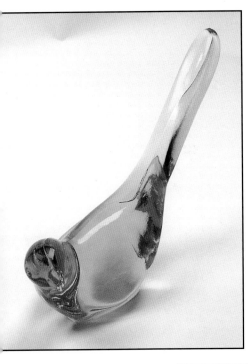

Petal Pink PN:
Happiness Bird,
5197, YOP: 1990-92,
$30-35.

Plum PL: Butterfly on Stand,
5170, $40-45. *Courtesy of Chuck
Bingham.*

Primrose DS, YOP: 1994: Bird, 5163,
$45-50; Cat, 5165, $50-55; Reclining
Bear, 5233, $50-55. *Courtesy of Laurie
& Richard Karman.*

Pink Pearl HZ: Sunfish, 5167,
YOP: 1991-93, $25-30.

Provincial Bouquet FS: Fawn, 5160, $50-55; Bear Cub,
5151, $55-60; Puppy, 5225, $50-55; Pig, 5220, $60-65,
YOP: 1987-88. *Courtesy of Bobbie & Harold Morgan.*

Pink Pearl HZ: Clown with Top Hat, 5217, YOP: 1991 only, $45-50;
Clown with Hands Up, 5218, YOP: 1991 only, $45-50; Clown with
Jester's Hat, 5219, YOP: 1991 only, $45-50; Clown with Head on
Hand, 5216, YOP: 1991 only, $45-50; Bird on Log, 5238, YOP:
1991-92, $40-45. *Courtesy of Bobbie & Harold Morgan.*

Provincial Bouquet FS:
Kitten, 5119, $50-55.
*Courtesy of Judy
Henselman.*

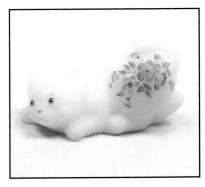

Pink Pearl HZ: Kitten, 5119,
YOP: 1993 only, $35-40.

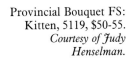

Rose Garden EG: Bear Cub, 5151, $50-55; Elephant, 5158, $45-50; Cat, 5065, $50-55; Playful Pup, $40-45; Small Bird, 5163, $40-45; Bear, Reclining, 5233, $55-60; Cat, 5165, $50-55. *Courtesy of Myers Mystique.*

Red Carnival RN: Unicorn, 5253, YOP: 1993 only, $45-50; Raccoon, 5142, YOP: 1993 only, $45-50; Fox, 5226, YOP: 1994 only, $50-55; Angel Figural, 5333, NIL, $45-50; Sitting Bear Club, 5151, YOP: 1991 only, $50-55; Reclining Bear Club, 5233, YOP: 1990 only, $50-55. *Courtesy of Bev & Jon Spencer.*

Rose Garden EG: Bear Cub, 5151, $50-55; Small Bird, 5163, $40-45; Cat, 5165, $50-55. *Courtesy of Laurie & Richard Karman.*

Red Carnival RN: Sitting Bear Club, 5151, YOP: 1991 only, $40-55; Fox, 5226, YOP: 1994 only, $50-55; Lion, 5241, YOP: 1990 only, $35-50; Raccoon, 5142, YOP: 1993 only, $45-50; Reclining Bear Club, 5233, YOP: 1990 only, $50-55; Unicorn, 5253, YOP: 1993 only, $45-50; Owl, 5258, YOP: 1996, $60-65. *Courtesy of Bobbie & Harold Morgan.*

Romance RW: Happiness Bird, 5197, YOP: 1997, $35-40. *Courtesy of Bobbie & Harold Morgan.*

Rose Garden EG: Cat, Stylized, 5065, $60-65.

Rose Garden EG: Doll, Brides-maid. *Courtesy of Myers Mystique.*

194

Rose Garden EG: Mouse, 5148, YOP: 1997, $50-55; Polar Bear, 5109, $55-60; Elephant, 5158, $45-50. *Courtesy of Laurie & Richard Karman.*

Sea Green Satin GE: Sun Fish, 5167, YOP: 1999, $25-30. *Courtesy of Myers Mystique.*

Rose Magnolia RV: Bear Cub, 5151, YOP: 1994 only, $50-55; Cat, 5165, YOP: 1994 only, $50-55. *Courtesy of Laurie & Richard Karman.*

Sea Mist Green LE: Bear Cub, 5151, $40-45; Fawn, 5160, YOP: 1991-92, $40-45; Cat, 5165, $40-45. *Courtesy of Bobbie & Harold Morgan.*

Salem Blue SR, YOP: 1990-92: Kitten, 5119, $40-45; Bear Cub, 5151, $40-45; Happiness Bird, 5197, $35-40. *Courtesy of Bobbie & Harold Morgan.*

Sea Mist Green Opalescent LO: Bear Cub, 5151, $40-45; Cat, 5165, $40-45.

Sea Mist Green Opalescent LO: Happiness Bird, 5197, YOP: 1991-92, $35-40.

Salem Blue SR, YOP: 1990-92: Kitten, 5119, $40-45. *Courtesy of Judy Henselman.*

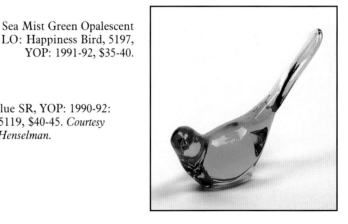

Shell Pink PE: Day Dreaming Bear, 5239, YOP: 1990-91, $45-50.

Shell Pink PE: Lion, 5214,
YOP: 1990 only, $30-35.

Shell Pink PE: Cat, 5165, $45-50.
Courtesy of Judy Henselman.

Teal Marigold OI: Bear Cub, 5151, YOP: 1988 only, $40-45;
Reclining Bear, 5233, YOP: 1989 only, $45-50; Small Bird, 5163,
YOP: 1989 only, $30-35; Cat, 5165, YOP: 1988 only, $45-50. *Courtesy of Chuck Bingham.*

Teal Royale OC, YOP: 1988-
89: Happiness Bird, 5197, $35-
40.

Spruce Carnival SI:
Alley Cat, 5177,
YOP: 1999, $75-80.
*Courtesy of Myers
Mystique.*

Thistle & Bows EW, YOP
1986: Fawn, 5160, $40-45;
Bear Cub, 5151, $40-45.

Trellis DX: Elephant, 5136, $30-35; Bird,
5163, $30-35; Bear, 5151, $45-55; Cat,
5165, $40-45; Squirrel, 5215, $40-45.
Courtesy of Laurie & Richard Karman.

Teal Marigold OI: Bear Cub, 5151,
YOP: 1988 only, $40-45. *Courtesy of
Bobbie & Harold Morgan.*

True Blue Friends IK, YOP: 1986: Bear Cub, 5151, $80-90; Pig, 5220, $75-80; Mouse, 5148, $100-125; Kitten, 5119, $75-80; Cat, 5165, $80-90; Fawn, 5160, $80-90; Mallards, 5147, $75-80 ea. Notice the difference in colors on the Mallards; this treatment proved difficult to produce! *Courtesy of Bobbie & Harold Morgan.*

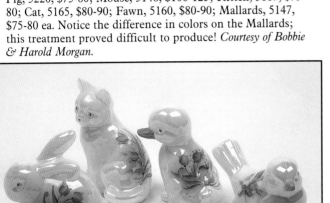

Tulips TL: Small Bird, 5163, $40-45; Cat, 5165, $50-55; Duckling, 5169, $40-45; Bunny, 5162, $40-45, YOP: 1990-91. *Courtesy of Laurie & Richard Karman.*

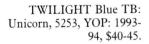

TWILIGHT Blue TB: Unicorn, 5253, YOP: 1993-94, $40-45.

TWILIGHT Blue TB: Cat, 5165, $40-45. *Courtesy of Judy Henselman.*

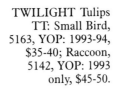

TWILIGHT Tulips TT: Small Bird, 5163, YOP: 1993-94, $35-40; Raccoon, 5142, YOP: 1993 only, $45-50.

TWILIGHT Tulips TT: Cat, 5165, YOP: 1993-94, $45-50. *Courtesy of Judy Henselman.*

Victorian Roses VJ: Puppy, 5225, YOP: 1987-88, $45-50; Hobby Horse, 5135, $45-50; Bear Cub, 5151, $55-60; Cat, 5165, $55-60; Fawn, 5160, $45-50. *Courtesy of Bobbie & Harold Morgan.*

Vining Hearts on Rose Pearl DW: Cat, 5243, YOP: 1993, $45-50.

Vining Hearts on Rose Pearl
DW: Cat, 5243, Side View.

Vining Hearts on Rose Pearl DW: Brides-maid Doll, 5228, YOP: 1993. *Courtesy of Fran & Bill Ersham.*

Violas on Petal Pink PU, YOP: 1994: Cat, 5165, $45-50.

Windflowers on Stiegel Green Stretch ST, YOP: 6-94-12-94: Sparrow, 5259, $40-45. *Courtesy of B & B Shop.*

Vining Garden on Sea Mist Green FP: Small Bird, 5163, YOP: 1993-94, $35-40; Reclining Bear Cub, 5233, YOP: 1993-94, $45-50.

Vining Garden on Sea Mist Green FP: Cat, 5165, YOP: 1993-94, $45-50. *Courtesy of Judy Henselman.*

Assortment of 5165 Cats issued in the early 1990s, $40-45 ea. *Courtesy of Laurie & Richard Karman.*

Watercolors PF, YOP: 1990: Cat, 5165, $55-60.

Assortment of 5165 Cats issued in the early 1990s, $40-45 ea. *Courtesy of Laurie & Richard Karman.*

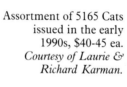

Bells

Fenton's first bell was made in the early part of the twentieth century in Carnival Glass. Later in the 1960s, they produced a bell in the Hobnail pattern. Shortly after that, several bell moulds were developed, were used throughout the 1970s and 1980s, and continue in use to this day many in the treatments and patterns that have been in, or are currently in, Fenton's regular line. In the mid-1990s, Fenton started a regular series of what was called "Designer Bells." These bells would be painted by many of Fenton's top decorators, highlighting different techniques that these decorators specialized in.

Items Not Pictured:

Arbor Blossoms on Petal Pink JY 1991-93: Bell, Petite, 9266, Bow & Drape, YOP: 1993 only, $20-25

Arbor Blossoms on Petal Pink JY 1991-93: Bell, 9667, Aurora, $30-35

Aquamarine AA 1999: Bell, 9265, Butterfly, 1999, $20-25

Autumn Gold AM 6/93-12/93: Bell, 8369, Barred Oval, $20-25

Black BK 1994: Bell, 9667, Aurora, $20-25

Buttercups & Berries on Red Carnival R1 1995: Bell, 6761, Paisley, $30-35

Champagne Satin PQ 1997: Bell, 8265, Lily of the Valley, $30-35

Cobalt Marigold NK 1985-87: Bell, 8361, Barred Oval, YOP: 1986, $30-35

Cobalt Marigold NK 1985-87: Bell, 9163, Famous Women, YOP: 1987, $30-35

Colonial Amber CA 1987: Bell, 9667, Aurora, $20-25

Colonial Scroll on Royal Purple N- 1998: Bell, Blown, 3271, $60-65

Dusty Rose DK 1984-94: Bell, 6761, Paisley, YOP: 1992-94, $30-35

Dusty Rose DK 1984-94: Bell, 846, Faberge, YOP: 1984-86, $30-35

Dusty Rose DK 1984-94: Bell, Petite, 9266, Bow & Drape, YOP: 1990-92, $30-35

Dusty Rose DK 1984-94: Bell, 9665, Beauty, YOP: 1985-89, $30-35

Dusty Rose DK 1984-94: Bell, 9763, Heart, YOP: 1993-94, $30-35

Floral on Spruce Carnival US 1999: Bell, 9066, Whitton, $30-35

Floral on Violet Satin XP 1999: Bell, 7568, Legacy, $30-35

French Cream FO 1986-87: Bell, 6665, YOP: 1986 only, $20-25

Hearts & Flowers FH 1988-93: Bell, Petite, 7662, YOP: 1988-93.

Irises on Misty Blue Satin LS 1997: Bell, 9667, Aurora, $30-35

Jade Opaline AP 1990: Bell, Petite, 9266, Bowl & Drape, $20-25

Jade Opaline AP 1990: Bell, 9268, Bow & Drape, $30-35

Kristen's Floral Bell, 6761, Paisley, $30-35

Lilac LX 6/90-12/90: Bell, Petite, 9266, Bow & Drape, $20-25

Minted Cream EO 1986-87: Bell, 6665, YOP: 1986-87, $30-35

Minted Cream EO 1986-87: Bell, 9466, Faberge, YOP: 1985-87, $30-35

Morning Glories on Sea Mist Green Bell, 9667, Aurora, $30-35

Mulberry MG 1989-92: Bell, Spiral, 6590, YOP: 1992 only.

Ocean Blue OB 1993-6/93: Bell, 9763, Heart, $30-35

Pastel Violets on Custard VC 1987: Bell, Petite, 7662, $20-25

Pastel Violets on Custard VC 1987: Bell, 7668, $30-35

Pearly Sentiments PT 1988-94: Bell, 9763, Heart, YOP: 1989-94, $30-35

Pearly Sentiments PT 1988-94: Bell, Large, 9764, Heart, YOP: 1989-93, $30-35

Peaches & Cream (Pink Opalescent) UO 1986-89: Bell, 6665, YOP: 1986-87, $30-35

Peaches & Cream (Pink Opalescent) UO 1986-89: Bell, 9466, Faberge, YOP: 1986-87, $30-35

Persian Pearl Opalescent XV 1992-93: Bell, 3567, Spanish Lace, YOP: 6/92-12/92, $30-35

Petal Pink PN 1990-94: Bell, 6761, Paisley, YOP: 1991-94, $30-35

Petal Pink PN 1990-94: Bell, Petite, 9261, Bow & Drape, YOP: 1990-93, $30-35

Petal Pink PN 1990-94: Bell, 9763, Heart, YOP: 1990-94, $30-35

Petal Pink PN 1990-94: Bell, Large, 9764, Heart, YOP: 1990-93, $30-35

Pink Pearl HZ 1991-94: Bell, 9560, Temple bells, YOP: 1991-92, $30-35

Pink Pearl HZ 1991-94: Bell, 9763, Heart, YOP: 1991-92, $30-35

Plum PL 1993-94: Bell, 6761, Paisley, $30-35

Plum PL 1993-94: Bell, 9763, Heart, $30-35

Primrose DS 1994: Bell, Petite, 7662, $20-25

Primrose DS 1994: Bell, 9462, Basket weave, $30-35

Provincial Blue OO 1987-89: Bell, 9560, Temple bells, $30-35

Provincial Bouquet FS 1987-88: Bell, 7668, $30-35

Red Carnival RN 1990-94: Bell, 9059, Sables Arch, YOP: 1992 only, $30-35

Red Carnival RN 1990-94: Bell, 9066, Whitton, YOP: 1994 only, $30-35

Red Carnival RN 1990-94: Bell, 9660, Fenton Trademark, YOP: 1993 only, $30-35

Rose Corsage MP 1989: Bell, 8267, Medallion, $30-35

Rose Magnolia RV 1993-94: Bell, 8265, Lily of the Valley, YOP: 1994 only, $30-35

Rose Pearl DN 1992-94: Bell, 8466, Faberge, YOP: 1993 only, $30-35

Ruby RU 1985-2000: Bell, 3369, YOP: 1987-89, $30-35

Ruby RU 1985-2000: Bell, 6760, Paisley, YOP: 1988-94, $30-35

Ruby RU 1985-2000: Bell, 9763, Heart, YOP: 1989-94, $30-35

Ruby RU 1985-2000: Bell, Large, 9764, Heart, YOP: 1989-92, $30-35

Salem Blue SR 1990-92: Bell, 6761, Paisley, $30-35

Salem Blue SR 1990-95: Bell, Petite, 9266, Bowl & Drape, $20-25

Sea Mist Green LE 1991-94: Bell, 9667, Aurora, YOP: 1991-92, $30-35

Sea Mist Green LE 1991-94: Bell, 9763, Heart, YOP: 1993-94, $30-35

Sea Mist Green Opalescent LO 1991-93: Bell, 9262, Rose, YOP: 1993 only, $30-35

Shell Pink PE 2988-91: Bell, 9560, Temple Bells, YOP: 1990-91, $30-35

Shell Pink PE 2988-91: Bell, Musical, 9762, Cross, $30-35

Steigal Blue Opalescent BO 1991-6/91: Bell, 9560, Temple bells, $30-35

Topaz Opalescent TS 1997: Bell, 9665, Beauty, $30-35

Thistle & Bows EW 1986: Bell, Petite, 7662, $20-25

Thistle & Bows EW 1986: Bell, 7668, $30-35

Twilight Blue TB 1992-94: Bell, 6761, Paisley, $30-35

Twilight Blue TB 1992-94: Bell, 7463, $30-35

Twilight Blue TB 1992-94: Bell, 9763, Heart, YOP: 1993-94, $30-35

Twilight Tulips TT 1992-93: Bell, 7463, $30-35

Victorian Roses VJ 1987-89: Bell, Petite, 7662, $20-25

Victorian Roses VJ 1987-89: Bell, 8267, Medallion, $30-35

Vining Hearts on Rose Pearl DW 1993: Bell, 9667, Aurora, $30-35

Vining Garden on Sea Mist Green FP 1991-94: Bell, Petite, 9266, 4.5", Bow & Drape, YOP: 1993-94, $20-25

Vining Garden on Sea Mist Green FP 1991-94: Bell, 9667, Aurora, YOP: 1991-94, $30-35

Violas on Petal Pink PU 1994: Bell, 1765, $30-35

Windflowers on Steigel Green Stretch 6/94-12/94: Bell, 9667, Aurora, $30-35

Anitque Rose AF: YOP: 6/89-6/90: Bell, 9667, Aurora, $30-35; Bell, Petite, 7262, $20-25.

Autumn Leaves on Black AW: YOP: 1994: Bell, 9667, Aurora, $40-45.

Bell Flowers on Ice Blue LH, YOP: 1999: Bell, 6864, Melon, $30-35.

Birds of Winter: Bell, 7667, "The Cardnial", YOP: 6/87-1988; Bell, 7667, "Downey Woodpecker", YOP: 6/89-1990; Bell, 7667, "Blue Bird in Snowfall", YOP: 6/90-1991; Bell, 7667, "A Chickadee Ballet", YOP: 6/88-1989, $65-70 ea.

Cobalt Marigold NK: Bell, 9063, Sydenham, YOP: 1986, $30-35.

Blush Rose on Opaline TE: Bell, 4568, $30-35.

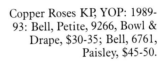

Copper Roses KP, YOP: 1989-93: Bell, Petite, 9266, Bowl & Drape, $30-35; Bell, 6761, Paisley, $45-50.

Cobalt Marigold NK: Bell, 3067, Wavy Hobnail, YOP: 1987, $30-35.

Cottage on Opal Satin ZB: YOP: 1993-6/94: Bell, 6.5", 7668, $65-75; Bell, 4", Petite, 7662, $50-55.

Dusty Rose DK: Bell, 9560, Temple Bells, YOP: 1989-91, $30-35; Bell, 9265, Butterfly, $30-35.

"Elizabeth" Silver Crest with Blue Floral ES: Bell, Spanish Lace, NIL, $45-50.

Country Cranberry: Bell, $75-80; Bell, Spiral, 6590, YOP: 1992-94, $75-80.

Country Garden on French Cream JF: Bell, 9667, Aurora, YOP: 1986-87, $30-35; Bell, Petite, 7662, $20-25.

Country Scene on Ivory Satin LT: Bell, 7668, YOP: 1990-91, $50-55.

"Elizabeth" Silver Crest with Blue Floral ES: Bell, 6761, Paisley, YOP: 1989-92, $45-50.

Golden Flax on Cobalt KG: Bell, 967, Aurora, YOP: 1995, $30-35.

Blue Royale with White Floral EM: Bell, 7463, $45. Elizabeth-Silver Crest with Blue Floral: Bell, Petite, 9266, 4.5", Bowl & Drape, YOP: 1990-91, $30-35; Paisley, YOP: 1989-92, $45-50. *Courtesy of Laurie & Richard Karman.*

Hearts & Flowers FH: Bell, 9462, Basket weave, YOP: 1988-93, $30-35.

Empress Rose CP: Bell, 9560, Temple Bells, YOP: 1998-99, $30-35.

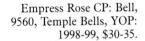

Floral Interlude on Sea Green Satin GG: Bell, 7688, YOP: 1998, $30-35.

Kristen's Floral: Bell, 9266, $30-35.

Light Amethyst Carnival DT: Bell, 9065, Sables Arch, YOP: 1991, $30-35.

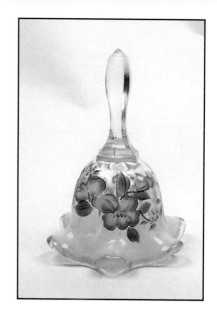

Martha's Rose AZ, YOP: 1999: Bell, 4694, $30-35.

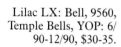

Lilac LX: Bell, 9560, Temple Bells, YOP: 6/90-12/90, $30-35.

Meadow Beauty: Bell, 4629, $30-35.

Meadow Blossoms on Opal Satin SF: Bell, 6761, Paisley, $30-35; Bell, Petite, 7662, $20-25.

Lilacs PJ: Bell, 2746, Paisley, $30-35; Bell, 2769, $30-35.

Misty Blue Satin LR: Bell, 1967, $25-30. *Courtesy of Myers Mystique.*

Persian Blue Opalescent XC: Bell, 3645, YOP: 1989-6/89, $30-35.

Morning Mist GG, YOP: 1999: Bell, 4769, $30-35.

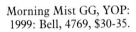

Provincial Bouquet FS: Bell, 7662, Petite, YOP: 1987-88, $20-25.

Pansies PF, YOP: 1996: Bell, 1145, $30-35.

Red Carnival RN: Bell, 6571, Columbus, YOP: 1992 only, $30-35; Bell, 9262, Rose, YOP: 1991 only, $30-35.

Red Carnival RN: Bell, 9560, Temple Bells, YOP: 1990 only, $30-35.

Rose Garden EG: Bell, 1773, $30-35.

Red Carnival RN: Bell, 9625, Butterfly, YOP: 1996 only, $30-35.

Rose Garden Bells: Special Issue Bells, $45-55 ea. *Courtesy of Bobbie & Harold Morgan.*

Rose Garden EG: Bell, Petite, Bow & Drape, $20-25.

Rose Magnolia RV: Bell, 3337, Hobnail, YOP: 1993 only, $30-35.

Sapphire Blue Opalescent BX:
Bell, 8265, Lily of the Valley, YOP:
1990-6/90, $30-35.

Teal Marigold OI, YOP:
1988-89: Bell, 8466,
Faberge, YOP: 1988 only,
$30-35.

Shell Pink PE:
Bell, 8185,
Faberge, $30-35;
Bell, 9761, Cross,
YOP: 1988-91,
$30-35.

Teal Marigold OI, YOP: 1988-89:
Bell, Spanish Lace, NIL, $45-55.

Star Flowers on Gold Pearl GF, YOP:
1992: Bell, 9667, Aurora, $30-35.

Teal Royale OC, YOP: 1988-89:
Bell, 9665, Beauty, $30-35; Bell,
9761, Cross, $30-35.

Tranquility AK: Bell,
4560, Strawberry,
YOP: 1999, $30-35.

Victorian Bouquet on Black
BT, YOP: 1995: Bell, 9667,
Aurora, $30-35.

Trellis DX: Bell,
1145, $30-35.

Vintage on Plum: Bell,
7463, $30-35.

Watercolors PF:
Bell, 9667, Aurora,
YOP: 1990, $30-35;
Bell, Petite, 7662,
$20-25.

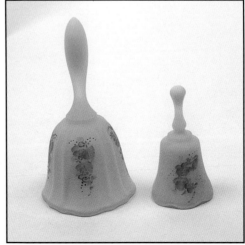

Tulips TL: Bell, Petite,
9266, Bow & Drape,
YOP: 1990 only, $20-25;
Bell, 9268, Bow &
Drape, $30-35.

Designer Bells Martha Reynolds: 7566 HT Iridescent Oval, YOP: 1999, $65-70; 1145 GF Butterflies, YOP: 1997, $65-70; 4564 IN Floral Medallion, YOP: 1996, $60-65; 2962 YD Topaz Swirl Paisley, YOP: 1998, $70-75. *Courtesy of Richard & Laurie Karman.*

Wild Flowers on Crystal F5: Bell, 9667, Aurora, YOP: 1991, $30-35.

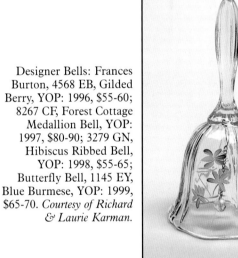

Designer Bells: Frances Burton, 4568 EB, Gilded Berry, YOP: 1996, $55-60; 8267 CF, Forest Cottage Medallion Bell, YOP: 1997, $80-90; 3279 GN, Hibiscus Ribbed Bell, YOP: 1998, $55-65; Butterfly Bell, 1145 EY, Blue Burmese, YOP: 1999, $65-70. *Courtesy of Richard & Laurie Karman.*

Designer Bells: Robin Spindler, 7562 PP Gardenia, YOP: 1996, $60-65; 9667 UJ Bleeding Hearts Aurora Bell, YOP: 1998, $75-80; 9862 BF Feathers Whitton Bell, YOP: 1997, $60-65; 6662 NI Gilded Daisy, YOP: 1999, $60-65. *Courtesy of Laurie & Richard Karman.*

Egg: Favrene HP ZN, 5140, Limited to 1,500, $55-65. *Courtesy of Laurie & Richard Karman.*

Designer Bells: Kim Plauche, 7667 HW, Wild Rose Bell, YOP: 1996, $45-55; 1145 QW, Fairy Roses, Rosalene, YOP: 1998, $65-70; 4629 AF, Roses on Ribbons Bell, YOP: 1997, $55-60; 7562 AG, Deco Fuchsia Bell, YOP: 1999, $60-65. *Courtesy of Richard & Laurie Karman.*

Eggs

Due to the success of the original 5140 eggs, issued along with many of Fenton's regular patterns in the 1970s, Fenton decided to create several other egg moulds in the early 1990s. The eggs produced off these moulds have become quite popular. Each year a number of limited edition eggs are produced by Fenton, besides many special series eggs. These eggs have become so popular that many sell out even before they actually hit the shelves, at both the Fenton Gift Shop and Fenton dealer stores.

Eggs, All 1997: Limited to 2500: Carnation on Blue Iridescent, 5145 7U HP, $35-45; Lighthouse on White Opal, 5145 7W, $35-45; Sea Mist Green HP Iris, 5145 7T, $35-45; Roses on Custard, 5145 7X, $35-45; Floral on Ruby, 5145 7V, $35-45; Rooster on Ebony, 5145 7Y, $35-45; Exotic Favrene Dolphin HP, 5145 7Z, $45-55. *Courtesy of Laurie & Richard Karman.*

1992 Eggs All, Limited to 2,500 Each: Pink Rose & Gold on White Opal, 5140 7V, $35-45; Floral on Rose Pearl, $45-55; Favrene HP, $55-65; Golfer Silhouette on French Opalescent Iridescent, $45-55; Floral on Sea Mist Green; Butterflies on Black, 5140 7W, $35-45; Unicorn on Cobalt, $35-45. *Courtesy of Laurie & Richard Karman.*

Egg, 5145 F6, Champagne Satin, YOP: 1996, $35-45; Egg, 5145, Floral on Rose Pearl, 5146, $35-45. *Courtesy of Laurie & Richard Karman.*

Eggs, All 1998: Limited to 3000: Ruby/Floral, 5146 D7, French Opal Dragon Fly/Floral, 5146 D6; Sea Mist Green Bountiful Harvest, 5146 D5; Misty Blue Floral, 5146 D1; Rosalene/Floral, 5146 D3; Cobalt/Ship, 5146 D4; Champagne Floral, 5146 D2. $45-55 all.

Buttercups & Berries on Red Carnival RI: Fairy Light, 8405, YOP: 1995, $65-70.

Eggs, Floral on Ebony, 5145, $35-45; Floral on Cobalt, 5145, $35-45; Scenic on White Opal Iridescent, 5145, $40-45; Hummingbird on Dusty Rose, 5145, $35-45; Floral on French Opalescent Iridescent, 5145, $35-45. *Courtesy of Laurie & Richard Karman.*

Fairy Lights

The fairy lights, sometimes called courting lights, were first made in the late nineteenth century. First patented by Thomas Clarke, these lights were produced in many beautiful Art Glass treatments, including Burmese and Peach Blow. As the Victorian era passed into the twentieth century, these lights lost popularity with the buying public and faded away. In the late 1960s, Fenton started to issue small fairy lights again, reminiscent of the Thomas Clarke lights. They again caught the collecting public's eye and have become very popular.

Items Not Pictured:

Aquamarine AA 1999: Fairy Light, 9404, Faberge, 1999, $40-45

Blue Royale KK 1988-90: Fairy Light, 9407, Strawberry, YOP: 1988-89, $40-45

Dusty Rose DK 1984-94: Fairy Light, 8405, Beaded, 1984-85, $45-50

Floral on Violet Satin XP 1999: Fairy Light, 5405, $45-50

Pink Pearl HZ 1991-94: Fairy Light, 8405, Beaded, YOP: 1992 only, $45-50

Provincial Blue OO 1987-88: Fairy Light, 9407, Strawberry, $30-35

Ruby RU 1985-2000: Fairy Light, 8405, Beaded, 1992-94, $40-45

Colonial Scroll on Royal Purple N4: Fairy Light, 3 piece, 1610, Limited to 2,950, YOP: 1998, $125-150. *Courtesy of Phyllis & Terry Sterrett.*

Cranberry Opalescent CR: Fairy Light, 3 piece, 3380, Hobnail 1994 only, $150-175.

Dusty Rose DK: Fairy Light, 9407, Strawberry, YOP: 1988-89, $35-40.

Hearts & Flowers FH: Fairy Light, 9304, Basket Weave, YOP: 1988-89, $50-55.

Hydrangeas on Topaz Opalescent TP: Fairy Light, 3 piece, 2040, Family Signature, YOP: 1997, $100-125.

Persian Blue Opalescent XC, YOP: 1989: Fairy Light, 3608, $45-50.

Misty Morn MM: Fairy Light, 7300, YOP: 1988-89, $75-80.

Pansies on Cranberry CW, YOP 1994: Fairy Light, 1700, $65-70.

Red Carnival RN: Fairy Light, 3 piece, 116, YOP: 1994 only, $80-90. *Courtesy of Norma & Melvin Lampton.*

Rose Garden EG: Fairy Light, 7300, $44-60. *Courtesy of Bobbie & Harold Morgan.*

Teal Marigold OI: Fairy Light, 8406, Heart, YOP: 1988 only, $35-40. *Courtesy of Bev & Jon Spencer.*

Shell Pink PE: Fairy Light, 8406, Heart, YOP: 1988-89, $45-50. *Courtesy of Bobbie & Harold Morgan.*

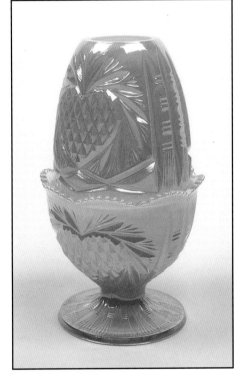

Teal Royale OC: Fairy Light, 9407, Strawberry, YOP: 1988-89, $30-35.

Floral/Butterfly on Opal, Fairy Light, 7300 HY, YOP: 1998, $55-65. *Courtesy of Bobbie & Harold Morgan.*

Lamps

Over the past thirty years, lamps have become a important part of Fenton's business. Prior to this, Fenton produced many lampshades and fonts for other companies to assemble. In the late 1960s they began to develop lamps to accompany their own lines. These lamps in many ways have become the backbone of the Fenton company. Every year Fenton's lamp division still produces fonts and shades for other companies, besides selling them at their own gift shop. Also, every year many different lamps are issued to accompany their lines or for their special series, such as the Connoisseur Line or their Christmas Series. In the mid-1990s Fenton began to issue special lamps each year; they would only be available to dealers, who would order so many of Fenton's regular lamps. These lamps, due to their limited number and distribution, have become very collectible.

Items Not Pictured:

Antique Rose AF 6/89-6/90: Lamp, 19.5", Student, 9308, $200-250

Aquamarine AA 1999: Lamp, 18", Student, 2809, Rose, 1999, $175-200

Autumn Gold Opalescent AO 6/93-12/94: Lamp, Student, 1520, $250-300

Bell Flowers LH 1999: Lamp, 20", 6702, Paisley, $175-200

Blue Royale KK 1988-95: Lamp, 20", 1400, Coin Dot, YOP: 1988-89, $200-300

Blush Rose on Opaline TE 1996: Lamp, 24", 1705, $350-400

Buttercups & Berries on Red Carnival R1 1995: Lamp, 20", 4605, Basket weave, $350-400

Champagne Satin PQ 1997: Lamp, 20", 9202, Poppy, $350-400

Champagne Satin PQ 1997: Lamp, 20", 9303, Poppy, $350-400

Cobalt Lamp, 18", Student, 5900, 1999, $200-250

Cottage on Opal Satin ZB 1993-6/94: Lamp, 16", Hammered Colonial, 7204, $300-400

Country Cranberry CC 1985-94: Lamp, 20", 1400, Coin Dot, YOP: 1982-91, $200-250

Country Cranberry CC 1985-94: Lamp, 17", 2001, Feather, YOP: 1985-92, $200-250

Country Cranberry CC 1985-94: Lamp, Pillar, 3108, Spiral, YOP: 1985-92, $250-300

Country Cranberry CC 1985-94: Lamp, 23", GWTW, 3504, Spanish Lace, YOP: 1994 only, $350-400

Country Cranberry CC 1985-94: Lamp, Student, 9218, Rose, YOP: 1989-94, $25-250

Country Scene on Ivory Satin LT 1990-91: Lamp, 16", Hammered Colonial, 7204, $300-400

Country Scene on Ivory Satin LT 1990-91: Lamp, 21", Student, 7209, $450+

Cranberry Opalescent CR 1970-1994: Lamp, 23.5", GWTW, 1800, Fern, YOP: 1991-93, $350-400

Cranberry Opalescent CR 1970-1994: Lamp, 15", Student, 3307, Hobnail, YOP: 1985-88, $300-350

Damask Rose on Red Carnival RC 1996: Lamp, 20", Student, 907, $250-300

Dusty Rose DK 1984-94: Lamp, 20", 6702, Paisley, YOP: 1992-94, $200-225

Dusty Rose DK 1984-94: Lamp, 10.5", Mini, 8202, YOP: 1987 only, $100-125

Dusty Rose DK 1984-94: Lamp, 11", Mini, 8303, YOP: 1987 only, $100-125

Dusty Rose DK 1984-94: Lamp, 9214, Rose, YOP: 1989-93, $125-150

Dusty Rose DK 1984-94: Lamp, 23", 9219, Rose, GWTW, YOP: 1992-94, $250-275

Dusty Rose DK 1984-94: Light, 8", Mini, 9600, YOP: 1990-92, $100-150

Empress Rose Lamp, 29", GWTW, 9219, Rose, 1999, $250-275

Floral on Gold Amberina AV 1999: Lamp, 24", 6150, Limited to 950, $450+

Floral on Spruce Carnival US 1999: Student Lamp, 20", F9307, $300-350

Gilded Star Flowers HV 1993: Mini Light, 7600, $100-125

Gilded Star Flowers HV 1993: Lamp, 19.5", Student, 9308, $300-350

Gold Pearl GP 1992: Lamp, 21", Student with Prisms, 3313, $350+

Golden Pine Cones VC 6/94-12/94: Lamp, 16", Hammered Colonial, 7204, $250-300

Irises on Misty Blue Satin LS 1997: Lamp, 18", 6700, Paisley, $300-350

Jade Opaline AP 1990: Lamp, 20", Student, 9128, Rose, $250-300

Kristen's Floral Lamp, 21", 2791, $300+

Lilacs PJ 1993-94: Lamp, 20", 6701, Paisley, $250-300

Martha's Rose AZ 1999: Lamp, 18", Student, 2791, $200-250

Meadow Beauty 1997: Lamp, 19", Student, 2719, $200-250

Meadow Blossoms on Opal Satin SF 1991-93: Lamp, 20", 6701, Paisley, $300-350

Morning Glories on Sea Mist Green Lamp, 20", 1600, $200-250

Morning Mist GG 1999: Lamp, 16", Student, 6505, $250-300

Pastel Violets on Custard VC 1987: Lamp, 19.5", Student, 9308, $250-300

Peaches & Cream (Pink Opalescent) UO 1986-89: Lamp, 25", G WTW Lamp 3308, YOP: 1988 only, $300-350

Peaches & Cream (Pink Opalescent) UO 1986-89: Lamp, 9", Electric 6602, YOP: 1986 only, $100-125

Persian Blue Opalescent XC 1989-6/89: Lamp 21", with prisms, 1413, Coin Dot, $250-300

Persian Blue Opalescent XC 1989-6/89: Lamp, 21", Student with Prisms, 3313, $250-300

Petal Pink PN 1990-94: Light, Mini, 9600, YOP: 1992 only, $100-125

Primrose DS 1994: Lamp, 20", 4605, Basket weave, $250-300

Provincial Blue OO 1987-89: Lamp, 10.5", Mini, 8202, $100-125

Provincial Blue OO 1987-89: Lamp, 11", Mini, 8303, $100-125

Provincial Blue OO 1987-89: Lamp, 23", 9214, Rose, YOP: 1989 only, $200-250

Red Carnival RN 1990-94: Lamp, 20", with Prisms, 6703, Paisley, YOP: 1993 only, $250-300

Rose Garden EG 1996-2000: Lamp, 21", Student, 7412, $250-300

Rose Garden EG 1996-2000: Lamp GWTW, 7583, 1999, $350-400, Rose Magnolia RV 1993-94

Rose Garden EG 1996-2000: Lamp, 21", Student with Prisms, 3313, YOP: 1993 only, $350-400

Ruby RU 1985-2000: Lamp, 16", Colonial Hammered, 3105, YOP: 1989-90, $200-300

Ruby RU 1985-2000: Lamp, 11", Mini, 8303, YOP: 1987 only, $100-125

Ruby RU 1985-2000: Light, 8", Mini, 9600, YOP: 1990-91, $100-125

Sea Mist Green Iridescent EZ 1991-94: Lamp, 20", with Prisms, 9260, Classic, YOP: 1992 only, $200-250

Teal Royale OC 1988-89: Lamp, 20", 1400, Coin Dot, $200-250

Teal Royale OC 1988-89: Lamp, 17", 2001, Feather, YOP: 1988 only, $175-200

Thistle & Bows EW 1986: Lamp, 16", Student, 7606, $250-300

Trellis DX Lamp, 18", 2793, $250-300

Tulips TL 1990-91: Lamp, 19.5", Student, 9308, $300-350

Twilight Tulips TT 1992-93: Lamp, 21", Student, 3210, $250-300

Victorian Roses VJ 1987-89: Lamp, 19.5", Student, 9308, $300-350

Vining Garden on Sea Mist Green FP 1991-94: Lamp, 21", Student, 3210, YOP: 1991-94, $200-250

Violas on Petal Pink PU 1994: Lamp, 20", 6702, Paisley, $250-300

Water Colors PF 1990: Lamp, 21", Student, 7410, $250-300

Country Cranberry CC: Lamp, 20", 6701, Paisley, YOP: 1991-94, $200-250.

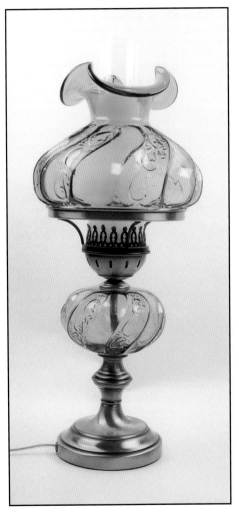

Colonial Amber: Lamp, 20", 6701, Student, Paisley, $75-80.

Colonial Scroll on Royal Purple N4: Lamp, 20", Student, 1509, Limited to 1450, YOP: 1999, $350-400. *Courtesy of Bev & Jon Spencer.*

Copper Roses on Black KP: Lamp, 19.5", Student, 9308, YOP: 1990-93, $450-500.

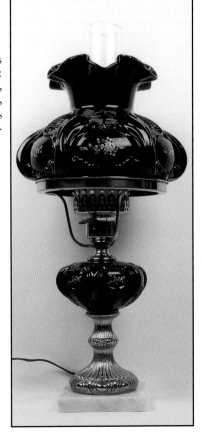

Cranberry Opalescent CR: Lamp, 21", with Prisms, 1413, Coin Dot, YOP: 1990-93, $450+.

Cranberry Opalescent CR: Lamp, 25", GWTW Hobnail, $450+.

Dragonfly & Flower on Rubina Verde BW: Lamp, 24", 1507, YOP: 1997, $400+. *Courtesy of Tina Boris.*

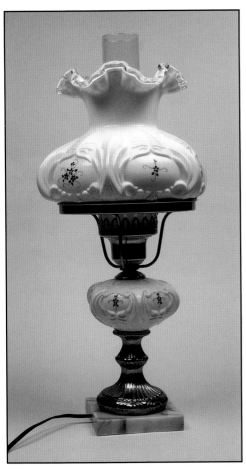

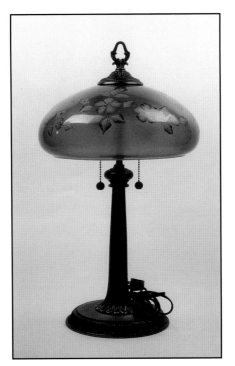

Evening Blossoms with Lady Bugs on
Mulberry MD: Lamp, 21", 5581,
Limited to 500, YOP: 1996, $450+.
Courtesy of Phyllis & Terry Sterrett.

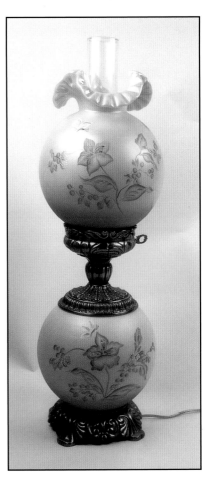

"Elizabeth" Silver Crest with Blue Floral
ES: Lamp, 19.5", Student, 9308, YOP: 1989-
92, $250-300. *Courtesy of Marylin & Dick
Treiwelter.*

Floral Interlude on Sea Green Satin
GG: Lamp, 24", GWTW 7511, YOP:
1998, $350+. *Courtesy of Cory Meyer.*

Left: Floral on
Violet Satin XP:
Lamp, GWTW
1602, YOP: 1999,
$300-350. *Courtesy
of Bobbie &
Harold Morgan.*

Center: Golden
Flax on Cobalt
KG: Lamp, 23.5",
1540, $300-350.
*Courtesy of Laurie
& Richard
Karman.*

Fuchsia EH: Lamp, 17", 2001,
Feather, YOP: 1994, $450+. *Courtesy
of Chuck Bingham.*

Left to right:
Grapes on Stiegel Blue Opalescent JU: Lamp, 20", 4605, Basket weave, YOP: 1991, $350-400. *Courtesy of Sarah Wells.*

Hearts & Flowers FH: Lamp, 19.5", Student, 9308, YOP: 1988-93, $300-350. *Courtesy of Bobbie & Harold Morgan.*

Opalescent TP: Lamp, 20", with Prisims2000, YOP: 1997, $350+. *Courtesy of Linda & Dennis Sowers.*

Light Amethyst Carnival DT: Lamp, 4603, Innovation, YOP: 1991, $175-200. *Courtesy of Connie & Aaron Patient.*

Minted Cream EO: Lamp, 9", Electric, 6602, YOP: 1986 only, $100-125. *Courtesy of Donna Hatch.*

Mulberry MG, YOP: 1989-92: Lamp, 20", Student, 9218, Rose, $400+. *Courtesy of Chuck Bingham.*

Left to right:
Mulberry MG, YOP: 1989-92: Lamp, Pillar, 30", Spiral, 3108, YOP: 1991 only, $400+. *Courtesy of Eileen & Dale Robinson.*

Mulberry MG, YOP: 1989-92: Lamp, 34", Coin Dot, 1415, YOP: 1989 only, $400+. *Courtesy of Linda & Dennis Sowers.*

Pansies PF: Lamp, 20", 6701, Paisley, YOP: 1996, $250-300.

Pansies on Cranberry CW: Lamp, $300-350.

Persian Pearl Opalescent XV: Lamp with Prisms, 1801, Fern, YOP: 1992-93, $350+. *Courtesy of Sarah Wells.*

Red Carnival RN: Lamp, Student with Prisms, 2792, YOP: 1994 only, $250-300. *Courtesy of Anne Musser.*

Rose Garden EG: Lamp, 18", 2791, $250-300.

Sapphire Blue Opalescent BX: Lamp, GWTW 1800, Fern, YOP: 1990, $350+. *Courtesy of Sarah Wells.*

Rose Garden EG: Lamp, GWTW 7583, 1999, $350-400. *Courtesy of Linda & Dennis Sowers.*

Sea Mist Green Opalescent LO, YOP: 1991-92: Lamp, 20", Student, 9218; Rose, $200-250. *Courtesy of Chuck Bingham.*

Top row, left to right:

Sweet Briar on Plum Overlay: Lamp, 20",
2800, $250-300. *Courtesy of Myers
Mystique.*

Vintage on Plum Overlay PV: Lamp, 17",
Diamond, 1706, YOP: 1993-94, $250-300.
Courtesy of Phyllis & Terry Sterrett.

Stiegel Blue Opalescent BO: Lamp, 4603,
Innovation, YOP: 1991, $150-200.
Courtesy of Kansas City Fenton Finders.

Trellis DX: Lamp, 24", 1703 GWTW,
1997, $300-350. *Courtesy of Laurie &
Richard Karman.*

Opposite page; bottom row left to right:

Sea Green Satin: Lamp, 24", 9204, Rose GWTW, $250-300. *Courtesy
of Elmer & Madonna Puskar.*

Sapphire Blue Opalescent BX: Lamp with Prisms, 1801, Fern,
YOP: 1990, $350+. *Courtesy of Sarah Wells.*

Shell Pink: Lamp, 19", 9208, Rose, YOP: 1988-91, $250-300.
Courtesy of Elmer & Madonna Puskar.

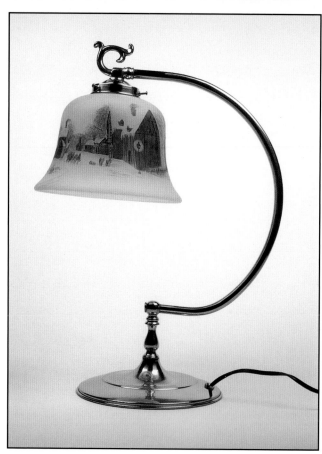

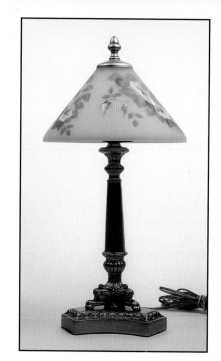

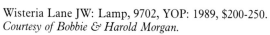

Wisteria Lane JW: Lamp, 9702, YOP: 1989, $200-250. *Courtesy of Bobbie & Harold Morgan.*

Limited Edition Lamp, 9872 XF, Burmese Wild Rose, Fall 1998, $400+. *Courtesy of Bobbie & Harold Morgan.*

Limited Edition Lamp, 5575 5X, Burmese, Fall 1996, $400+. *Courtesy of Bobbie & Harold Morgan.*

Logos

First issued in the late 1970s and early 1980s, these glass signs (deciphering the Fenton logo) have become very popular with collectors. Some colors and treatments that they have been issued in are very rare. When first issued, they were intended for dealers who were selling Fenton or were made for the FAGCA (Fenton Art Glass Collectors of America) for their conventions. They quickly became so popular that they were regularly issued in many of Fenton's regular lines.

Items Not Pictured:

French Cream FO 1986-87: Logo 9799, YOP: 1986-87, $40-45
Light Amethyst Carnival DT 1991: Logo 9799, $60-65
Rose Magnolia RV 1993-94: Logo 9799, YOP: 1994-94, $55-60
Sea Green Satin GE 1999: Logo, Oval 9499, $35-40
Stiegel Green Stretch SS 1/94-6/94: Logo 9799, $45-50

Opaline TE: Logo, Oval, 9499, YOP: 1996, $50-55.

Sapphire Blue Opalescent BX: Logo, 9799, YOP: 1990, $50-55. *Courtesy of Sarah Wells.*

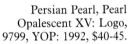
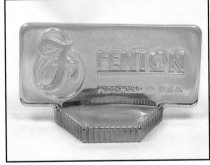

Persian Pearl, Pearl Opalescent XV: Logo, 9799, YOP: 1992, $40-45.

Shell Pink PE: Logo, 9799, YOP: 1988-89, $50-55.

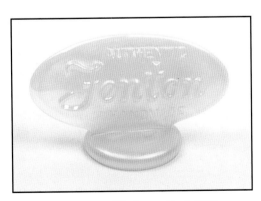

Topaz Opalescent TS: Logo, Oval, 9499, YOP: 1997, $50-55.

Bibliography

Fenton Art Glass Collectors of America. *Caught in the Butterfly Net*. Williamstown, WV: Fenton Art Glass Club of America, Inc., 1991

Heacock, William. *Fenton Glass: The 2nd Twenty-Five Years*. Marietta, Ohio: O-Val Advertising Corp., 1980.

_____. *Fenton Glass: The 3rd Twenty-Five Years*. Marietta Ohio: O-Val Advertising Corp., 1989.

Measell, James, ed. *Fenton Glass: The '80s Decade*. Marietta Ohio: Antique Publications, 1996.

_____. *Fenton Glass: The '90s Decade*. Marietta Ohio: Antique Publications, 2002.

Walk, John. *Fenton Compendium 1940-70*. Atglen, PA: Schiffer Publishing, 2001.

_____. *Fenton Compendium 1970-85*. Atglen, PA: Schiffer Publishing, 2001.

Walk, John & Joe Gates. *The Big Book of Fenton Glass 1940-70*. Atglen, PA: Schiffer Publishing, 1998.

Whitmeyer, Margaret & Kenn. *Fenton Art Glass Patterns: 1939-80*. Paducah, KY: Schroeder, 1999.

Periodicals

Fenton Art Glass Collectors Of America. *Butterfly Net*.

Koch, Nora & Terri Steele, eds. *Depression Glass Daze: 1980-1997*.

National Fenton Society of America. *Fenton Flyer*.

Richardson, David, ed. *Glass Collector's Digest*: 1986-1997.

Schaeffer, Barbara, ed. *Glass Review:* 1978-1987.

Internet

Fenton Fanatics: www.fentonfan.com; John Gager; Webmaster

Biography

John Walk, owner of Memory Lane Antiques, has been in the antiques business for over twenty years, doing antique shows and flea markets. He currently travels a thirty state area regularly, both buying and selling, while logging over one hundred thousand miles a year. When home, he sells on the internet, both on his web page (www.walkmemorylane.com) and on Ebay.

He first became aware of Fenton Art Glass through a friend over fifteen years ago and fell in love with it shortly thereafter. He has collected and specialized in Fenton for the past twelve years, and quickly became aware of the rising interest of Fenton Art Glass from the 1940s to the 1980s. He also became aware of the lack of references available upon the subject about ten years ago.

John started doing research on this book, first edition, around eight years ago, in an attempt to inform his customers on what was available in the patterns they were collecting. As he became involved with this project, he soon saw the need for a full colored identification guide with prices.

John lives on the dairy farm he was raised on, near Mulberry Grove, Illinois, when not traveling. While he's on the road, his parents, who live with him, take care of his mail order business.